Although both monarch and nation mourned the tragic death of Henry Havelock in 1857, while at the peak of his military triumph, his passing sealed his own life-long ambition – to show that a Christian could also be a meritorious soldier, and be both soldier and saint. Just as Henry Havelock inspired his own generation, John Pollock's biography will inspire today's generation to strive professionally, not only to become men among men, but also to be known spiritually as men of God.
Brigadier F.R. Dannatt MC,

Way To Glory is unusually instructive, and John Pollock's warm, authoritative style captures most attractively the adventure of the Christian life in the setting of a military epic. It is rare to read a biography in which the subject emerges with such godly proportions in his professional, domestic and spiritual responsibilities as does Havelock. This is the most inspiring biography of a Christian officer it has been my privilege to read.
Brigadier W.I.C. Dobbie

This is an outstanding biography of an outstanding soldier, General Henry Havelock. News of his death drew tributes from Victorian Britain second only to the death of Nelson. What set Havelock apart was his great professionalism combined with his evident Christian character, a model for each of us to study and emulate.
Major General Sir Laurence New

For
Brigadier Ian Dobbie

Way To Glory

The Life of Havelock of Lucknow

John Pollock

Christian Focus Publications

© J. C. Pollock
ISBN 1-85792-245-X

First published by John Murray, 1957

This edition published in 1996 by
Christian Focus Publications,
Geanies House, Fearn, Ross-shire,
Scotland, IV20 1TW, Great Britain.
Cover design by Donna Macleod

Printed and bound in Great Britain by
The Guernsey Press Co. Ltd., Guernsey, Channel Islands

Contents

FOREWORD

It is just short of 150 years since Sir Henry died and yet there is a fascination in his name for me that brought an immediate response to the publisher's request that I should write a foreword for this account of his life.

During my early years I was frequently in the congregation of the late Reverend William Grant, the Free Presbyterian Minister of Halkirk in Caithness, who made frequent references in his sermons to General Havelock that fired my curiosity. Mr. Grant, who served as an officer in the London Scottish during the First World War and suffered substantial damage to himself in consequence, greatly admired the Christian character coupled with the martial skills displayed by Havelock and he transmitted this admiration to me. In consequence the account of Havelock's life which was available in our home was an early part of my reading.

This account of Havelock's life is a much more detailed narrative than that which I knew. For those interested in the military history of the Afghan wars and the Indian Mutiny there is a great deal of first hand description of the situations with which Havelock was confronted and the manner in which he dealt with them. His skill as a soldier won him reluctant admiration from those who were not in sympathy with his Christian views. The nature of that skill is well described as the reader is caught up in the tensions of the battle. Havelock's life was often in dire danger in these battles, but miraculously he was preserved through them, and although horses he was riding were killed underneath him he lived on.

For those interested in the personal relationships of people at the top of an organisation there are insights into the command of the armies in India at the time from which a great deal could be learned which is relevant to running an organisation today. If a person is put in charge he should be allowed to control. The danger of not doing so is vividly illustrated in the problems encountered in the attempts to relieve Lucknow.

But the central interest of this book is surely the Christian character of the hero. In a time when it was seriously doubted whether a Christian could be a good soldier, Havelock demonstrated that the practice of Christianity made a huge contribution to being a good soldier. He showed that being a Christian was not inconsistent with being a strong disciplinarian. But he showed also that being a Christian in the times in which he served put obstacles in the way of his merits being recognised.

He obviously believed wholeheartedly that British rule was essential for the well-being of the Indian people of his day. It is against this background that this volume gives us a picture of a Christian living out his principles in very difficult situations. There is much in this volume, a good deal of it Havelock's own words, to illustrate Christianity in action, in the service of his country, in the concerns for his family, in the heat of battle, and in the special problems for the British in India at that time, which will enlighten, encourage and counsel those who aspire to be practising Christians in the very different situation in Britain and the world today as we approach the second millennium of the Christian era.

The Lord Chancellor,
Lord MacKay of Clashfern

PREFACE TO NEW EDITION

His statue stands in Trafalgar Square and his story is timeless.

For much of his life Henry Havelock was known only to soldiers and officials in India until he swept to international fame for his brilliant campaign which saved the raj at the height of the Indian Mutiny. He recaptured Cawnpore, scene of the massacre which had appalled Victorian Britain. He fought his way through to Lucknow, where a small garrison and the surviving European women and children were besieged in the Residency. All would have been slaughtered had it fallen.

The nation took the little old general to its heart, not least because of his extraordinary power to inspire his troops under terrible conditions. He reached the Residency, where his battle-worn force, too weak to lift the siege, held out for nearly two months until the Second Relief of Lucknow. Then, 'with the suddenness of a thunderclap' came the news of his death. 'General Sir Henry Havelock is dead,' wrote the *Daily Telegraph*, 'and a whole nation mourns his loss. No words less emphatic would express the profound and universal sorrow created by the announcement of his untimely fate and which will long abide in the hearts of millions. The people had adopted him ... they had ranked him amongst the noblest in England's history.'

Nor was this grief confined to the British. In New York and Boston flags on public buildings and the shipping in the harbour were flown at half-mast for a day, 'a purely voluntary tribute,' commented the *New York Times*, 'which even the Duke of Wellington did not command, and which we believe was never before paid to a foreigner.'

Queen Victoria, forgetting the disparity of age and that she had never met Havelock, said she felt she had lost a brother. Plans were at once announced for the statue in Trafalgar Square.

On the Sunday following, the pulpits in almost every church and chapel 'gave forth a funeral eulogy on his merits and his worth'. A funeral sermon was preached in Westminster Abbey. At the Baptist Church in Bloomsbury, which Havelock had attended when on leave, a thousand people had to be turned away and the sermon delivered again the following Sunday. 'If,' wrote Havelock's brother-in-law to the General's son, Harry, who had been with him at his death, 'there can be any consolation to us who are bereaved it is to be found in the nation's sorrow.'

Havelock's name remained secure in the national affection until all that generation passed away. Nearly every town in England has its Havelock Gardens, Square or Road. Yet it was not merely his military achievements at a time of calamity which secured his lasting position: 'It is as a Christian soldier that his memory is cherished by the Christian world in England, as a man who mixed the highest military genius with the sincerest Christian piety.'

This gives him a timeless appeal. The military authorities had slighted and overlooked him, despite his heroism and strategic skill in the earlier campaigns described in this book. Yet he went quietly on, and even if his great opportunity and fame had never come, he should be honoured as a pioneer of the social and spiritual welfare of the Army, and for his outstanding faith and dedication.

Soon after Havelock's death a spate of tracts was followed by the first, unofficial *Life*, which sold forty-six thousand copies, an enormous sale for the mid-nineteenth century. The official biography when it came in 1860, John Clark Marshman's *Memoir of Major-General Sir Henry Havelock, KCB*, remained in print for nearly fifty years.

Havelock was fortunate in his biographer. His brother-in-law not only was a historian and man of letters but had long lived at the centre of Indian affairs as a foremost authority. Marshman, however, showed the public what it wanted – a hero in pure white marble. He gave scant indication of Havelock's warm and attractive humanity or his sense of humour. He held to contemporary tradition in smoothing away his subject's foibles and weaknesses, and in treating him as a public man whose private life should be discreetly veiled. Since Havelock's widow and children were very much alive he could say nothing of the love story, nor of Havelock's remarkable relations with his eldest son. In public matters, especially about Outram, Marshman was equally guarded.

Nearly a century after the Indian Mutiny and Havelock's death, I was looking for a subject of fame and vibrant faith whose private papers had never been fully used for a biography. I had always been interested in Havelock as many of my family had served in India: two of them come into the story (see pp 96 ff. and 110).

I approached Havelock's descendants and found that several boxes of unpublished manuscripts were in the cellars of his late grandson's home. Through the kindness of the Havelock-Allans I was able to study Havelock at leisure. The brave little man came alive as I handled the wafer thin letters from India.

This was my first full length biography, written less than ten years after the independence of India and Pakistan. Both factors may perhaps be detected in the writing but apart from a few minor corrections it seemed best to reprint and not rewrite.

This, then, is the story of little Henry Havelock, 'every inch a soldier and every inch a Christian.'

John Pollock
Rose Ash, Devonshire
April 1996

ACKNOWLEDGEMENTS

In the first edition (1957) I was very glad to express my thanks fully to the following, some of whom are no longer living.

The Executors and Trustees of Sir Henry S. M. Havelock-Allan, 2nd Baronet, and his widow, Doris Pamela, Lady Havelock-Allan; Sir Henry R. M. Havelock-Allan, 3rd Bt; Sir Anthony Havelock-Allan, 4th Bt.

The County Archivist, North Riding of Yorkshire (Mr C. K. Croft-Andrews, F.S.A.).

In India and Pakistan (Research tour 1956): The Rt Rev A. J. Dain; Dr M. B. Fox (Lucknow); Sir Henry Holland, CIE FRCSE (Quetta); Mr and Mrs Alan Norrish (Landour); Mrs Stewart (Serampore); the Rev F R Thompson and Mr and Mrs Kenneth Willcox (Kanpur).

The Curator of the Regimental Museum, Somerset Light Infantry (Lieut-Colonel A. C. M. Urwick); Colonel F. M. Bailey, CIE; Mr F. S. McCarthy.

Sir John Murray, KCVO and the Hon. George Kinnaird of John Murray, Publishers.

I would add my warm thanks to the publishers of this new edition, especially Willliam Mackenzie and Malcolm Maclean.

Note on Indian names: I have standardized spelling of persons and chief places to the forms generally familiar to western readers.

PART ONE

The Neglected Lieutenant

1

Disgruntled Young Man

A disgruntled young man sat in the parlour of a small house at Henbury near Bristol, reading the news of Waterloo.

Henry Havelock, only five foot five in height ('and five-sixteenths', as he liked to point out) but well proportioned with clear cut features and chestnut hair, felt that life had deceived him. Born with a silver spoon, the spoon had been rudely snatched away. For five years, since 1810, he had received nothing but shocks, and now, at twenty, was left without a future.

He had been born at Ford Hall, Bishop Wearmouth on the outskirts of Sunderland, on Easter Day, April 5th 1795, second son of a successful shipbuilder. In 1800, Mr Havelock's fortune being made, the growing family had come south to the spacious luxury of Ingress Park on the Thames, between Dartford and Gravesend.

They were a high-spirited crowd and Ingress Park gave them ample scope, with a window on the world as they watched the battered *Victory* bringing home Nelson's body, or the fine East Indiamen sailing up to London Pool, with the wealth of the far-off empire in the East. Will Havelock, the eldest, 'wildest of the wild', with very light blue eyes and fair hair, was leader in their romps and expeditions. Henry, pugnacious enough when roused, was more studious, and as he grew older would browse for hours in the library. Their father, a clever but hot-tempered man, meant little to them; but to their mother, a delicate gentle woman, they were devoted.

They were both sent to Charterhouse in the city, and the roughness of an early nineteenth-century public school proved congenial. William found all he wanted – cricket, fencing, the peculiar ball game in the cloisters which was to develop into 'soccer', frequent opportunities to use his fists; and, according to Henry, 'not only spent the best part of his vacations in head-long career in the wake of a pack of foxhounds but indulged in day dreams of the beloved past-time when he ought to have been poring over Homer or Euripides'.

Henry developed differently. His small size gave him more than his share of bullying, but neither this nor the rigours of fagging could deflate his high spirits; he could be as rowdy as Will when he chose. His delight, however, was less in games than in scholarship. With Dr Raine, the Headmaster, he burrowed deep into classics and philosophy, earning the nickname 'Phlos'. With four kindred spirits he even ran sufficiently counter to good form occasionally 'to read a sermon by stealth in the dormitories'.

As a future lawyer – for so his mother intended – Henry Havelock had his feet firmly planted on the right ladder. Then came the first shock, the sudden death of his mother early in 1810. The boys were urgently called down from Charterhouse, being told no more than that their mother was seriously ill. They arrived at Ingress Park after dark. 'Henry hastily opened the door,' recalled his sister Jane, 'rushed upstairs without a question, entered her room and asked the nurse if he might see his mother. She withdrew the curtain, he bent over her, supposing her to be asleep, kissed her cold lips and not till then discovered she was no more.'

That summer, when news of Wellington's retreat in the Peninsula was disturbing England, William Havelock, now seventeen, was sent by his father across the ferry at Gravesend to ride with a business message to Colchester. To old Havelock's rage and disgust, for he had promised his wife that none of their sons should enter the army, the groom returned with the news that the young master had 'slipped away with a draft of the 43rd', and was already on his way to the war.

In August 1811, Dr Raine died and a twenty-five-year-old assistant master, John Russell, was given the school. Dr Russell's new methods of teaching gave Charterhouse an unprecedented prosperity, though his attempt to replace flogging with fines was defeated by the boys, but Henry Havelock took an intense dislike to him and asked to leave. His father refused, and an acrimonious argument developed until Mr Havelock at last took both Henry and Thomas away and left them to pursue their own education unaided at Ingress Park.

They had not been at it long when William, for whom his father had grudgingly bought a commission, reappeared from the Peninsula, ill with fever, having been bundled on a battery-cart a hundred miles to the coast. And then Mr Havelock's ship-building business failed, he sold Ingress Park and the impoverished dejected family migrated to Clifton and thence to Brighton.

Henry persuaded his father to let him now enter the law and was put, to save expense, into the chambers of a special pleader, the prosy and pedantic, but exceedingly skilful, Joseph Chitty. The legal idyll was soon rudely broken. In 1814 Henry Havelock and his father had another and more violent quarrel. The cause is nowhere revealed. Jane was passionately convinced that Henry was 'the *innocent* sufferer', but both father and son were obstinate and opinionated, and the father held the trumps; he withdrew financial support and Henry was forced to abandon his career. Depressed and ill he rejoined the family at Brighton, and with them, moved again to Clifton and thence to Henbury.

William had earned such a reputation for devil-may-care courage under fire and hard riding to hounds between battles, that he was known throughout the army in Spain as Young Varmint. At the Peace of 1814 he had been home, resplendent in magnificent uniform and twirling mustachios. His success made Henry's failure more galling.

And now, in June 1815, Henry sat reading of the great battle at Waterloo, and saw William's name in the despatch as aide-de-camp to the Hanoverian General von Alten. William was already famous, while Henry, at twenty, had no profession and no prospects. Life had lost its humour.

THE WATERLOO DESPATCH opened an unexpected way out. William had his grateful general's promise of a commission for anyone he should name and offered it to his brother. Henry was still set on the law, but Mr Havelock was 'inexorable', and thus, 'though unwillingly', as Jane recalled, Henry 'as an alternative became a soldier'.

William's best friend was the Harry Smith who had won romantic fame and a beautiful Spanish wife at the taking of Badajoz; after Waterloo they had 'set on foot a pack of fox-hounds... a capital one', with Smith as Master and Havelock as Whip. It was in Harry Smith's regiment, the 95th Foot (the Rifle Brigade), that Henry Havelock was commissioned as Second-Lieutenant on July 22nd 1815.

The traditions of the Rifle Brigade, eyes and ears of the infantry, and with unusual emphasis on individual responsibility in every rank, suited a young man who, if he must be a soldier, was determined to practise his profession as a science, while the strange green uniform was kind to such a diminutive officer as Havelock. At Shorncliffe, however, the Rifle Brigade had drifted back to the stiff unimaginative routine of peace time. Havelock loved the parade ground, being a natural disciplinarian; he enjoyed the balls and routs at which he and his brother officers dazzled the young ladies of Kent, though Havelock had to make do on the pittance of an allowance. But he dreamed of generalship; he studied and analysed the campaigns of Napoleon, Frederick and Marlborough; he talked of military glories. And the other subalterns would have none of it. Bursting in on him as he sat absorbed in the Battle of Blenheim, or in the poetic delights of Wordsworth, they would throw the books out of the window and playfully sit on his head. Who had ever heard of a soldier reading poetry or the classics? If in the mood, he would join the rag gaily enough. But sometimes, conscious that the others were intellectually so much his inferiors, he would feel that they joined his after-dinner arguments about battles long ago merely to make him lose his temper.

In 1818 he was rescued by Harry Smith. 'When I was a boy,' wrote Havelock years later, 'he was one of the few people who ever took the trouble to teach me anything; and while all the rest around me would have persuaded me that English soldiering consisted in blackening and whitening belts with patent varnish and pipe-clay... he pointed my mind to the nobler past of our glorious profession.'

In Harry Smith he at last found someone on whom to lavish his fund of affection. Smith thought Havelock 'a clever, sharp fellow', and they became close friends. When the regiment was in Glasgow during the year of Peterloo, Havelock had his first 'action', escorting an arrested house-load of workers' delegates through a violent mob, while 'brick-bats, stones etc were flying among us, half as bad as grapeshot', as Smith assured his young subalterns.

Old Mr Havelock had been using his much reduced fortune to speculate in mortgages and life annuities through a firm in Burlington Gardens, Haward and Gibbs. In 1820, the firm failed and he was reduced almost to penury. He moved, with his two unmarried daughters, Helen and Jane, to live in genteel poverty at Teignmouth in Devon. For his sons the financial crash was disaster. Promotion depended almost entirely on purchase, no officer could live in England on his pay, and therefore their careers were, in Henry's word, 'blighted'. William, already with his extravagant tastes, heavily in debt, decided to exchange into a regiment serving in India, where active service might bring promotion without purchase. He sailed in 1821 with the 4th Hussars for Bombay. The next year their youngest brother, Charles Frederick, left for Bengal as a cornet of the 16th Lancers.

Henry also decided on India. But whereas William had no interest beyond soldiering and horses, Henry, characteristically, determined to equip himself by learning Persian, the language of government and diplomacy, and Hindustani, the hybrid of Hindi and Urdu which Europeans in India used for normal dealings with the natives. In October, he took extended leave, purchasing a half-pay lieutenancy, and enrolled at the Oriental Institute in Leicester Square under Professor Gilchrist, a fiery, avaricious, eccentric Scot and a rabid republican, but the best Hindustani pundit in London, who, a year later, passed him proficient 'with the O mark of a full *munshi*'. Havelock had heard that the 13th Foot[1] was about to be formed into a corps of light infantry in which his Rifle Brigade training would not be wasted, and was under orders for Bengal. He had already exchanged his half-pay for a full-pay lieutenancy, paying the difference, and now obtained an exchange into the 13th.

He fitted out in Regent Street with the scarlet coat with gold collar and wings, the dark grey close-fitting trousers and the tall shako, topped with the green ball, which was the regiment's uniform in all climates and weathers. On January 3rd 1823, after a brief Christmas with the family at Teignmouth, he embarked with the 13th Light Infantry at Gravesend, close to the luxurious home of his childhood, in the *General Kyd* Indiaman; an impecunious and rather dissatisfied lieutenant in his twenty-eighth year.

HAVELOCK, NOW THAT he had come to full manhood, was small but very erect, rather spare but with straight shoulders. His face, framed by luxuriant hair and whiskers, was long rather than oval, with a broad forehead, large and somewhat penetrating blue eyes, a nose more aristocratic than his lineage allowed, and a determined mouth. Despite an inward longing for affection, he was not easy to know, though amiable enough to acquaintances. His humour was gentle rather than boisterous, but he was quickly enraged, was very sure of his own opinions and would not brook contradiction. He was intensely ambitious, proud of his intellectual and literary interests, and scarcely concealed his contempt for the 'follies' on which his brothers (and many of his brother-officers) squandered their pay, and he could

---

[1]The Somerset Light Infantry, now the Light Infantry.

not suffer fools gladly. He made a fetish of punctuality and discipline.

As the *General Kyd* ran down the Channel and across the Bay, Havelock was able to gauge his new regiment. Half of the 13th, with Lieut-Colonel McCreagh, the Commanding Officer, was three days ahead in the *Kent*. His own contingent was under Major Robert Sale, second-in-command, a stocky, red-faced man in his early forties who had already seen much action in India and was a byword for courage, and whose bluff good-humour made him popular with officers and men.

Of those with whom he must be cooped for over five months in the confined space of an East Indiaman, Havelock was attracted most to a Lieutenant James Gardner, 'a humble, unpretending man', just twenty-one, whose quiet ways contrasted with the puerilities of some of the others. Through this unknown man Havelock made a decision which shaped and coloured his whole career.

They had not been long out when Gardner discovered Havelock's knowledge of Hindustani, and suggested that some of them should pass the time and improve their prospects by sitting at his feet. An officers' class was formed. With mock ceremony Havelock was installed as professor, and Gardner was amused to see how seriously he took his duties.

As the voyage lengthened and despite the disparity of age, their friendship deepened; Gardner and Havelock lent each other books. Gardner pressed on Havelock an appropriate book for a *munshi*, the life of Henry Martyn, the brilliant chaplain of the East India Company who had translated the New Testament into Persian and Hindi and the Prayer Book into Hindustani, and had died at the early age of thirty-one, only eleven years before. John Sargent's *Memoir of the Rev Henry Martyn* seemed particularly apposite, for in 1805, Martyn had sailed the seas they were now sailing, but in wartime convoy with the troops who were to capture the Cape before proceeding to India. Moreover, Martyn's early character 'would in the eyes of the world be con-

sidered to have been admirable and commendable. He was out-
wardly moral; was with little exception unwearied in application; and exhibited marks of no ordinary talent. One exception
to this statement is to be found in an irritability of temper...' It
might have been, Havelock thought, a pen portrait of himself.

Before he left Cambridge, Martyn had undergone a definite
'conversion' – a word Havelock had been taught to despise and
suspect. Martyn wrote of 'truly experiencing the love of God',
and referred to Christ in a curiously personal way. Havelock
read of Martyn's efforts to convert Indians to Christ despite the
settled opposition of the Company, and followed the story to its
end in the loneliness of an Armenian caravanserai, with Martyn's last entry in his journal a few days before death: 'I sat in
the orchard and thought with sweet comfort of the peace of my
God; in solitude my company, my friend and comforter...'

When asked about the book, Havelock admitted his interest
but rejected Martyn's doctrines. If Gardner supposed Havelock
to be as irreligious as most of their brother officers, he was
wrong; Havelock told him of his mother's Bible teaching and of
the surreptitious sermon reading at Charterhouse. He outlined
the conclusion to which his wide reading in philosophy had led
him, a nicely-ordered world in which man must aspire to the
highest, Christ was no more than the greatest human teacher,
and 'enthusiasm' or 'methodism' such as Martyn's, however
sincere and worthy, was false.

Gardner lent him another book, Thomas Scott's *The Force of
Truth*, a best-seller in excruciatingly small print in which the
great biblical commentator described his spiritual journey from
a position similar to that which Havelock held.

At first Havelock could read with detachment; Scott's character in youth had been unsavoury. The description of his ambition as a young clergyman was nearer the mark: 'I sat down',
ote Scott, 'to the study of such subjects as I considered most
'ful in order to lay the foundation of my future advance-
I was full of proud self-sufficiency.' He denied Christ's

divinity, even in the pulpit – and such denial made an easy doctrine, 'a soft pillow on which to lull myself to sleep'. Very slowly Scott was led by his neighbour John Newton, the hymn writer and ex-slave trader, whom Havelock could remember as an old man sometimes to be pointed out in the streets near Charterhouse, to see the emptiness of such typical eighteenth-century semi-paganism, and began to feel an 'anxious desire to know what it was to be "born again", or "born of the Spirit"'. Eventually, Scott realised without question that Christ was the Son of God, that in His great love He had died in the sinner's place so that the sinner might be freed from the penalty of his sin and able to stand, in Christ's name, unashamedly in the presence of a holy God. And that the risen Christ, alive and at work in the world, though invisible, could become the sinner's dearest, closest friend, making effective in his heart and character all that the sacrifice of the Cross had won. This was eternal life. To reject Christ was eternal death, in this world and the next. 'Thus has the Lord led me, a poor blind sinner, by a way that I knew not.'

Havelock was still not convinced that such an intimately personal faith was either necessary or desirable, and put his views vehemently as Gardner and he sat under the awnings in the tropical sun as the *General Kyd* neared the Line. Yet there was an inner sense, despite intellectual disbelief, that Gardner and Martyn and Scott were right; and that their faith would meet his deepest needs. He began to realise, as he put it, that the Spirit of God had come to him with His 'offer of peace and mandate of love'.

He let Gardner lead him through the relevant passages in the Bible, and at last reached conviction that Gardner was speaking truth. Convinced now with his mind, Havelock saw that a clear-cut decision of the will must be made. As he saw it, Christ had died for him on the Cross and now patiently sought admittance into his life. If he yielded, he must face the consequences – new aims and new responsibilities, a certainty of ridicule and a possibility of unfavourable discrimination. It was accepted belief, to which Havelock subscribed, that no one could be both a true soldier and a true Christian or, as he would have said until now, a 'methodist'. Yet if he did not yield, he would not know peace.

But the 'offer of peace and mandate of love, though for some time resisted, at length prevailed'. Writing in the third person over twenty-five years later Havelock could go on to say: 'then was wrought that great change in his soul which has been productive of unspeakable advantage to him in time, and he trusts has secured him happiness in eternity'. He was conscious at last of 'a dear and merciful Saviour', as he once described Him, 'who will never cease to be kind to those who come to Him in faith...'

THE 13TH LIGHT INFANTRY reached Calcutta in June 1823. The *General Kyd* made her way up the Hooghly river, through swamps and tiger-infested jungle, into the sudden beauty of Garden Reach with its mansions standing back from the shore, the river bending once again to bring her to the ghat a short distance below the ponderous mass of Fort William.

After over five months at sea India was enthralling, with noise and colour and innumerable servants making respectful salaams and unintentionally confusing their 'griffin' masters by shaking heads when a westerner would nod. But the 13th did not find Calcutta pleasant. They had arrived at the worst season with the heat at its highest, followed shortly by the rains which brought swarms of insects and made books and equipment mildewy and blistered. The perpetual damp which gave all but the best-kept houses a decayed and rotted look, the squalid streets in the native city, the sacred cows and Brahmini bulls rucking in the garbage, the whining beggars, formed a depressing backcloth to the discomforts of gastric disorders and prickly heat, that irritating rash so frequently brought on by close-fitting military tunics.

Soldiering at Fort William imposed few demands and leisure

was plentiful. Calcutta society spent much of its time in enormous meals and heavy drinking, regardless of the climate; books were scarce, polo was still unknown, tiger shooting in the hinterland was beyond the means of subalterns and there were few amusements except horse racing, a rather lewd theatre, and native girls, though the wilder young officers could run up heavy enough debts as Havelock was to discover to his cost a few years later.

Havelock now had better interests. His most interesting contact, as the months slipped by, was with William Carey and his missionary brotherhood at Serampore, the Danish enclave fourteen miles up the Hooghly from Calcutta which had received the missionaries when the East India Company would have none of them, some twenty years before. Havelock found himself welcome in the spacious college they had built, with its colonnaded porch and wide steps facing across the blue river, about as wide as the Thames by Greenwich, to the Governor-General's country palace at Barrackpore. Carey, although somewhat pacifist and in times of fever inclined to hallucinations of redcoats descending to hell, showed him his numerous translations of the Scriptures into Indian languages; Ward showed his printing press, and the Marshmans took him round their schools, the main school where European boys and girls were educated (one of the sources of funds for the missionary work) and the native day school in the town which was Mrs Marshman's own.

With the Marshmans he became close. Dr Marshman, once a weaver and later a schoolmaster in Bristol, was self-educated, brilliant and rough-grained. His wife, a competent woman of inexhaustible good humour, was house-mother to the whole community. Their eldest son, John Clark Marshman, a year older than Havelock, could give him the intellectual companionship which Gardner could not, for he was a historian and lawyer, a Chinese and Sanscrit scholar, a journalist who had founded and now owned and edited the *Friend of India*, most influential of Calcutta journals, and seemed to know everyone in the government. He was a Baptist, as were they all, but despite Havelock's prejudice against Dissent, so natural in that age, he found that a common faith made differences trivial. 'He is one of the kindest and best of men I have ever known,' was Havelock's considered verdict, 'and a most liberal, amusing, intelligent and useful man.'

Havelock spent weekend leaves at Serampore, stimulated by the missionaries' vision of a Christian India, and, as John Marshman could recall, 'he often entertained his friends by fighting over again, when the cloth was removed, the most memorable battles of Marlborough and Wellington, of Frederick the Second and Napoleon, calling up from his tenacious memory the strength and disposition of the different divisions, and tracing their evolutions on the table, till he came to the critical moment when the fortune of the day was decided by some masterly movement'. The Marshmans would amuse Havelock by reading out letters from their fourteen-year-old daughter Hannah, at school in England, a sprightly young miss who could not spell and whose escapades were a little too wild for a missionary's daughter.

Havelock came to the conclusion that he ought, in his own words, 'as a solemn Christian duty, to devote his time and attention to the spiritual welfare of his men'. The one chaplain on the station was responsible for the troops and all the European civilians, and his spiritual oversight could not be more than nominal.

Havelock decided to hold informal religious meetings for such men as were 'well disposed'. He would read to them from the Bible and lead them in prayers and the singing of hymns and psalms – an unprecedented step for an officer. His brother officers were appalled. They were convinced that even in Havelock's hands such proceedings would be subversive of discipline; Gardner himself had lacked courage to run so counter to accepted usage. He now, however, gave his support, and the meetings began.

But, still dreaming of generalship, Havelock pined for active service. In February 1824, rumours of troubles on the eastern frontier crystallised into a definite declaration of war against the King of Ava. The 13th were to form part of an expedition to seize Rangoon and penetrate Burma, an almost unknown country, and punish the King. Havelock was selected for the staff, a sure tribute to his efficiency, and appointed Deputy Assistant Adjutant-General to the force.

Gardner had been ill and could not go to the war. As Havelock left their 'chummery' for the last time he turned to him and said, 'Give me your hand. I owe you more than I owe any man living.'

2

The Court of Ava

Delayed by staff affairs and adverse winds, Havelock reached Rangoon a few days after its fall following a brief bombardment and a British landing without casualty. Since the King of Ava had conquered the area only recently and was hated, the Commander-in-Chief, Sir Archibald Campbell, had expected a ready welcome from the populace. But the Burmese had imposed a total evacuation and the city was empty. The troops saw grisly remains of recalcitrants who had been crucified naked with splints through their tongues, to die from the flies, ants and heat.

Havelock found Rangoon no worse than the dreariness of Calcutta, despite the ravages of the victorious troops who in a drunken orgy on the night of their arrival had burnt down much of the town. The poorer houses were 'raised on wooden piles, constructed chiefly of wood, and have roofs of thatch, tile or wood', so that the space underneath formed a 'receptacle of filth of every description and is selected by the dogs, cats, pigs and poultry as their favourite promenade'. The centre of Rangoon was protected by that peculiarly Burmese defence work, 'a stockade, as it is the fashion to call it', which Havelock thought was 'most like a park paling in England, forty or fifty feet in height and loopholed at the top, and fabricated by massive timbers instead of plank'.

Nearly forty ships rode at anchor alongside the town, including the redoubtable *Diana*, the first steamship ever to see active service, whose paddles and belching smoke had terrified the enemy more than the guns of the cruisers. The troops and staff had taken up quarters in houses and pagodas outside the town, on a hill which rose gently from clumps and groves of bamboo, acacia and fruit trees, and was topped by the massive gilded spire of the Shwe-dagon. The bells tinkling in the breeze made Havelock homesick for the downs and for 'flocks grazing in the thickets'. Inside the pagoda which housed the 13th someone had stuck the regimental colours into the arms of a large Buddha, cross-legged and serene, and the latest joke was 'to introduce you to the new ensign'. The Shwe-dagon itself, a wide platform of shade trees, temples and shrines dominated by the huge gilt pagoda which shimmered in the sun, was occupied by General Headquarters and Havelock's billet was in the deserted house of a Buddhist priest.

While the army was inactive except for outpost forays, the duties of Deputy Assistant Adjutant-General were not arduous, though Havelock and all but the very senior slept every night in their clothes. Off duty, Havelock sought out the two American missionaries, Wade and Hough, who had been rescued from beheading by the British bombardment and were now again in their home ('it would be called a shed in England') below the British positions on the hill of pagodas. Both were married, 'Mr Wade to an exceedingly pretty woman', and Havelock helped with the housekeeping by procuring passes for their servants. Their small flock had fled with the Burmans, and their leader, the great Adoniram Judson, had been caught up-country by the outbreak of war.

No chaplain had been attached to the force though nine English regiments were on the field, nor was one sent from start to finish of the two years' war. The missionaries did what they could. 'About thirty non-commissioned officers and privates and a few officers attend Divine Service at their house on Sunday mornings', wrote Havelock, and he also, though now on the staff, resumed his informal meetings with men of the 13th. On certain evenings, as the headquarters mess turned to cards or backgammon, Havelock would slip away to the side-temple which he had obtained permission to use, to find his men awaiting him. And thus another officer of the expedition once had an experience he never forgot: wandering in the precincts of the Shwe-dagon after dark he was astonished to hear the sound of distant psalm-singing. Tracing it through the warren of passages in the pagoda he found himself in an inner temple. Small Buddhas were ranged round the walls. On their laps were placed little oil lamps which threw shadows on to the gilded and carved ceilings. In the centre, the light flickering on scarlet uniforms, were a number of soldiers of the 13th standing in a circle singing a hymn, with Havelock at their head.

ON JUNE 10TH 1824, Havelock at last found himself in action. A force set out, three thousand strong, with ladders and howitzers and a flotilla to support them from the river, to capture the fortified village of Kemmendyne, two miles up river. Years later, with his incurable romanticism, Havelock described the thoughts of a novice awaiting baptism of fire: 'The ideas are wonderfully concentrated, and visions of glory and of slaughter, of distant home and its endearments, of duty sternly performed and nobly rewarded, of wounds, death – and of judgment, pass rapidly through the brain'. But if he had any such 'thrilling sensation' early on June 10th 1824 it must have soon evaporated as the force plodded and sweated through the steaming sludge, manhandling the guns, two miles in five hours. They came on a stockade, battered it with artillery and flung themselves on the remains. Havelock was with Sale, now commanding the 13th, who 'led his men most boldly and entered sword in hand, the very first man. The affair cost us fifty men.' They trudged on a further mile and bivouacked for the night not far from the main Burmese position, with rain pouring down and thunderstorms vying with bloodcurdling yells from the stockade. The next day, after further battering with artillery, they carried it in triumph, to find nothing but an old woman within.

After a month of further forays and heavy rain, Havelock, with most of the army, was down with disease. For weeks he lay in his bunk on the hill of pagodas, racked with pain, maddened by mosquitoes, feeling a revulsion to food and beset with that loneliness and depression which so often accompanies tropical illness. Evacuated to Calcutta, skilful treatment, and a long sea voyage to Bombay to visit his brothers, combined 'to repair the ravages of toil, care, famine and the fury of the elements upon this pygmy frame', as he wrote to Gardner now returned home.

In July 1825 he rejoined Campbell and his tattered, dirty but high-spirited army at Prome, two hundred and fifty miles up the Irrawaddy from Rangoon. Shortage of officers brought Havelock, in addition to his staff post, the command of a company of the 13th, now under Sale, and part of the division of Brigadier-General Willoughby Cotton. Cotton, a tubby officer of forty-two with whose career Havelock was to be closely linked, was an unusual character to be found serving in comparatively low rank in the India of the eighteen twenties. Of high birth, as a youth he had been a page to the Prince of Wales ('and was in truth,' said Havelock, 'rather an adroit courtier and clever man of the world') and after a dissolute period as a young guards officer, he had served as aide-de-camp to Sir Arthur Wellesley in the Peninsula. But something seldom hinted at had driven him east.

Havelock restarted his religious meetings, no longer in a pagoda, but in a hut on the banks of the Irrawaddy. His action surprised and annoyed some of his brother officers who did not think that such activities should be resumed so deep in enemy territory; he was also conscious of the jealousy of those who resented his reappointment to the staff.

In October negotiations for peace were followed promptly by a renewed Burmese advance, and by the third week of November, the troops in Prome, who not long since had believed the war to be victoriously over, knew that the enemy were slowly closing round in great numbers. Reconnaissance parties sent into the jungle reported stockades rising nearer every day, and stumbled on the disconcerting holes in which the Burmese skilfully entrenched themselves. Enemy forays were increasing. Bodies of sentries caught unawares would be discovered shockingly mutilated. Campbell found his men jittery and occasionally out of hand, and matters were not improved by the appearance of three wild prophetesses in the Burmese ranks, whose frenzied screams heard at night from the jungle were too eerie for joking. Nights and days were harassing.

It was then that an incident occurred which became something of a legend in the Army: an outpost was set on at night and a runner came back to headquarters for instant support and Campbell thereupon sent an orderly to the next company on the roster. The orderly reappeared with the company officer, who had to confess that half his men were drunk. Campbell swore roundly and turned to his aide-de-camp, 'Then call out Havelock's saints,' he roared, 'they are always sober and can be depended on and Havelock himself is always ready.'

Breaking out of Prome on December 1st, Campbell conducted a gruelling campaign in scorched country, with a British army dwindling daily through disease until, early in February 1826, the King of Ava sent his prisoners, Adoniram Judson and Dr Price, the American missionaries, to sue for peace, which was signed at Yandabo, forty-five miles south of the capital.

Campbell agreed not to bring his victorious army to Ava – to their disappointment, for it lost them the prospect of loot – but three commissioners were to proceed there to receive the King's cession of provinces and treasure. Campbell selected Captain Lumsden of the Horse Artillery, Staff-surgeon Knox, and Havelock.

EXCEPT FOR TWO brief visits by envoys and the more recent penetration of Judson and Price, no westerner other than a few luckless prisoners of war, had ever reached Ava. On historical grounds and from his interest in missionary work, Havelock was delighted to be setting out as one of the first Englishmen to meet the Burmese King, and he kept a journal of his experiences.

The three commissioners were rowed steadily through a pleasant countryside in Burmese warboats, the rhythmic splash of oars and the chant of the boatmen providing a drowsy background to the first rest they had had for weeks. When night fell they expected to be in Ava at first light but at four o'clock the next afternoon they had only reached Yapadaing, half way, where they were invited to land and treated with great ceremony, but their protests at delay politely brushed aside.

At sunset they believed they were near Ava, but it was not until nearly midnight that 'first the appearance of blazing lights and then of a vast collection of boats of every size moored along the bank', convinced them. The night was cold and, as they swept on, impenetrably dark. An uncanny silence surrounded them. They began to be impatient and when next they saw lights and heard voices the Englishmen stopped their boat and jumped ashore, finding a guardhouse where they were told that a deputation awaited them at a landing-place on a small tributary higher up. Returning to the boats, a quarter of an hour later, they saw 'by the light of numerous Chinese lanthorns the figures of Dr Price and thirty or forty Burmese in dresses which marked them as men of distinction'.

After the reception, they entered the silent city through a 'ponderous gate cased with iron' and the torches showed them a broad, clear street of wooden houses. They passed the dungeon where the missionaries had been confined and Price shuddered as he pointed out a grating over which victims were held for mutilation or execution. They reached the house of the Burmese noble who was to be their host to find a banquet, although it was already in the small hours. 'The dishes were numerous,' records Havelock, 'wines and liquors were produced in profusion. The guests were noisy and voracious, the host talking louder and more tediously than all the rest', while a crowd of attendants and spectators stood gaping at the English uniforms. The three men were glad to escape at last to their camp beds.

The next morning, March 1st, the Master of Ceremonies arrived and with 'the most scrupulous exactness' took down every conceivable item about them and settled points of etiquette. They formed up for the procession to the palace, but a messenger announced that the King had retired for a rest. Suppressing their vexation at 'this ill-bred trifling' one of them politely remarked that they could do with a sleep themselves 'and wished the monarch sound and peaceful slumbers'. They retired back to their room.

Late in the afternoon the King was ready and the procession reformed. By some miracle the two officers had preserved their full dress more or less intact and Lumsden appeared in the plumed helmet and laced jacket of the Horse Artillery and Havelock in his feathered hat and embroidered coat of the Adjutant-General's department. Knox was in plain clothes. As the procession moved through the streets the awed populace gasped at the white faces and strange uniforms and murmured, 'Kyet-toung-bo', 'Kyet-toung-bo' – 'Cockfeather Chieftain'. In front was the vast royal palace rising to a gilded spire.

'At length,' records Havelock, 'the moment of presentation arrived.' As they advanced, the gate swung silently open. They passed two further gates and 'then the full splendour of the golden place stood unveiled'. Colonnades of gold and scarlet pillars enclosed a great courtyard in which were drawn up four thousand guards in green war-jackets, with bayonets fixed on their muskets ('which is seldom seen in oriental armies', thought Havelock) and three large batteries of variegated guns. Beyond, a wide staircase led up to the palace, with the gold roof and spire 'glittering in the rays of the setting sun'. As the British walked forward, drums beat and cymbals clashed, together with 'the shrieking of pipes and the drowsy thrumming of a kind of guitar'.

They passed slowly up the staircase and removed their boots as arranged. They entered the grand gallery and a second band struck up, joined by the soprano voices of a hidden choir, while at either end 'a dancing girl richly attired and loaded with orna-

ments was displaying her fascinations'. Now they were in the
throne room, a shimmering haze of white and gold, filled with
the princes and chivalry of Burma ('they were all coarse-fea-
tured men with an unpleasing expression of countenance'). The
throne – a bare platform railed with gold, immediately beneath
the spire – was empty.

The music ceased. Buddhist priests entered and chanted a
hymn in praise of the King, and every time they cried 'Phra!
Phra!' the whole assembly except the three Britons sitting at the
end of the hall, opposite the throne, bent their bodies to the
ground. The chant ceased and a long silence ensued. Every
Burmese head was touching the ground. 'The whole assembly
seemed spellbound with servile awe', was the contemptuous
impression of the subjects of George IV. The fluttering of sacred birds in the rafters made the only sound or movement.

Suddenly the gilded panels behind the throne flew open 'with
a thrilling crash'. The bodies sank deeper and a murmuring
'Phra! Phra!' rose from the assembly. Craning forward, Havelock
saw a figure rising from below, beyond the throne. 'In a moment it had mounted the platform' and came forward, the royal
footsteps distinct in the silence. The King, noted Havelock, 'was
of middle stature. His head was bound with a plain and slight
fillet of white. His hair and beard were sandy, he wore no mous-
taches. He had on a vest of white muslin, and a loongee of variegated silk, in which bright red was the predominating colour.
Around his neck was the golden tsalo of twenty-four small
chains, a large jewel appended to it rested on his breast. His legs
were bare, his feet shod with scarlet sandals.' Across his chest
he held a heavy gold-sheathed sword. And, not unnaturally in
the circumstances, he looked sulky. 'Suddenly he stopped, bent
both knees mechanically and sunk at once on to a cushion, sitting with folded legs.' Havelock was quite surprised at the speed
of the movement.

A slave crept forward and placed a betel-box in the royal
reach. The British officers bowed their heads three times. The

Master of Ceremonies made a formal speech, during which the King indulged 'in a long stare of uncontrollable curiosity'. Captain Lumsden formally asked for ratification and was given it with expressions of gratification which no one believed. Compliments were exchanged and trays of sweetmeats placed before the British while the King sat immobile. A fresh set of trays arrived, each officer receiving a roll of silk and a gold ring set with a large ruby; Havelock lost his stone at Rangoon on the return.

Then the Commissioners were created nobles of Ava. A Burmese officer came forward and placed on their foreheads a fillet of gold leaf, inscribed in Burmese characters. As each was invested, the Master of Ceremonies proclaimed his title, which they were told meant 'Valorous Renowned Rajah'. And there they sat, the trays of presents and sweetmeats before them and their foreheads bound with gold leaf.

A bare quarter of an hour passed. As Havelock watched, the King, now formally bereft of seven provinces and a crore of rupees, 'sprung suddenly upon his feet with remarkable agility, faced about, stalked with much dignity to the head of the concealed staircase, fronted, gazed steadily for a few seconds upon the scene, then faced about again.

'And as he descended in the midst of the same reverential silence which had marked his appearance, the panels closed again with a mystic sound.'

3

Hannah

On June 13th 1828 the thirty-three-year-old Lieutenant Henry Havelock, Adjutant of the Royal Depot at Chinsura on the Hooghly, twenty-five miles above Calcutta, author of a highly competent, commercially unsuccessful and, from the viewpoint of frowsty superiors, somewhat impudent book on the recent campaign in Burma, wrote a letter to young Miss Hannah Marshman, aged nineteen, fresh and bright from England.

His constant visits to Serampore, a dozen miles off, had swept his heart away. In the second week of June, he had twice gone there with a purpose, but, twice by accident, Hannah had been absent. And so now he wrote a letter beginning, 'Dear Miss Hannah Marshman', in which he declared in a sentence of some eighty words, 'the sentiments of very great regard which I have learned to entertain for you...' 'After this declaration declared in so long a sentence,' he continued, 'I might perhaps be permitted to pause a while; but I cannot help further adverting to the very great satisfaction it would give me to believe that I was fortunate enough to have secured ever so small a portion of your esteem...'

He sealed and despatched this letter with a covering note to Mrs Marshman, from whom he was confident of support, and waited impatiently for a week. In reply, he received from Miss Hannah a note, 'short and penned in a spirit of *very exemplary caution*', but sufficient to give 'much encouragement and consolation'. Mrs Marshman also wrote encouragingly, but referred to his poverty and said she could not allow a definite engagement until Dr Marshman returned from Europe in the cold weather. Havelock thought this 'a little cruel' and wondered why John Marshman could not act on his father's behalf.

The following weekend Havelock was able to get down to Serampore and knew without a shadow of a doubt that his love was fully returned and that whatever Dr Marshman might say, the family looked on the two as engaged. 'I would not exchange for half the years which I have lived, the evening of Sunday last', he wrote to Hannah, when he had returned to his damp and lonely bungalow at Chinsura. 'It is necessary that you should first have seen and felt all the calamity and vicissitude which I had witnessed; and been conversant as I have been with jealousy, calumny, strife, debate and turmoil before you could comprehend as I did in that happy hour, the joy of having peace and consolation and love spoken to me by one nurtured in the purest piety, and of feeling that the affection and fidelity which was then promised me was not that which could cease with time but such as would survive and continue to bless on into eternity.'

Hannah was all for their marrying without waiting for Papa's return, but Havelock recognised that this was unseemly. Nor would Mrs Marshman allow it.

The pains of Burma were now catching him up again and constant depressing liver attacks combined with 'a fever of petty avocations' to damp his elation; 'a wrinkled, careworn, crazy-looking grey headed little man' was his self-description to Hannah. One delay after another prevented a fresh visit to Serampore, and for the rest of July they had to make do with letters. A further attempt to get the date settled was firmly snubbed by Mrs Marshman and by John, who added insult to injury by announcing the date of his own wedding.

To make matters worse, early in August Havelock had 'letters from another part of India of so distressing a character as really to unfit me for everything. I have been acting, writing and trying to think with my thoughts wandering from the subject and full of bitterness and distress.' The trouble was his younger brother. His elder brother Will, having horsewhipped a brother officer, had been dismissed from the service and had gone home with his newly-wedded wife, 'a very sweet creature'. But if Will was in disgrace, Charles was in debt, so hopelessly that bankruptcy and the loss of his commission seemed inevitable. He had won more prize money in Combermere's brief campaign at Bhurtpore than Havelock in two years of Burma, but like so many other young officers in India, the money slipped through his fingers. And now, faced with ruin, he besought the aid of Henry.

After a week of worry, Havelock was able to act. 'I am to leave for Calcutta as soon as the tide turns', he wrote to Hannah by express messenger on the morning of August 12th, 'to try to extricate my younger brother from the hands of the Jews. You will believe that this is not the most pleasant undertaking in the world; but if you knew the young chevalier for whom I am undergoing the task you would think him worth the effort, for he is a gallant and gay young cavalier; as different therefore as can be imagined from your future lord and master.' His budgerow would pause at Serampore and Hannah was to be on the ghat so that Havelock could 'gaze two whole minutes on those little lips of coral. I know I must not touch them, such being contrary to the canons of Serampore.' But it was after dark when he reached her so that they were able, after all, to kiss; for the next day he was writing from Calcutta, 'What a morning I have spent among Jews and Gentiles, 10% and life insurances! Nobody however spoke of a *love* insurance; and if they had I would not have effected it, seeing that I carried it away with me last night signed, sealed and attested; yes! sealed with that *coral* seal which is to me more precious than diamonds.'

On the way back Havelock was able to spend several days at Serampore. Whenever he was with Hannah his tendency to depression was blown away by her gay bantering. 'So your mother thinks you were really too severe upon me,' wrote Havelock, a few days after he had again left her, 'and that I must be furiously enraged at your sarcasms. I am shocked that she does not know that if I am kept clear of soldiers and Hindustani domestics, I am in all other relations of life the most patient, clement, sweetly merciful and enduring personage in existence. There is not an instance on record of my having been angry with anyone of higher rank than a sergeant or a servant,[1] and as for taking offence at witticisms they are the things of all others which I dearly love, and I take no exception against them whatever because they happen to be pointed against myself. Besides, whatever you may venture to write, I at least have the power to close the *lips* of such little satirists as you, rosy though they be.'

Hannah could talk religion also, but he was too blind with love to realise that she was, in fact, dissembling.

Late rains and an attack of toothache made the last week of August dismal to a lover who was still not allowed to name the day. 'No papa yet – nor any letter or news of him? How slowly these ships sail, wafted slowly or delayed by pitiless breezes and steered by men who never loved anybody but themselves.' Charles' difficulties continued, though the worst seemed averted. 'I had sad sacrifices to make to assist him,' Havelock told Hannah, 'but he is young, and has given up all his extravagant habits, so that from a brother the best efforts were due.' Charles knew too well the way to Henry's heart.

The weeks dragged by. 'Everything here is damp and dull as ever,' he wrote, 'send me a letter full of smiles, consolation and content. We have after all many sources of happiness: hope, trust in God, love, mutual and unalterable, consciences not void of offence, but lightened and brightened by the merits of a Redeemer.' Hannah complied, and also hopefully sent a prescription, with unfortunate results. 'You are the best of young gentlewomen,' wrote her betrothed, 'but the very worst of physicians. I think your prescription would kill me in a lunar month or thereabouts.'

On October 17th Havelock attended John Marshman's wedding, though far from well and rather sore that Hannah and he were still in suspense. A fortnight later his misery was intense.

---

[1] He actually used a Hindustani word, but what he called 'my villainous autograph' is quite illegible at this point.

'Medicine scarcely seems to promise me any relief, and corporal uneasiness is accompanied by a daily increasing dislike and distaste for company or conversation. Fortunately I am not severely tempted in either point having next to nothing to do, and few persons to intrude upon my solitude in which alone I find a release from weariness and disgust. This is not despondency for my mind rises fully above the many vexations I have to encumber and dread; but it is physical depression acting with uncontrollable power on the spirits.'

But the nadir was passed. By November 12th he was physically better. And a few days later, Dr Marshman being indefinitely delayed at sea, Mrs Marshman at last allowed John to act as head of the family and give consent to the match.

AT SERAMPORE, THAT November, occurred an event which was to ensure the very depth and height of future happiness. Hannah sat down at her table and put her thoughts in a letter which she then sent across to her mother's room. 'My beloved Mama,' she wrote, 'I fear you have been grieved too frequently at my silence on the subject of religion. But since you last spoke to me, I have acquired the courage which I had not known before and I declare that throughout this year I have felt and suffered more than I can describe on account of my alienation from God. The Bible has afforded and continues to afford me peculiar satisfaction. And though many of its truths are not less awful than correct they have not deterred me from seeking the Saviour, and I am sure it will give you pleasure to know that your *example* has caused me to put my trust in Him, to fly to Him, and to believe that if I seek Him with my whole heart He will be found. In comparison with the future I have not yet suffered one hardship, not one bereavement, not one denial of a single comfort; and if I do not now choose God for my friend when my hour of distress is come I shall find it a hard struggle to pass through it, without any other than human support.' As a Baptist, Hannah had not yet been baptised, having not made open profession of faith.

Now, before marriage, it was her 'earnest and most particular desire to come forward and dedicate myself to Christ and in His name to be baptised... Though I have so long neglected His call of mercy I pray that I may not be cast off.'

To the missionaries at Serampore the most vital matter was not baptism (by immersion) but the trust in Christ and the cleansing and rebirth of which baptism was a symbol. Havelock, though a member of the Established Church, found fullest Christian fellowship among them. For some years he had been drawn increasingly towards their denomination. Whenever he met Baptists, ordained or lay, they were thoroughgoing Christians; but regrettably the majority even of the few chaplains of the Church of England in the Company's service, with some notable exceptions, were not ornaments to their faith. In Burma Havelock had discussed matters with Adoniram Judson, a Baptist, though not by birth, but it was not until his engagement that the matter came forward seriously. John Marshman claimed in his *Memoir* of his brother-in-law that when Havelock raised the question at Serampore, 'it was the only topic on which his friends were unwilling to enter', since their mission was to the heathen and not to convert Christians to their sectarian views. In December 1828, however, they were at it hammer and tongs. 'You and he,' Havelock was writing to Hannah, 'both fight for the Front Parlour[1] with all the zeal of anti-episcopalians. Nevertheless, do not take it unkindly that I ask to be permitted to take the opinion of one person before I give up the Cathedral.' At length, early in 1829, he parted with the Church of England and was re-baptised by John Mack, the Serampore chaplain. Such was the feeling against Dissent that several of Havelock's Anglican friends henceforth abjured him. Yet denominational loyalties, the 'husks and shells of creed' never came before what

[1]The front parlour of Carey's original house at Serampore had been turned into the chapel, the vestry being the room where his mad first wife had been confined, raving and moaning.

he called 'the precious kernel' of sincere faith in Christ.[1] If a man had in him 'the root of the matter' Havelock called him brother and was prepared to 'fraternise with every Christian who held by the Head and was serving the Redeemer in sincerity and truth'. Hannah even thought at one time years later, though quite wrongly, that he was contemplating return to the Established Church.

THE DATE OF the wedding was fixed for January 19th 1829. 'I cannot tell you how much happier I am since something definite has been arranged,' Havelock told Hannah, 'but when I look round my humble position here, and my gloomy dwelling, uninfluential situation in the world, poverty and shattered health, I almost tremble.' Hannah wanted his portrait. 'As you have not the remotest chance,' he replied, 'of ever being permitted to take your own way after your union with so absolute a person as myself, so it would seem hardly more than fair to let you choose your own course for this once before it.' And the portrait was done.

Ill health struck again late in December – 'a beautifully swelled face from cold, which renders me peculiarly amiable in look and temper', and pains in the right side which would not yield to treatment. The day was postponed three weeks, being fixed finally for Wednesday, February 4th 1829. As it approached, the affair of the improvident and impenitent Charles loomed large again, and with it an awful possibility. Havelock, with John Marshman to assist, struggled with the moneylenders of Calcutta in the last week of January. On Monday, February 2nd, he wrote to Hannah, 'Pray without ceasing for me until we meet, for I am full of care.' On Tuesday evening he reached Serampore, staying at the hotel. The news he dreaded followed him and he was forced to postpone the ceremony indefinitely and take boat for Calcutta.

---

[1] Which is one reason why an Anglican is happy to write his life.

Two days of suspense, and late on Friday evening, instead of her betrothed, Hannah received a letter, written from the nearby hotel. 'My dearest Hannah,' began the familiar scrawl, 'I sit down with a heavy heart just quietly to explain that we, that is you and I – are ruined.'

Picking her way through the crossings-out, Hannah learned that Havelock had 'after all in every probability to be answerable for the whole of the sum to be made up to my brother's creditors, which will swallow up every rupee I possess in the world.' An expected additional post at Chinsura, with its emolument, was going to another. 'Thus I shall find myself at the outset in debt, a debt which must be increased before we can be established with any comfort; and this while my health is daily declining.'

There was only one thing she could do, he said, 'Loving me as you do, you ought to make an effort, perhaps more than can be expected from a female heart; you ought even at this late and delicate moment, to sacrifice every feeling to the calculation of necessity – and to save us both from interminable miseries; consent to dissever the obligation that binds us. But if you cannot do this it shall never be said of one of my name that he performed less than his promise. I will make the vows which I have engaged to make, and pray to heaven for grace to keep them; but I shall do so knowing that I seal the misery of two persons. But if you have the magnanimity to make this sacrifice then I ask no promise from you, but solemnly vow never to be united or seek to unite myself to any other. The last words of love I shall ever speak have already passed my lips. Henceforth I abandon myself without a murmur to my solitary lot, only let me be spared scenes, in which I might make shipwreck of my honour...

'Now decide quickly – let me receive your answer before midnight. Will you be a happy, free and tranquil girl or a wretched, ruined wife? Let at least no consideration of what the world may say affect your decision. It has said what it pleased of me for thirty-four years and so long as there has been no upbraiding within I have found its censures wholly innocuous... Decide quickly, and may God direct your heart to the decision which shall truly tend to your happiness and peace.'

Whether Hannah flung on her wrap and hurried round to the hotel, or whether it was too late for a European girl to venture on the streets and she had to make do with a note until morning, is not revealed. But there was only one answer to give.

The weekend was on them. The ceremony was fixed at last for the Monday, February 9th. Yet still there was an obstruction. An order arrived for Havelock to serve on a Court Martial at Fort William at midday on Monday. Havelock said that he must obey it. The Marshmans argued that his own wedding was surely sufficient excuse and that no other officer would think twice about it, but Havelock insisted that as a soldier he was 'bound to obey orders, regardless of his own convenience'.

They were therefore married first thing in the morning at the Danish Church, with its royal monogram above the portico and its slightly incongruous spire added at the expense of Lord Wellesley, who had said that the view across the river from Barrackpore would remind him of an English village. From the ceremony the bridegroom sped down the blue Hooghly to the Court; and returned to his bride and the long-suffering guests in the afternoon.

4

Havelock's Saints

Their third wedding day found Havelock and Hannah on the River Jumna approaching Agra on the north-west frontier of the Presidency. With them were their little boy Harry and the baby, Joshua, born on the river six weeks earlier; Toy their dog; Lucy, Hannah's Indian Christian maid from Serampore and Nance the ayah, another Christian convert; and Seib the bearer, a south country Muslim who ate opium on the sly. That day they saw the Taj Mahal for the first time. 'We saw it in the morning at the distance of eight miles, like a white cloud, and as we approached the sight became more and more imposing.' As they turned the final bend the Taj was in full beauty, set off by the great red fort in the background to the right and the melons growing on the sandbanks below.

Havelock had rejoined the 13th Light Infantry, on the extinction of the Chinsura depot in 1831, at Dinapore in Bihar, an isolated cantonment on the Ganges. Hannah had hated it. 'I was never in a duller and more stupid place than Dinapore,' she had written to her sister Rachel, 'and if it were not for the real pleasures that my own home affords me I dare say I should exceedingly regret the want of such gaieties as are absent here.' There was nothing to do but call and be called on, or to drive out in the evenings under the mango trees in which parakeets fluttered or to picnic on Ganges bank and watch the heavy-laden barges sailing down the wide river or returning empty, towed by coolies. The one occasional consolation was a fleeting glimpse, when the rains had settled the dust and the weather was clear, of the far-away snow-covered Himalayas.

All this had changed when a few months later the regiment

was ordered to Agra. They had left in pouring rain on December 1st. Nearing Benares, half-burned bodies floated by, and as the transports sailed opposite the teeming waterfront, Hannah and Havelock could see the thraldom from which Serampore and others were working to release the land. No widows were burning alive for Suttee had been outlawed two years earlier, but scores of pilgrims were bathing in the sacred river and a noisy, tight-packed mass crowded the ghats, with here and there the wide coloured umbrellas under which priests painted worship marks on devotees; behind, an imposing backcloth, rose the temples of the gods and the minarets of Moghul mosques.

Near Chunar, Joshua was born, and so at last they came to Agra. The Havelocks found 'a very large bungalow' still under repair by the new owner who had let it to them. The tall rooms, each opening out of the other, were arranged round 'a long stone chamber built for a mussulman tomb. It has an arched roof and much filigree work.' On one side was waste land and on the other the garden, at present 'in confusion' but with apples and peaches coming into blossom as the days warmed up.

Scarcely was the regiment in quarters than the Governor-General, Lord William Bentinck, arrived to receive the independent Rajah Scindia of Gwalior. The two camps scattered themselves on the plain between the fort and the Taj, the red stone pavilions in the Taj being used as banqueting and audience hall. 'Henry is dining with the Governor-General', Hannah wrote home on March 15th. 'He arrived here yesterday and held a levée and the ladies' drawing rooms. I wished much to have been presented but it was not possible as they are so far off that I must have been absent for four or five hours and I could not leave my little Jos for half so long a period. For the same reason I have not been able to go to the dinner party.'

She did, however, get a view of the Mahratta irregular horse which accompanied Scindia, 'their riders most singularly accoutred with matchlocks and spears; on their head, a small helmet of steel, on their feet native shoes, a Korch (?) for a whip, and patches of red and yellow cloth made into saddle and bridle, and in this loose way they ride like wildfire and accomplish such feats'.

They were at Agra four years. Their home was renowned throughout the cantonment for happiness. Havelock's despondencies had blown away and his physical condition improved under the influence of Hannah's 'kind heart, on which I entirely rely for affection and sympathy in every circumstance and condition of life'. There was no question who wore the breeches. Hannah was fourteen years younger than her husband and without a tithe of his brains. Despite the difficulties of Havelock's work the days passed in a whirl of delight. 'We are all happy together', Hannah wrote to Serampore.

Each day began with family prayers, by no means yet common even in England, and on one such occasion an Irish servant, daughter of one of the men in the regiment, provided a tale long current. Havelock's extempore prayer had reduced the girl to tears, and as she rose from her knees she blurted out, 'Oh, Misther dear, you're not fit for a soldier. It's too tinderhearted you are. Sure you was born a praist, and a praist it is you ought to be.'

Havelock would be back for tiffin after which Hannah rested and would then play with her children, watch the *mali* watering their little lawn, or receive or pay calls. In the evening, in the short cool hour before dark, 'Henry gives me such nice long drives'. Sometimes he would sit with her in the carriage, more often he rode alongside. Leaving their bungalow, bright with bougainvillea, they trotted down the wide Mall greeting their friends; or, lords of the land, made way for with salaams, went to the caravanserai to see the camel trains in from the north, though here the beggars were tiresome. The spacious Mahratta fort with its ivory palaces and view of the Taj, pink in the setting sun, made a pleasant stroll. They often visited the Taj, especially in moonlight, the marble still warm from the heat of the day.

Sometimes they went to the bazaar – also best seen at night, but not for a European woman. Leaving the carriage, they walked up the noisy narrow street lined with booths, the roof-tops almost touching above. Avoiding a rolling beggar as he came down the slope (gaining merit) they stopped to watch the famous marble-workers before calling at a silk seller's booth where Hannah fingered the fine gay-coloured stuffs, leisurely displayed before her, heedless of the crowd of staring urchins. Then they admired a sweating craftsman rhythmically beating out long strips of toffee, and next bought some of Agra's succulent *pethe*, the vegetable-marrow candy, before rejoining the carriage.

Hannah was friends with all her neighbours. 'Mrs Colonel Sale who has a splendid garden sends me every morning a beautiful bouquet of flowers, large enough for two flower-pots. And Mrs Stehelin, my old friend with the yellow bonnet, sends me very very often a quantity of fresh-made butter and new-laid eggs. Others send me books and others send me a dolly...'

WITH THIS BACKGROUND of domestic happiness, Havelock, though a mere subaltern again, was working far harder than most, and for a definite purpose: 'It was the great object of my ambition to be surpassed by none in zeal and determination in the path of my duty, because I was resolved to put down the vile calumny that a Christian could not be a meritorious soldier.'

The 13th Light Infantry was made up of drafts typical of the recruits which England despatched to the East – the refuse of London streets and jails. When Havelock had first rejoined, indiscipline was rife, officers were stabbed and Sale was once shot at. Again and again the regiment would attend punishment parade to see a man strapped to the triangle, naked to the waist, to receive two or three hundred lashes. Sale won through and by the time they reached Agra the 13th were reported by the divisional general 'one of the finest corps I have seen in India; and its very high state of discipline does great credit to the zeal and ability of its commanding officer'.

Off duty the men were treated as in any other regiment – serfs to be fed and housed, but not otherwise the responsibility of their officers. In the hot weather, parades were early in the morning and in the evening. During the heat of the day from nine to five, the unmarried men were confined to their barrack rooms and verandas with nothing to do, most not even knowing how to read.

Liquor was cheap and plentiful, and though the ration in the canteen was strong enough more could be obtained from native vendors or unscrupulous sergeants' wives, drunkenness thus being the commonest crime. When not drinking, many would wander into the bazaar to frequent the houses of ill-fame where low-caste women were ready to satisfy the lusts of men whose blood was stirred by the warm climate. The policy of placing in one barrack room men of varying ages and service made it difficult for a young soldier to retain any high ideals. As a private of the 13th wrote a few years later, 'In many instances the lips of sergeant and private teemed alike with pollution, and their horrible oaths and execrations coupled with expressions of obscenity pained my ears tenfold more than the shrill screaming of the troops of jackals that came nightly from the graves and tombs to prey upon the offal of the camp.' There was one custom which inevitably degraded. Every week the doctor went the rounds of the barrack rooms and held an inspection for venereal disease, mere lads and hardened lechers alike parading stripped, each being examined in the frankest manner in sight of the rest.

With men under such conditions Havelock re-started his Bible meeting. A few survived of his earlier group, the chief being a sergeant, George Godfrey. Not unnaturally Godfrey and his fellows followed their leader into Baptist allegiance, and at Dinapore they had built a makeshift chapel. At Agra, Havelock decided on a more permanent structure, and Godfrey 'collected a great deal of money for the new chapel from officers and men of the 13th and residents' while Havelock endowed it by buying land at Chitaurah, twenty miles away, which he cleared with convict labour borrowed from the magistrate, and then leased.[1]

The small group of thoroughgoing Christians met daily for hymn-singing, Bible-reading and prayer. The chapel also provided an opportunity, not then otherwise allowed for in a military cantonment, of 'small places for retirement for private devotion, to which many resort', as Havelock wrote to Dr Marshman in Serampore. On Sundays, after the men had attended the obligatory parade service, 'there is public worship before noon, and in the evening. I think', continued Havelock, 'the congregation on the latter occasion fluctuates between fifty and sixty, sometimes the frequenters of this chapel are reckoned among the best behaved men in the regiment.'

Havelock was content for a while to read a printed sermon of some contemporary divine, but this seemed 'a spiritless action, which does not move and awaken as does the declaration of his own views in an address indited by the speaker', and he began to write and read out his own sermons – a clear break of the stiffly regulated conventions of the early nineteenth century. He found that 'the men listen gladly', and Dr Marshman encouraged him to continue. Marshman even approved his administering the Sacrament to those who scrupled to attend the Church of England, until the arrival at Agra of a Baptist padre, a Reverend Mr Grayson – who, so Hannah wrote, 'though a very good man, wants a label round his neck marked "To be well shaken", and always looked moreover as if he had just heard a thunderclap'. Grayson was a member of the Baptist Missionary Society; as an officer of the *raj* it was almost impossible for Havelock to do any direct missionary work, but he proved his love of India by good treatment of his servants, by encouragement of men such as Grayson, and by unstinting gifts, year by year, to Serampore and other missionary work.

His personal efforts were limited to his soldiers. And thus

---

[1] It is still the property of the Baptist Missionary Society. The chapel is now known as Havelock's Chapel.

young men who had almost forgotten childhood attendance in an English country church, or who since earliest days in slum streets had never had the chance of hearing the Christian gospel, would risk the ribaldry of their friends and take a seat at the back of the chapel on a Sunday evening.

The palm-mats were rolled up and the room open to the hot still air. Round the walls vegetable-oil lamps guttered and flickered. The singing and prayers done, the men sat stiff and erect. Havelock spoke. He knew what they needed, and told them in clipped, simple phrases: 'Time is short, and eternity at hand,' he would begin, and the men remembered the dozen or more of their comrades buried in the past six or nine months, 'so I must not delay to speak to you on the most important of all subjects – the care and prospects of your immortal souls. Do not suffer yourself to be deceived by the false names which men give to things; but look steadily at the abiding truth, that mankind are divided into two classes – the children of God, and the servants of the world and its prince Satan. Make at once your choice for that good part which shall not hereafter be taken from you. Come to the Lord Jesus Christ, and ask Him for instruction and enlightenment of mind, and change of heart; and then do all that He commands you, and you shall be happy for ever... Learn to regard Jesus Christ as personally your Friend and Benefactor, to come to Him for all that you need, to feel assured that all your sins are laid on Him...'

When the service was over he would, if a man so desired, speak with him individually, showing from his Bible the way in which he might 'have Jesus for your Friend'. For those moments the relationship of officer and ranker was forgotten, to be resumed inexorably when they left the chapel.

HAVELOCK'S CONSTANT WORK in spare time was costly for his wife, who once remarked to her mother that 'Henry is at his office all the morning and I do enjoy his society so much when he comes home that I am quite jealous of the time he spends among his soldiers'. But she gave him all support in her power, starting a Sunday School for the regiment's children, teaching the men to read, and encouraging Havelock when his chapel was the target of violent criticism. 'I trust,' she wrote, 'that my dear Henry will be spared to continue to use all his efforts to be useful to the soldier, among whom he is greatly beloved.'

All this voluntary service for the welfare of his men was done, so Havelock wrote, 'in the very teeth of ridicule and opposition'. Officers of the 13th, though acknowledging Havelock pleasant enough a man with a good record of soldiering, considered that he was making himself ridiculous. Nor did criticism come only from the empty-headed topers such as were to be found in every mess at a time when the only antidote for heat and boredom was believed to be brandy. The gossip went round and round and when, in their absence, officers and their wives were discussing the Havelocks, they were able as so often in religious controversies to summon considerable moral indignation: Havelock did not receive pay in order to interfere with the private lives of the men – his constant consorting with them was bound to subvert discipline and put notions in their heads – he demeaned himself by social intercourse with his inferiors – for a King's officer not to belong to the Established Church smacked of disloyalty; and as for a layman preaching and conducting services, it was thoroughly unseemly. He should stick to the work for which he was paid, and leave the men to see to their own amusements. And thus a course of action which to later generations appeared commendable, was criticised in the pioneer.

One couple alone stood quietly for Havelock – Robert Sale the commanding officer, and Florentia his masterful and determined wife. Sale, indeed, though not following Havelock in all things was thoroughly content with him, as he showed on one occasion in no uncertain manner. When Havelock once was ill, a 'saint', one of his own company, was reported drunk, to the merriment and jubilation of the critics. On return to duty Havelock demanded an investigation before the Commanding

Officer. His man was produced and he had no difficulty in proving that the defaulter was of the same name in another company. The accusers thereupon shifted their ground and illogically complained that the fellow was a Baptist anyway, at which Sale lost his temper, thumped the table (the story was told all over India) and exclaimed, 'Baptists! Baptists! I know nothing about Baptists. But I know that I wish the whole regiment were Baptists. Their names are never in the defaulters' roll and they are never in the congee-house.'[1]

WHILE AT AGRA, Havelock took a step which had far-reaching results. He and his men had chafed at the compulsory Church parades which, by the Articles of War, Roman Catholics were excused while Dissenters were not. In October 1832 Havelock drew up a Memorial to the Commander-in-Chief at the Horse Guards petitioning that the liberty accorded Roman Catholics in the Army be extended to Dissenters. Sale forwarded the Memorial to the Governor-General and in due course it reached London and for seven years filtered through the appropriate channels until in July 1839 Havelock's request led to liberty of worship for the whole British Army.

Shortly after the despatch of the Memorial the 13th went under canvas to escort the Governor-General on a state visit to Gwalior, some seventy miles away. 'The 13th are to escort his lordship to Gwalior as there is much to be feared from the Mahrattas,' Hannah told Rachel. 'They will be away about a month and as I shall not find it pleasant to be left here along with my boys, for the jungles are infested with dacoits who are kept in check only by the soldiers, I am persuading Henry to take me with him.' A surprise was in store. Lady William Bentinck, who knew the missionaries at Serampore and whose husband gave them more support than previous Governor-Generals, attached Hannah to her suite as interpreter. By easy

---

[1] Indian army slang for the cells.

stages camp and escort marched from the plain and across the rough country of the River Chambal, until the long flat-topped sandstone ridge of Gwalior Fort came in sight, dominating the landscape. The Bible meetings continued regularly, in a tent or under a tree. Bentinck, whose reforming zeal had been intrigued by Havelock's Dissenters Memorial talked with him on occasions, and when a deputation from the Kingdom of Ava which had hopefully tracked the Governor-General all the way from Calcutta was received with pomp and a deliberate display of military power, Havelock was by the Governor-General's side to renew acquaintance with his fellow 'valorous renowned rajahs'.

Not long afterwards the Adjutancy of the 13th fell vacant and Havelock applied. He knew the opposition he had aroused and had little hope of the post. He was nearly forty and still a lieutenant. Whenever a vacancy had occurred Havelock had been unable to raise the money and had been passed over – 'by three sots and two fools'. Only vacancy by death or by an increase of establishment, highly improbable, would give him promotion without purchase, and an attempt to purchase with money loaned by Marshman had been thwarted by the Calcutta commercial crisis. Havelock had taken a temporary post as interpreter with a regiment at Cawnpore in order to provide for his growing family.

Hannah was down at Serampore where she had taken their third son, a sickly infant, in the vain hope of saving his life. Hearing of the Adjutancy she determined to take matters into her own hands.

She sat down at her bureau, boldly wrote a letter to Lord William Bentinck and sent it to Barrackpore. Shortly afterwards a red and gold liveried servant called at the mission house with a request from Lord William that Hannah should do him the goodness to call. She stepped into the Governor-General's barge and was carried swiftly across the river to the fine park with its zoo and artificial hills.

Lady William Bentinck received her. They sat in the wide windows looking over to Serampore, the portico of the college clearly visible and the spire of the church where the Havelocks were married peeping above the trees, and talked merrily about old times in Gwalior. Lord William entered, smiling, and carrying a bundle of letters. 'About that letter you wrote me, madam,' he began, 'I am going to read you a few other letters I have received on the subject from your husband's regiment.' Hannah was all of a flutter. Lord William said, 'Before I allude to this correspondence I give you the assurance that I have bestowed the Adjutancy of the 13th on your husband because he is unquestionably the fittest man for it.'

Hannah subsided with relief, and Lord William began to read out from the letters. One called Havelock a methodist and a fanatic. Another begged the Governor-General to realise that Havelock's 'character as an officer was lowered by familiar intercourse with the men', and a third respectfully intimated to his lordship that strong religious views would destroy an adjutant's impartiality.

Lord William said he had made enquiries and was convinced that Havelock's men were the most sober and well disciplined in the regiment. 'Give your husband my compliments and tell him he must continue his religious exertions, and if possible convert the whole regiment. He can baptise the lot if he likes.' (A Bishop of Calcutta had cryptically described Lord William as 'more of a Christian than a Churchman'.) 'But,' he added with a smile, tapping the letters, 'the *Adjutant* must not preach.'

The adjutancy was gazetted on December 30th 1834. An inspecting general in 1835 reported that 'the greatest uniformity seems to prevail among the officers of the regiment'. As for the men, 'I and others,' Sergeant Godfrey could say, 'often witnessed his aim to do justly towards all.' Havelock was a martinet, in the accepted style of the day, but he was not a bully. And he once gave his son, when an adjutant twenty years later, succinct advice on which, presumably, he had acted himself: 'keep well with the lady; and do your duty *zealously*; and give no opinions'.

EARLY IN 1835, while Hannah was desperately ill after the birth of their first girl, the 13th left Agra to transfer to Karnal, north of Delhi.

They were over a month on the road, with Havelock so busy that he could not find time to let Mrs Marshman know whether Hannah was alive or dead, 'and much reproof I got about it'. They marched to Delhi, through the Moonlit Mile and under the walls of the Red Fort and out through the Kashmir Gate. Along the new Grand Trunk Road the passing caravans pulled close in under the shade trees as the scarlet column swung by in its cloud of dust, at its head Sale and Havelock riding, the Adjutant's straight back disguising his lack of inches, and at its tail the carriages of the officers' wives, and the bullock carts and disdainful camels of the baggage train, and a straggle of camp followers in the rear. They came in sight of the hills, a blue haze on the far horizon; on Wednesday, January 20th 1836, Hannah, now well again, wrote to her sister, 'we left our last halting ground and heard the "general" sound for the last time (a bugle which at half past four a.m. orders us to strike our tents and march away and at the sound of which Lucy always wakes the children) and marched half way when we met H M 31st Foot, the regiment which has just left Karnal to make way for ours. And it was a very pretty sight indeed and one that I have never seen. The 31st drew up all in a line on one side of the road presenting its colours, being the junior regiment, while the 13th marched past them in style, and also in dead silence, the band playing and colours flying!'

They liked Karnal even better than Agra. The garrison was bigger and the place neat and clean, 'and would you not feel a wish', wrote Hannah to Rachel, 'to see the cloud cap't towers, as I do on a clear day, and would you not like to be only 80 miles distant from the foot of the highest mountains in the world! We can see the pass by which to ascend them, and I am wishing for wings to flee away and perch as high as I can on them.'

Karnal became oppressive in summer, especially for women

and children in petticoats, stays and spine-pads which convention and tropical medicine imposed, and Havelock arranged with his brother Charles that their wives and families should share a house in Landour, the nearest hill station. In mid-April they travelled by dawk into the foothills and through the lovely valley of the Doon until on the third day they reached the little village of Rajpur nestling right under the mountains. At Rajpur Hannah and her sister-in-law Mary and the children transferred to jampans, palanquins for two carried by teams of sturdy, smiling little hillmen. Old Seib the bearer marched beside them, while the brothers rode mountain ponies and the baggage was strapped on the backs of coolies. The twisting track climbed steeply up the scrub-covered mountain, 'nowhere wider than six feet and with a precipice on one side'. They had left Rajpur at three in the afternoon and after two and a half hours were in sight of Mussoorie, 'the place', wrote Hannah, 'where all the fashion and beauty reside, but it is only 5,000 feet high and by no means as healthy as Landour'. A thunderstorm overtook them as they climbed the last steep steps and they reached Landour drenched, but 'a comfortable fire soon set all things right again'.

Their cottage, Oakville, had the best view in Landour. On the brink of a precipice, a little below the crown of the mountain, from their garden they could see what no one else could – both the plains and the unexplored Himalayas, 'the snows perpetual on the north', so Hannah described it, 'the valley of the Doon in beautiful ripeness on the south; on the west, part of the snowy range and the interior, and on the east Mussoorie and the plains... in this delightful climate I hope to reap great advantage to myself and also to be able to carry out the education of my dear boys very greatly'.

That summer Hannah was supremely happy, though she had to content herself with a wistful gaze down across the sparkling ribband of the Ganges into the haze where Havelock toiled in the heat. But she had her baby, and the boys were full of fun, 'both capital climbers and by six every morning they are climb-

ing with old Seib up steeps where I cannot go without slipping.'
There were walks and rides along the Tehri road with its surprising corners and steep edges, and picnics up near the
Pepperpot, and laughter at the antics of the grey baboons, and
in the evening a book beside the fire, or work on the collection
of her stuffed birds, or perhaps a letter from Henry.

DOWN IN THE plains Havelock, now a brevet captain ('East Indies
only') had begun a new work. The Divisional General at his last
inspection had commented on the 'many courts martial which
proceeded from habitual drunkenness... but I trust the exam-
ples that have been made and the certainty of punishment for
their crimes will prevent a repetition of them for the future'.
But drunkenness continued.

In the garrison at Karnal Havelock met an old friend, Edward Wakefield of a Native Regiment. They discussed this problem together and Wakefield mentioned an abortive attempt in a
battalion of the Buffs at Fort William in 1833 to start a Temperance Society, a British and Foreign Temperance Society having
recently been formed in England. Havelock passed the idea to
Sale, remarking, 'We've tried everything else.' Sale approved
and a Regimental Temperance Association was formed, of men
pledged to abjure alcohol. To expect them to honour such a surprising and original pledge was impossible unless a counter-
attraction was provided; Sale therefore secured the Commander-
in-Chief's permission to allocate £90 from the Canteen Fund
for the building of a Coffee Room, such as had never been seen
in an Indian cantonment.

When it was built, Sergeant Godfrey, advanced in years, was
placed in charge. 'We put him at the bar of the Coffee Room,'
recalled Wakefield, 'his wife made the coffee and he distrib-
uted it. We gave them a good cup of coffee for a pice.[1] We gave
them the *Penny Magazine* and other papers to read, and we had
meetings.' 'By pure moral persuasion', as Wakefield put it, the

---

[1] Less than a penny.

13th soon had strong membership for the Regimental Temperance Association. Within a few months Brigadier-General Duncan officially reported its strength at 'two hundred and seventy-four persons'. 'Havelock's crochet', as the men called the Temperance drive, had caught on.

More was required. Though no toper Havelock had drunk wine in moderation like anyone else, total abstention among gentlemen being then almost unknown. To further the Temperance work he now took the pledge himself. Wakefield demurred. Havelock said, 'I know you are a perfectly temperate man. Can you talk to men to get them to leave off what they abuse when you yourself indulge in the use of it?' Wakefield then took the pledge, though most of the officers did not.

Other units on the station became interested. Wakefield remembered, one of many instances, an artilleryman who had seen a friend die of delirium tremens and who came to the Coffee Room. Havelock was sitting bolt upright at a table, Wakefield beside him and the man at attention before them. 'Well, my good man,' said Havelock, 'you wish to take the pledge?' 'Yes, sir.' 'Well, do you think that you can do it in your own strength?' 'No, sir!' 'If you really do come here solemnly and conscientiously desiring to get free from it, feeling that you have no strength of your own, in God's name, He will help you. Put your name down.'

The scheme gradually expanded. A Savings Bank was established. 'Mrs Sale joined in and we had our monthly meetings for the wives of the men and their children, and we gave them buns and cakes, and they enjoyed themselves.' Havelock wrote to Adjutants of other British regiments in India, and in course of the next two years some thirty units formed Temperance Societies; reports from them were read out at the monthly meetings in the 13th. By June 1838, when General Duncan again inspected the regiment, he reported a definite improvement. 'Courts martial continue to be numerous, but they appear all to be held on the same set of men for habitual drunkenness.'

IN THE LAST week of October 1836 a runner arrived in Karnal from Dr Robertson in Landour. Oakville had been burnt down. Hannah and the baby were dying of their burns, the ayah was dead and Lucy the maid unlikely to survive.

He set off for the hills at once. By the time he arrived Hannah was out of danger, though still in great pain and dreadfully scarred. The baby had just died 'after ten days and about two hours of sad torment', and they showed him the pathetic little corpse. Lucy was also dead. Mary Havelock in the other part of the house had escaped and had even saved some property. Dr Robertson had taken them all in.

Bit by bit Havelock was able to piece together the tragedy. Hannah had been woken about two in the morning by the noise of flames. 'I rushed out of bed, called the ayah, gave her the baby, snatched up both boys out of their beds and rushed into the passage.' Wherever she looked were flames and 'I had no alternative but to rush through them.' In fact, one side was clear; 'but I had lost my reason for I saw myself surrounded by flames and I had three children to save'. She fell twice, the second time right into the flames. Seib rushed in and dragged her to safety and went back for Harry, while Mary's bearer rescued Jos. Hannah lay in agony, but in a coherent moment gasped 'Baby!' and the gallant Seib rushed back into the bedroom, to find the ayah and her own child on the floor in the flames and Hannah's baby on the burning veranda, her skull fractured. 'The silly woman instead of rushing out as I had done remained bemoaning their fate until the very roof of the house began falling about their ears.'

For some time it seemed that Hannah's hands or feet might be contracted and her face permanently scarred ('I trust I should not have loved her less if it had been,' said Havelock) but she steadily improved in body and nerves and by January was convalescent. They buried the baby out in the wilds, 'in the still valley of the wolf and the leopard, full in sight of the loftiest pinnacles of nature'.

They had lost many of their possessions, from furniture and clothes to the gold fillet of nobility from Ava. They returned to Karnal in mid-January 1837. Immediately on their arrival a deputation of men of the regiment asked to be allowed to make up the Havelock's loss by contributing each a month's pay.

IN JUNE 1838, through the death during a cholera epidemic of a company commander, 'a dear friend', Havelock at last got his substantive captaincy without purchase.

War was again in sight. Lord Auckland, a man of peace but afraid of Russian encroachments in Central Asia and suspicious of Dost Mohammed, Amir of Afghanistan, had been led by his advisers to unearth a former Amir, Shah Shujah, who had lived in exile in India for twenty-two years. An expedition, 'the Army of the Indus' was to penetrate to Afghanistan, remote beyond the independent Sikh kingdom of the Punjab, and replace Shah Shujah on the throne of Kabul.

For a while Havelock feared he must serve as a company commander, 'nearly as absolute a cypher as a lance corporal', for the adjutancy had lapsed on his promotion and though Sale, to command a brigade on the expedition, asked for him as Brigade-Major, the Commander-in-Chief gave the appointment elsewhere. But at the last moment the Bengal division was given to Sir Willoughby Cotton, now fat, old and somewhat slow. Cotton found all staff appointments filled, but with action in prospect he required Havelock's brains, and took him on his staff with the title of Second Aide-de-Camp.

In November 1838 Havelock, who had once fervently assured Hannah, 'I would rather spend one hour in your dear society than win a battle', trotted merrily off into the West.

PART TWO

Gates of the West

5

The Rising

In bright moonlight the headquarters of the Bengal division of the Army of the Indus, Havelock riding beside Sir Willoughby Cotton, left Karnal at 3 a.m. on November 8th 1838 for this most disastrous of all Indian wars.

The division was to rendezvous near Ferozepore on the Punjab frontier where the Governor-General would hold court with his ally Ranjit Singh, the wily and bloodthirsty Sikh Maharajah. During the march to Ferozepore Havelock learned from Cotton that Shah Shujah and the Bengal division were not to be allowed by their allies the Sikhs to cross the Punjab and approach Afghanistan by the shorter route through the Khyber. They must descend the Sutlej and Indus rivers through the independent amirates in Sind and Baluchistan and, after joining the Bombay division, led by Keane, Commander of the whole expedition, fetch round across desert and mountain to Kandahar, the Afghan southern capital.

By now, after fourteen years, Havelock knew Cotton well, 'His best qualities were dignified and polished manners, the shrewdness and tact which long intercourse with the world imparts, rapid decision and prompt despatch of business. His defects were an irritable temper and a nervous dread of responsibility', and as for his strategic abilities, so Havelock wrote years later, he had 'those confused and nervous views' typical of most generals in the British Army, 'many of whom are men of action, and practically clever in small matters – few, very few of sufficient grasp of mind to plan a campaign or comprehend the true principles of great combats'.

At Ferozepore Ranjit Singh and Lord Auckland displayed their glories in enormous encampments on either side of the frontier river. Sikh horsemen in splendid armour charged each other in tournament, and Havelock caught a glimpse of Ranjit Singh as the elephants lumbered by, 'an old man in an advanced stage of decrepitude, clothed in faded crimson, his head wrapped up in folds of cloth of the same colour, his single eye still lighted up with the fire of enterprise'. That evening the Maharajah's camp gave a display of fireworks, while some remarkably plain nautch girls ('choral and dancing prostitutes', Havelock called them) ogled and gyrated in front of Lord Auckland and his sisters and the British staff.

On December 2nd Shah Shujah, with his army of irregulars led by British officers, set out from Ferozepore, followed ten days later by the Army of the Indus, an enormous spread-out mass – the compact scarlet and blue of British and sepoy infantry; cavalry and guns kicking up clouds of dust; twenty-five thousand camels; innumerable servants and camp followers; and herds of cattle and long-haired sheep and goats for slaughter on the march.

Four months later, on April 12th 1839, on the summit of the Khurjak Pass, seventy miles north of Quetta, Havelock stood beside Keane the Commander-in-Chief and gazed at the magnificent view of the plains of Afghanistan. 'We looked down upon a winding road through a narrow *ghat*. Beyond it was descried an extensive plain. It was filled with mist, although the sharp wind of the mountain kept all serene around us; but we could see in the extreme distance with the telescope two little eminences, which some of the inhabitants boldly affirmed to be immediately in front of Kandahar.'

Behind them, across a thousand miles of river bank, desert and mountain passes, were scattered the bones of tens of thousands of camels, and of several hundred soldiers dead of disease, starvation or thirst, but not, save for a few, of enemy bullets or knives.

Through the gaunt yellow oven of Baluchistan the Bengal contingent had struggled. In pouring rain they had climbed the

Bolan Pass, threading their way up between the steep jagged mountain sides speckled with scrub, crossing and recrossing the shallow Bolan River, and filing through defiles which would have made perfect ambuscades, had the local chiefs opposed them. Once, during the climb, Havelock found himself for a short time near the 13th. 'They halted a few moments to close up the rear of their column after crossing the nullah and then advanced by bugle signal, which rung amidst the caverns and lofty peaks.' As he looked at these 'finely grouped figures in the mountain picture, the soldiers with their shoes off, and trousers tucked up to their knees after fording, their bronzed countenances and drenched and faded uniforms', Havelock was swept with pride and homesickness. He had not had opportunity to bring his saints together on the campaign; but he started the day as he always did, another officer going so far as to record that Havelock 'invariably secured two hours in the morning for reading the Scriptures and private prayer. If the march began at six he rose at four; if at four he rose at two.'

At Quetta in springtime they had been faced with starvation, through the treachery of a Khan who was supposed to be Shah Shujah's ally. Keane and Macnaghten, Auckland's imperious Envoy who considered himself the real commander of the expedition, had joined them with half a Bombay brigade, the Shah and his private elephants, and they had marched on to the head of the Khurjak Pass. Keane bungled the steep ascent and a determined enemy could have finished the campaign on the spot. The plain proved a waterless waste for forty miles but Kandahar was surrendered without a shot. On April 25th Headquarters 'advanced across the plains towards the capital. Our camp, during the cool and moonlight night', records Havelock, 'had been perfumed by the fragrance of a wild flower which grows in profusion on the wilds around. In scent and appearance it resembles mignonette'. From rising ground Havelock could see 'a plain of brilliant green, in the midst of which are white buildings', with a background of small isolated brown hills with odd-shaped razor-edges. The walled city was flanked by gardens, orchards and fields. 'As we approach the western capital, therefore, our opinion of Afghanistan becomes a little more favourable.'

The army spent two months in Kandahar waiting for reinforcements and supplies before they could march north to enthrone Shah Shujah at Kabul, and the prolonged stay was unpleasant. The dirt and the beggars were worse than any city Havelock had seen in India. No grain had been found and the army had gorged itself on mutton, and on mulberries, plums and apricots, followed as the season advanced by grapes, melons and apples which no one had seen since England. Such a diet, and the damp climate, thinned the ranks by fever, dysentery and jaundice.

The Bombay Division had reached Kandahar early in May (and with them Captain James Outram of the Company's service, whom Havelock thus met for the first time) but the lines of communication in Baluchistan and Sind were under constant attack, and the camel convoy was the first to fight its way through Afghan horsemen who refused to acknowledge Shah Shujah as King and raided almost to the gates of the city. A young officer who stayed out after nightfall had been murdered.

Keane had to march or starve. Havelock was not impressed by Sir John Keane, an Irishman in whom 'the shrewdness and quick perceptions which so often fall to the lot of his countrymen were united to a selfishness and self-will that manifested themselves in command in the grossest partiality and a contempt for truth, justice and common honesty. His open parade of private vices, and affected coarseness of language and manner were only a cloak for darker features of his character, and the most malignant personal animosities. He was a man of tried courage and an apt, clever officer but hardly deserved the name of general.' The Bombay division was the apple of his eye, while the Bengal division 'was under an indiscriminate ban of exclusion from his confidence'. And 'so unfortunately did his favouritism act upon the public service' that he nearly brought the force to disaster. Kabul lay three hundred and sixty miles north through easy and well-watered country. Only one fortress lay on the path – Ghazni, reputed to be impregnable, but which Macnaghten and Sir Alexander Burnes, his assistant, were confident would surrender to Shah Shujah without a fight. Keane therefore determined to leave his siege guns behind because their commander, a Bengal officer, was the senior gunner in the force and if they were left at Kandahar command of the artillery would devolve on a Bombay officer, who would thus reap the rewards and prize money.

On hearing of Keane's decision Havelock reported to him that his own information, gathered from contacts with Afghans of all classes, pointed to Ghazni being held in force; the siege guns would be essential. Keane impatiently brushed him aside. Havelock thereupon ventured to remind the Commander-in-Chief that 'Napoleon at Acre, Wellington at Burgos, Lord Lake at Bhurtpore had each found cause to rue the hour in which they attacked fortifications unprovided with a sufficient number of guns of breaching calibre'. But Keane had no time for book-learning.

The force advanced on June 27th. The road wound through well-watered valleys scattered with woods and little forts. The men remained on half-rations until ripe corn was found in abundance half way to Ghazni. During the second week of the march the troops' supplies of rum ran out for the first time on the campaign, and no more could be obtained. Havelock recognised the hardship of this 'sudden withdrawal', but welcomed an opportunity of proving his temperance theories. 'I am fully persuaded,' he said, 'that when the soldier has by a few weeks' use become habituated to the change, his physical powers will gain strength, whilst his discipline improves under this system of constrained abstinence, and the troops will enjoy an immunity from disease which will delight those interested in their welfare. It is probable that we shall not find the means of replenishing our stock of ardent spirits until this important experiment has been fairly tried.'

Eleven miles south of Ghazni a young Afghan chieftain, 'well dressed and mounted', with a small escort, came down the road towards Cotton, who was leading the van. He excitedly asked for the Shah, and rode off in a cloud of dust without revealing his identity. He proved to be Abdul Rashid, a nephew of Dost Mohammed and a useful traitor.

Keane and Macnaghten were convinced that the fortress was empty. Abdul Rashid would not give an opinion. 'Thus we continued to march on in uncertainty', records Havelock, 'until the grey walls and lofty citadel were full in view.' In front were walled gardens and the river, and rising behind the city were wooded hills with a spur running down to the north edge of the city. With Sir Alexander Burnes and Abdul Rashid the staff moved forward, and saw Afghan horsemen on guard by the garden. Havelock felt that 'this did not look like an intention to evacuate the fortress'. Keane soon saw that he was faced with the problem of Ghazni's capture. He had three days' food for the army and could not afford a siege. And since the heavy guns had been left at Kandahar he could not breach the walls. Abdul Rashid offered a suggestion. The Kabul Gate was not fully built up when he had absconded. If it was still in disrepair it could be blown in and serve as a breach.

The same evening the force marched round to the north of the city. Darkness fell, and blue lights constantly flickered from the ramparts, answered by fires from the plains and hills. The next day a body of screaming horsemen, with pennants and scarves of a jihad, or holy war, galloped down from the hills to attack the camp of the Shah who was returning to power on the arms of infidels and 'feringhis'. The attack was beaten off and British officers were disgusted to find the Shah's executioners hacking the prisoners to pieces with refined brutality ('they were laughing and joking and seemed to look upon the work as good fun').

Keane's plan, 'calmly and quietly circulated on Monday evening' but known at once to every camp follower, since he had told it in confidence to Macnaghten, who had told it in confidence to the Shah, was 'bold and brilliant'.

As the sun rose the next morning, two hours after the Kabul Gate had been blown up, and following a stiff assault in which Sale and the 13th had greatly distinguished themselves, Keane and Macnaghten led Shah Shujah in triumph to the citadel in the centre of Ghazni.

A whole day stretched ahead. If the British soldiery ran true to form, after taking a city by storm the officers would be hard put to get them together, prevent looting and rape and a sacking such as had disgraced Campbell's troops at Rangoon or Wellington's at Badajoz. But no sack took place. 'Let it be recorded to the honour of the captors', wrote Havelock in his *Narrative of the War in Afghanistan*, published in England the next year, 'that though Ghazni was carried by storm after a resistance stout enough to have roused the angry passions of the assailants, the Afghans were everywhere spared when they ceased to fight; and it is in itself a moral triumph that, in a fortress captured by assault, not the slightest insult was offered to one of the females found in the zenana within the walls of the citadel.'

And Havelock had no doubt of the cause: 'The self-denial, mercy and generosity of the hour may be attributed to the fact of the European soldiers having received no spirit ration since the 8th of July, and having found no intoxicating liquor amongst the plunder of Ghazni. No candid man of any military experience will deny that the character of the scene in the fortress and citadel would have been far different if individual soldiers had entered the town primed with arrack, or if spirituous liquors had been discovered in the Afghan depots.' And he hoped that Ghazni would open a new era. 'Since, then, it has been proved that troops can make forced marches of forty miles, and storm a fortress in seventy-five minutes without the aid of rum, behaving after success with a forbearance and humanity unparalleled in history; let it not henceforth be argued that distilled spirits are an indispensable portion of a soldier's ration'.

A FORTNIGHT LATER, on August 7th 1839, Havelock rode with Cotton in Shah Shujah's train at the state entry into Kabul. Dost Mohammed 'the Usurper' had fled. Well fed and in highest humour the British army was camped among the orchards and fields of the rich Kabul Valley, with its pleasing background of hills and distant snow-capped mountains. Even Havelock had dismissed the warning they had heard long ago in Quetta: Shah Shujah, a Baluchi chieftain had said, 'ought to have trusted to the Afghans to restore him to his throne; whereas he is essaying to deluge the land with Hindustanis, an insult which his own people will never forgive him. This will never do. You English may keep him by main force for a time on the throne; but as soon as you leave the kingdom, your Shah Shujah will be driven beyond its frontiers.'

TWO YEARS LATER Havelock had cause to remember that prophecy. He had been back to India to see Hannah and the family, at Serampore, and to write his account of the Afghan War, now supposed to be over – a book as unsuccessful as his *Campaigns in Ava*.

In June 1840, the Occupation Army in Afghanistan being still unable to withdraw, with safety to Shah Shujah, he had set off again for the North-West in command of a draft of recruits for the Kabul garrison. Many were Light Infantrymen for the 13th; and neither the young soldiers nor their draft commander knew what they were to go through together. On the way up river he met, after nearly twenty years, Harry Smith, now Adjutant-General, Queen's Troops, and basking in the fame of his great ride in Kaffirland. At Ferozepore he stayed with Henry Lawrence, a man of like faith who became one of his greatest friends. He also found General Elphinstone, who had been selected to command in Afghanistan, a most amiable man though he had not seen action since Waterloo, but a martyr to gout who had only accepted the post because he believed that the Governor-General's urgent order took precedence of his own sense of unfitness. Elphinstone appointed Havelock his Persian Interpreter. In April 1841 they were in Kabul.

The Army of Occupation amused itself with horse racing and cricket in summer and skating and plays in winter. The men wrestled and threw weights with Afghan champions and crowded to cockfights in the bazaar where the betting was high. Lady Sale (Robert Sale had been knighted for Ghazni) and other officers' wives had arrived. The rankers grumbled that their wives were not sent them, but the Afghan women were not then in purdah and instead of being shapeless white-draped figures as in India, openly displayed their charms. Sir Alexander Burnes remembered the best brothels from a previous visit. Men of all ranks followed his example and others were found in respectable zenanas, more than one murder resulting.

And the men drank. Kabul produced a particularly potent brew from grapes. On the British arrival in 1839 the Commissariat had contracted immediately for regular supplies in place of the exhausted Indian rum. Havelock had commented that 'it is to be feared that the Afghans, like other nations invaded by our armies, will soon be taught the difference between Britons drunk and Britons sober'. And since then Colonel Dennie had been obliged in regimental orders to call on 'the soldiers of the 13th to consider... that of nearly one hundred men who have perished within the last year the remote, if not the immediate cause of their disease and death (with few exceptions) has been liquor... The new liquor of this country has been found to be more poisonous than that of Hindustan... For your own sakes, for the honour of your regiment, abstain from the beastly vice of intemperance.'

There was no chaplain with the force. Havelock immediately set about to supply the need. The survivors of the 13th Light Infantry 'saints' formed a nucleus and the services were open to all. Queen's officers were still little interested but evangelicals were found in the Company's service, especially in the Engineers and Artillery. 'Havelock was able to meet the men again,' recalled Sir John Login of the Bengal Artillery, 'and, assisted by some officers of the Artillery he was able to assemble them on Sabbath evenings for Divine Service, and to meet them occasionally during the week in a tent which had been set apart for the purpose. On many of these occasions I had the satisfaction of being present during my stay in Kabul, up to September 1841, and I have to this day a very vivid recollection of the fervour with which all joined in the service, and the heart with which they sung the hymns which Havelock read out to them.'

Macnaghten and the politicals were in continual friction with the military. Elphinstone, constantly ill, hoped that Auckland would allow him to resign. The second-in-command, Shelton, was a one-armed, cantankerous bully who quarrelled with his colleagues and was detested by the men.

Shah Shujah, meanwhile, finding Sale, Macnaghten and others with their wives, decided that he would have his. The royal harem ran to six hundred women (including relatives), with very many attendants and two or three score of children. George Broadfoot, an energetic and forthright Madras engineer seconded to the Shah's service, had been sent to fetch them. Macnaghten gaily allowed the Shah to turn out the British troops from the Bala Hissar and make it his harem. This building, the old citadel, dominated the city. In 1839 Havelock had noted that 'all depends, in a military point of view, on a firm hold of the Bala Hissar. It is the key of Kabul'. He now said, and many others agreed, that Macnaghten's act was 'an absurdity'.

LATE IN SEPTEMBER 1841 Havelock attended a durbar at which Macnaghten received the mountain chiefs of the Ghilzai passes between Kabul and Jalalabad.

Macnaghten, appointed Governor of Bombay, had arranged

to leave shortly and Elphinstone also, illness having reduced him 'to a state of the most pitiable debility of mind and body of which he was painfully conscious'. Lord Auckland's government had found the bill for Afghanistan so much heavier than the estimate that retrenchments had been ordered. Sale's Brigade was to be withdrawn. Macnaghten prided himself that all Afghanistan was at last quiet and now had called the mountain chiefs to inform them of an additional economy; their annual subsidy, a traditional bribe paid by the rulers of Kabul to prevent them plundering the caravans was to be heavily reduced. The Ghilzai chiefs had fulfilled their bargain – 'they had', as Havelock commented, 'prevented even a finger from being raised against our posts, couriers and weak detachments' – and this was their reward. They salaamed, expressionless, and retired. Macnaghten continued with his packing.

On October 2nd a terrified merchant rode into the Kabul bazaar reporting that a caravan had been plundered in the passes. On October 7th an officer who had narrowly escaped with his life on the way up reported that a loyal Afghan had warned him that the country was about to rise, which Macnaghten dismissed as absurd. On October 9th the leading detachment of Sale's Brigade, the 35th Native Infantry (Lieut-Colonel Monteith) with cavalry, two guns and Broadfoot's sappers (Afghan irregulars whom he ruled with ferocious discipline and who worshipped him almost as a god), received orders from Macnaghten to start for India, making a 'demonstration' against the 'impudent rascals' as they crossed the passes. Before they left Macnaghten had refused to say whether serious opposition was to be expected; he had insulted the Commander-in-Chief and lost his temper with Broadfoot, while Elphinstone, in excruciating pain, had feebly and ineffectually protested.

Early next day a runner reported that Monteith had been heavily attacked at night in his camp at Butkhak ten miles away at the foot of the Khurd Kabul Pass. Sale was ordered to move at once with the remainder of his Brigade, and clear the passes on his way out of Afghanistan. The flint locks of the 13th were old and condemned, but when Sale asked for an issue of the new detonating muskets, he was told 'they were not necessary to a force on its march to India'.

Havelock, anxious for action, obtained a few days' leave to accompany the force. And thus, casually, began the great adventure.

Sale's detachment marched out of the Lahore Gate below the Bala Hissar, and along the Jalalabad road through the glades and under the low, abrupt and jagged Sia Sang Hills, across the race course and away on to the plain. Havelock on his favourite charger Feroze, rode beside Sale. Dennie led the 13th, but the tramp of the men and of the two hundred jezailchis (Afghan irregulars) behind them was drowned by the mooing and shuffling of four thousand cattle trailing in the rear as food for the march to India. A train of baggage camels strung out in the distance could be seen dimly through the dust.

At Butkhak Monteith, the wig on his bald head carefully brushed and his body scented, reported that he had not been attacked again. The next morning Sale flung his men at the Khurd Kabul Pass. The yellow-brown sides, speckled with bushes, rose almost perpendicularly from the steep narrow path through which a rivulet was running down towards the plain. At the first turn a hot fire poured from the Ghilzai rebels who could be seen sheltering behind rocks, the sun glinting on the barrels of their long jezails. Rocks hurtled down as skirmishers of the 13th deployed rapidly up the heights, stopping to fire and reload and clambering on, while the light mountain guns fired shrapnel and grape, the reports echoing and re-echoing in the valley. Havelock, as always when under fire, dropped his usual taciturnity and was chatty and bright, advising Sale at each turn and cantering with him where the fire was thickest to urge on the men, until Sale was badly hit. One by one the turns of the Pass were cleared. The rebels disappeared up the mountain side, the smoke cleared away and the valley was still.

Sale, lying in great pain on a doolie, ordered Havelock to ride back to Kabul and personally urge on Elphinstone and Macnaghten the need for reinforcements. At daylight on the 13th Havelock mounted Feroze and cantered across the plain, passing on the way Captain Macgregor the political agent, 'handsome, with ready smile and calm, cautious, courteous conversation', as he once described him, who had been out in the north and was to direct Sale's political contacts (and, if Macnaghten had his way, to direct Sale). Havelock went at once to Elphinstone, and to Macnaghten who grumbled, 'I suppose we shall have to thrash the rascals after all'. Fortunately both General and Envoy were anxious that trouble in the Passes should not postpone their journey homeward. The necessary troops were ordered but the guns were not ready.

Havelock now wondered whether his duty was to stay with Elphinstone or 'to offer my services again to join Sale and assist him in his operations'. He reflected on 'certain vague intimations I had received of the coming storm, in the shape of an awful insurrection then concocting'. But Kabul 'on the surface, was in perfect tranquillity'. Macnaghten remained complacent and Sir Alexander Burnes, impatiently waiting to step into his shoes, assured Havelock that there was no fear of disturbance. He therefore obtained leave to return to Sale.

Early on the morning of the day the reinforcements were to march from Kabul, Havelock went out when it was scarcely light, while the servants were noisily packing his baggage, to the mulberry grove where he could enjoy in the quiet his customary time with his Bible. It happened he had been reading Jeremiah, a chapter a day, and had reached chapter thirty-nine. As he read the end of the passage the closing verses, apparently so inappropriate, seemed to stand out from the page: 'Thus saith the Lord of hosts, the God of Israel, Behold I will bring my words upon this city for evil, and not for good; and they shall be accomplished in that day before thee. But I will deliver thee in that day, saith the Lord; and thou shalt not be given into the hand of the men of whom thou art afraid. For I will surely deliver thee, and thou shalt not fall by the sword, but thy life shall be for a prey unto thee: because thou hast put thy trust in me saith the Lord.' These words often reoccurred to him in the days ahead, and he never forgot the incident.

Late that same evening Havelock re-entered Sale's Camp with additional sepoy infantry, another squadron of native cavalry and Abbott's battery of horse artillery. Sale was still in pain and unable to walk. At daylight camp was broken and the force marched up the valley.

Seventeen miles of defiles were passed without incident, though here and there the glint of a jezail could be seen high up among the rocks, until the advance guard toiled up the final ascent of a deep gorge towards the curious natural pudding-stone column at the entrance to the valley of Tezin, where the enemy were seen mustered in full force. Backhouse and Abbott hurriedly unlimbered and a few rounds of shrapnel sent the Afghans flying, their puggarees streaming in the wind and their longees tucked up between their legs. As the brigade entered the valley the enemy were hovering on the heights. Dennie ordered a detachment of the 13th to scale them but did not think it necessary to unlimber the guns again. Firing was heard and, to the horror of all, the 13th were seen running for their lives, the Afghans after them and a young officer left dead on the rocks.

Somewhat shaken, Sale called Havelock to his doolie and they planned an attack for the next day on the principal fort in the valley, but the chief tendered his submission. For two days Macgregor and the chief sat in durbar. The young officer was buried in a lonely grave and the cattle and camels spread out foraging. Occasional activity was noticed on the heights. Bribes were offered by Macgregor and hostages by the chief and cavalry orderlies went to and fro between Macgregor and Macnaghten until on Tuesday, October 25th a convention was ratified. The rising was evidently over.

Sale ordered his reinforcements back to Kabul. Havelock

made ready to go with them to rejoin Elphinstone but Sale, 'lying on his pallet suffering intense agony from the wound he had received at Khurd Kabul', was aghast. He distrusted his own judgment. 'When he heard of my intention to return he at once interposed, represented to me that, rendered helpless in some measure by the severe fracture he had sustained, and invested with an important command, he could not consent to be deprived of the services of an additional staff-officer... My remonstrances were perpetually met and overborne by the same arguments. Finally, General Sale, loading himself with all the responsibility of the measure, told me that I *must* accompany him.'

The march was resumed, the Ghilzai hostages riding with the column. Flanking parties marched on the edges of the valley and though the scenery was grandly imposing the road was not difficult. On each of the three days the cumbersome rearguard was attacked. The hostages loudly assured the irate Sale that the perpetrators were undisciplined and disobedient tribesmen. Havelock felt that 'our bane throughout has been our superfluous baggage and heavy camp equipage, which may, and must in Afghanistan, be reduced in quantity and form'.

Nearing Jagdalak on the third day Havelock remembered riding two years earlier through the 'Fairy Glen', a 'terrific defile, the rocks of which, said to be granite and sandstone, were piled one on the other in dark and frowning strata, sloping down on either side towards a mountain rivulet for which they scarcely left room to flow'. He strongly advised an alternative route and later it was found that an ambush had been laid in the Glen. Spending the night of the 28th at Jagdalak, among the almond and mulberry trees and aromatic grass, the brigade started up the rough three mile ascent of the Jagdalak Pass, the mountains, wooded with holly trees and pine, bristling with armed parties which skirmishers had to dislodge. Below the crest lay the valley of Gandamak, wide and fertile, where a detachment of the Shah's Irregulars were stationed at the little town at the far end.

As the descent began Dennie complacently hurried forward, leaving a widening gap between the main column and the baggage, with its escort of two companies of the 13th and some sepoys. Then, as Havelock wrote, 'a perfect ocean of baggage began to flow over the mountain and the rebels took heart, resumed the initiative in their fashion and fell upon the rear'.

Those in the main column, looking back, saw that an unsavoury panic had developed and sent back supports. When all was over, just as darkness fell, it was found that the young soldiers of the 13th had again begun to run away, that Captain Wyndham of the 35th, trying to rescue a wounded man, had been hacked to pieces and that the courage of a few officers, led by Broadfoot, his spectacles jammed on his nose and his fair hair waving in the cold wind, had alone saved a disaster. The next day, Sunday, October 30th, the brigade trailed into Gandamak and sat back to lick its wounds.[1]

---

[1]Havelock was mentioned in despatches for his part in these actions near Tezin (October 22nd) and near Jagdalak (October 29th).

6

Jalalabad

Sitting in his hut among the mulberry trees at the Gandamak cantonment, shadowed by the mountains already topped with snow, George Broadfoot was writing letters to India on November 4th. 'I grieve to say', he wrote, 'that with all but old Havelock, not to be daunted, and Sale, who does not know the details and is a bold man moreover, except Monteith also and some of the 35th officers, a strong feeling of depression has been produced among men and officers of the European and native infantry and regular cavalry.' As to Havelock he went on, 'it is the fashion, especially in his own corps to sneer at him; his manners are cold, while his religious opinions seclude him from society; but the whole of them together would not compensate for his loss. Brave to admiration, imperturbably cool, looking at his profession as a science, and, as far as I can see or judge, correct in his views.'

No couriers had come through from Kabul for three or four days and the local inhabitants were buzzing with rumours. For four more days no official word came. On November 10th Macgregor at last received a letter from Macnaghten informing him that Burnes (and Broadfoot's brother) had been murdered and that all Kabul was up. Sale must return. But Elphinstone also wrote, to Sale, giving him an option not to return if he could not provide safely for his sick and wounded. Sale called a council of war. Emotionally he had every wish to help Kabul, where his wife and daughter were in danger; but he hesitated.

The council of war argued late and long. Havelock, as Sale's personal staff officer, had no vote but spoke freely and 'urged the most forcible reasons against such a movement'. 'It was evident', run the notes of his speech, as he gave them to Marshman afterwards, 'that the British hold on Kabul was

81

shaken, if not from the force of circumstances yet by the loss of moral courage in those who were at the head of affairs. How was the garrison of the cantonment to be aided, since it apparently could not and would not aid itself? Yet, how again could it be in peril? It consisted of between five and six thousand men, having a good artillery and immense munitions of war.'

As for Sale's Brigade, Havelock pointed out that a hard winter had already set in and that if Gandamak was cold enough, the passes would now be freezing. 'The force was badly clothed; it had lost a great portion of its camp equipage; its camel-drivers had nearly all deserted with their animals. It had not cartridges for more than three battles, and might have to fight its way every march out of eight. The morale of the troops was yet low... Finally, it was not possible to deposit the sick and wounded in safety. They exceeded three hundred in number, and to leave them at Gandamak was to abandon them to certain destruction.'

Havelock swung the vote; the Brigade could not retire to Kabul. The next question was whether to remain at Gandamak. Havelock pointed out that the water and supplies of the position could easily be cut off, while Macgregor reported that he had received intelligence that the tribes around Jalalabad were about to occupy or destroy it. The loss of Jalalabad would isolate the army in Afghanistan whereas, Havelock argued, for Sale to secure Jalalabad would be an 'immense advantage'. 'It would place the communication with Kabul on the one side and Peshawar on the other on a more secure footing; it would create a well-defended fortress on which the Kabul garrison might retire, and would prove the key of Eastern Afghanistan if the Government should send means and reinforcements across the Khyber'.

The next day, the Brigade marched for Jalalabad. The inhabitants of the one village on their route watched them demurely and even waved a Union Jack, but as soon as the rear guard was through opened fire from behind. From the edges of the wide valley tribesmen poured down into the plain. A running fight developed and Dennie cleverly trapped a horde of them into a cavalry ambush. The Brigade reached the walls of Jalalabad by nightfall and on the morning of November 13th 1841 took possession of the town unopposed.

TWO YEARS EARLIER Havelock had described Jalalabad as 'a town of houses of mud surrounded by a very poor wall of the same material; it may contain some ten thousand inhabitants. The Kabul river flows within a mile of it, a rapid and clear stream about one hundred yards in width but here, at this season,[1] so shallow as to be navigable only on rafts. There are extensive plains around the city. To the northward are seen a secondary range of mountains running parallel with that of the Indian Caucasus;[2] to the southward and westward, the Tirah chain with the same high boundary, which obstructs the route to Peshawar.'

When the Brigade entered the town on November 13th 1841, most of the inhabitants fled. Sale discovered that the walls, long disused, were so crumbled and covered with rubbish and meandered so far through gardens, old forts, the richer houses and the assortment of ruins found in the suburbs of every eastern town that they were not proof against a vigorous assault, even if there were sufficient men in the Brigade to hold the whole line. Meanwhile the plain was swarming with Afghans, some creeping near enough to snipe at the sentries who took cover behind camel-saddles and any shelter that came to hand.

They occupied two little hills which threatened the southwest angle of the defences, and on one of them they could be seen dancing jigs to the sound of the pipes, in anticipation of massacre and loot; the troops promptly named it Pipers' Hill. During the night the cantonment built by Macnaghten was burned down and with the sky red from the flames Sale laid plans for an assault at dawn.

Monteith was in command. All the cavalry, two guns and seven hundred infantry emerged from the South Gate in the half

---

[1] He was writing of the same time of year.
[2] i.e. Hindu Kush.

light and deployed across the plain. Havelock accompanied Monteith and the attack was delivered with such vigour that the Afghans fled, leaving some two hundred dead. By noon the plain was clear of tribesmen, and the villagers soon trundled their bullock carts up to the Peshawar Gate to sell forage and food to the garrison.

Day after day followed, with no Afghan rebels seen on the plain. Broadfoot, using the tools he had extracted at Kabul from an unwilling Macnaghten, took command of the rebuilding of the defences. Havelock undertook all correspondence for Sale, who was rapidly recovering from his wound. No one knew how long would be the respite or what was happening in Kabul. Cossids (native runners) had been able to leave by the Peshawar road and contact Ferris, holding a post with Irregulars twenty-five miles to the east, where messages and letters could be sent through the Khyber Pass to the small force in Peshawar, ninety miles from Jalalabad, and thus to India, but Ferris, his Irregulars deserting, was compelled to escape for his life to Peshawar. Only one armed post now remained in the Khyber hills though cossids could still get through.

A letter came from Elphinstone at Kabul. Writing in French in order to deceive English-speaking Afghans, Elphinstone approved Sale's move but, strangely, in view of the forces at his disposal to rush the rising, wrote 'Notre peril est extreme', and implored Sale to come to the rescue if he could leave his sick and wounded in safety. When Havelock read the letter he wished he could be in both places at once. To his family, after these depressing messages from west and east, he wrote: 'God's special Providence alone can extricate us from these difficulties. We trust through His goodness that our spirits will rise instead of sinking under them, and that we shall be strengthened to retrieve gloriously.'

On November 27th the Afghans returned to the valley. On December 1st heavy firing broke out from the Afghan positions, and since Sale refused to allow reply, for his ammunition was low, the Afghans triumphantly advanced. The sappers stopped work on the defences and took to arms and Dennie was sent out with a strong assault column. The Afghans fired one volley and fled, and the cavalry chased them across the plain and into the river while the infantry seized supplies and shepherded sheep and goats back to the town. Once more the villagers returned, content to do a lucrative trade in food regardless of politics.

DECEMBER 17TH WAS a day of ugly rumours. The commanders in Kabul were said to have signed a treaty with Mohammed Akbar, Dost Mohammed's son who was leading the revolt, to evacuate the country at once. 'There are certainly indications of something extraordinary having occurred', noted Havelock, 'these are to be traced in the renewal of the attempt to tamper with our sepoys, and the hints dropped in the bazaars. If a compact has been entered into, no faith will be kept by the Afghans, and our troops will be attacked in the passes; but whatever be the result of that contest, it is our duty to die behind the walls of Jalalabad rather than abandon the country.'

On the last day of 1841 a spy brought astonishing news. Macnaghten had been treacherously murdered by Mohammed Akbar himself during a conference in the open air; the British troops had capitulated and were immediately to retire through Jalalabad to India. Macgregor carried the news to Sale and Havelock. Other officers gathered. None could believe, whatever the truth about the murder, that five thousand British and sepoy troops would meekly surrender. It had not occurred in Indian history.

Two days later, on January 2nd 1842, the facts were confirmed in a letter from Eldred Pottinger, Macnaghten's acting successor, written on Christmas Day. Pottinger wrote of 'a sad comedy of errors, or rather tragedy here'. Mistake after mistake, it seemed to Sale's officers, had brought the Kabul garrison to near starvation. Attacked by the rabble and entangled by Akbar in parleys which should never have been allowed, they were now negotiating a capitulation and were to set out, in the depths of winter, women and children included, to cross the passes to Jalalabad. 'We may expect opposition on the road,' Pottinger concluded, 'and we are likely to suffer much from the cold and hunger as we expect to have no carriage for tents and superfluities.'

The officers of the Brigade were aghast. Much sympathy was offered Sale whose wife and daughter might even now be enduring the horrors of a march in such conditions, but the uppermost thoughts were indignation that an Army of which the Brigade was part should be licking the boots of an Afghan, and a determination that the retreat should go no further than Jalalabad. 'There is a force at Jalalabad', Havelock wrote to Harry Smith, urging him to get command of an army of revenge, 'which would I trust, sooner bury itself under its ruins than be saved by a convention, and which ardently desires, when reinforced, to be led against the treacherous and sanguinary foe which has butchered our ambassador and must be defeated if we would save our own in India.'

To Marshman, who he knew would publish in the *Friend of India* the substance of his reports and was in touch with the highest authorities in Calcutta, Havelock detailed the reinforcements needed and added, what was much in his mind, that 'we have no chaplain or minister of God's word in this country. This aid ought to be afforded us. An active unencumbered man who would really labour to disseminate religious instruction among our soldiers would be useful. He must be one who would not disdain to offer his exhortations in any kind of hut, house or tent, or the open air, sooner than lose his opportunity. I do not build much on divine service parades but they are a part of our military system as it stands, and must not be neglected. But great good is to be expected from the voluntary attendance of soldiers on effective preaching; and there is a disposition in this force to take advantage of such openings, and I am happy to say that it is manifested by some of the best soldiers we have.'

On January 8th a cossid arrived from Kabul with a letter in bad French from Pottinger to Macgregor beginning 'Notre situation devient perilleuse de plus en plus', and telling him that the capitulation was signed, without much faith in Akbar, and the Jalalabad garrison was not to move without further orders. But the next day three Afghan nobles haughtily rode up to the Kabul Gate and handed in two official letters, one from Elphinstone and one from Pottinger, ordering, under the terms of the capitulation, the evacuation of Jalalabad.

Sale called for his staff and commanding officers and a lively discussion began. Broadfoot and Havelock urged that no obedience was due to a general who acted under duress and that by capitulation Elphinstone had surrendered his right to command. The defences of Jalalabad were now adequate and reinforcements were believed to be already entering the Khyber. As for Akbar's promise, Havelock had previously received a copy of a proclamation in Persian in which Akbar called on the inhabitants of the valley to destroy the Brigade as it retired.

An answer was therefore prepared, with an eye to its being read by Akbar, and to gain time. In this Elphinstone and Pottinger were informed of Akbar's proclamation to the valley and were politely requested to 'point out the security which may be given for our safe march to Peshawar'.

Sale loudly declaimed that he would not move without orders from India. 'This is all right', scrawled Broadfoot to his relations in India, 'but the trying time will be when the force (if ever) comes down. We must then encourage the old General[1] by every means to hold out...' While Broadfoot was writing, a cossid came in from Brigadier Wild, who had been sent across the Punjab with one weak brigade, to say that he was no further than Peshawar and had insufficient strength to come on. Jalalabad must look after itself.

This gloomy news was followed by a pitiful letter from the

---

[1] i.e. Elphinstone.

Kabul force, written soon after the march had begun, saying that the guns had been surrendered, the treasury was empty and morale was at its lowest. Dennie, on reading the letter remarked, to Sale's anguish, that not a soul would get through but one – to tell of the destruction of the rest.

January 12th was a miserable day. Rain fell, off and on, and the roads and ramparts were sticky with yellow mud. An eerie gloom pervaded the whole garrison; soldiers and sepoys on guard or off duty or working on the defences were unnaturally quiet. Foreboding of disaster, for no apparent reason, stifled all jokes and chatter, and the thoughts of every officer and man were westward to the passes where snow would be falling. A cossid rode in through the rain, and Havelock and Macgregor brought Sale the letter – a scribbled line, several days old, saying that the Kabul force had not yet been allowed to enter the Khurd Kabul Pass, that distress was great and that Akbar was raising the whole countryside against them.

January 13th was a Thursday. The rain had stopped. At about two in the afternoon Havelock and some officers were on the roof of the highest house in the town and looking out towards Char Bagh, a house and garden some 4 miles to the west. 'One of them', noted Havelock in his journal, 'espied a single horseman riding towards our walls. As he got nearer it was distinctly seen that he wore European clothes and was mounted on a travel-hacked yaboo which he was urging on with all the speed of which it yet remained master. A signal was made to him by someone on the walls, which he answered by waving a private soldier's forage cap over his head. The Kabul Gate was then thrown open, and several officers rushing out received and recognised in the traveller, who dismounted, the first and it is to be feared the last, fugitive of the ill-fated force at Kabul in Dr Brydon. He was covered with slight cuts and contusions and dreadfully exhausted. His first few hasty sentences extinguished all hope in the hearts of the listeners regarding the fortune of the Kabul force. It was evident that it was annihilated. Countenances full of sorrow and dejection were immediately seen in every corner of Jalalabad; all labour was suspended; the working parties recalled; the assembly sounded, the gates were closed and the walls and batteries manned and the cavalry stood ready to mount. The first impression was that the enemy were rapidly following a crowd of fugitives in upon the walls, but three shots only were heard; and when the effervescence in some measure subsided not an Afghan could be discovered. But the recital of Dr Brydon filled all hearers with horror, grief and indignation.'

The exhausted Brydon told in broken phrases how they had left Kabul, five thousand troops and hundreds of followers, on the Thursday previous. On the Saturday, in the Khurd Kabul Pass, 'great numbers had been killed'. Lady Sale had been wounded, but Akbar had carried her away, with the married officers and their wives, Elphinstone, Shelton and the politicals, as 'hostages'. Three days of rear-guard fighting, treachery and bad management had brought the force, a starving, weakened rabble, to Jagdalak. Yesterday morning they had started up the Jagdalak Pass: 'the confusion was now terrible; all discipline was at an end'. He was wounded and staggered on. After that it was a ghastly memory of hunger, thirst and massacre, gibbering sepoys freezing to death, 'men running up the hills on the side of the road, throwing away their arms', a few of the European soldiers making a gallant stand till cut down where they stood. By daybreak that morning Brydon and seven European officers and a few soldiers were at Gandamak, 'and had lost all traces of those in our rear'. They pushed on; several were trapped and killed by villagers. Three had ridden forward and he had not seen them again. Eventually he was alone, and broke through a last knot of armed villagers, his sword broken, his pistol lost, until he had seen Jalalabad in the distance. 'Suddenly all my energy seemed to forsake me, I became nervous and frightened at shadows, and I really think I would have fallen from my saddle but for the peak of it.' But by then Sinclair of the 13th and others were riding out to meet him.

While Brydon was being fed and his wounds dressed (his pony was taken to a stable, lay down and died), cavalry was sent out to scour the plain for survivors. Havelock and most of the officers were standing above the Kabul Gate, 'the poor General looking out with a spy-glass Kabul-ward', when Broadfoot came up to the ramparts and called Havelock aside, urging him to make the General and Macgregor see the gravity of their position, 'knowing them both to be in the habit of keeping away the belief in danger, rather than of estimating and preparing for it', and to settle at once either to hold out to the last man, as he hoped, or to retreat on Peshawar that very night while it was still possible. Havelock spoke to Sale who said he would stand his ground.

Cavalry patrols were sent out again in the evening and found nothing but the bodies of three British officers. When darkness fell a bright light was set burning on a bastion near the Kabul Gate, and for three nights long, at half-hour intervals, the garrison heard their bugler sound, as a signal to possible survivors, the 'Advance', its rousing notes strident and cynical. A battered and dying European merchant came in on the third night, and one sepoy Lance-Naik some days afterwards.

Close investment was certain. 'We can no longer trust our Afghan Irregulars', Havelock wrote to Marshman, after telling him of Brydon's arrival, 'and are getting rid of them. We must, by God's help, strive to defend an extensive *enceinte* of which the parapets are not simply cannon proof, with an insufficient supply of ammunition which can last only by being husbanded; and only two, not strong, regiments of infantry, one European and the other native, a good artillery and 200 horse. We have full six weeks' provisions but forage for only about three weeks longer than we can command the country around us. We have embodied camp followers already to upwards of a thousand, and are arming them with muskets, jezails, swords, spears, and even stones for the defence of the walls... I think we can, by God's blessing, if besieged with guns protract our defence full forty days. We are resolved on every effort to save for Government Jalalabad and Eastern Afghanistan. If it cannot then relieve us we sink, but we shall I trust die like soldiers.'

The whole force was awed and shaken by the proximity of a disaster unparalleled in British Indian history. On the Sunday, January 16th, Havelock, who had maintained his informal Bible meetings with such men as were off duty, suggested a partial cession of work in order that Divine Service might be held. Sale invited him to read the service.

The European officers and men assembled in a square of the Bala Hissar, with the Union Jack fluttering overhead from the tower. 'Everyone came as usual, with sword and pistol or musket and bayonet', wrote Captain Thomas Seaton of the 35th NI, 'and with sixty rounds in pouch, ready at a moment's notice to march to battle. To me it was an affecting sight to see those great rough fellows of the 13th, with their heads bowed, humbly confessing their sins before God, and acknowledging their dependence on His goodness and mercy.' The familiar Church of England morning service sounded moving and impressive as Havelock read, in his clear, rather abrupt voice. For the psalm of the day he substituted Psalm 46, 'which', he had remarked, 'Luther was wont to use in seasons of peculiar difficulty and depression', and the men all joined in the words: 'God is our hope and strength, a very present help in trouble. Therefore will we not fear... The heathen make much ado and the kingdoms are moved: but God hath shewed his voice and the earth shall melt away. The Lord of hosts is with us: the God of Jacob is our refuge... Be still then, and know that I am God: I will be exalted among the heathen, and I will be exalted in the earth. The Lord of hosts is with us: the God of Jacob is our refuge.'

ON JANUARY 25TH a formal letter arrived from Kabul. Written in official red ink by the munshi of Shah Shujah's court, it pointed out that the Brigade was still, despite the treaty, in Jalalabad and asked what were its intentions? A letter came also from

Mohammed Akbar informing Sale that Lady Sale and the other hostages were his prisoners in the Lughman valley, forty miles across the hills to the north, and that he was prepared to negotiate the evacuation of Jalalabad and the restoration of his father to the throne.

Macgregor was much with Sale throughout the day and on January 26th the officers commanding were summoned to a Council of War in Sale's room in the Bala Hissar. Havelock, and Hamlet Wade the Brigade-Major, attended as Sale's staff officers to take down the minutes, but had no vote. Sale sat at the head of the table with Macgregor beside him. Dennie and Monteith, commanding the 13th Light Infantry and the 35th Native Infantry, Colonel Oldfield commanding the cavalry, Captain Abbott the Company's artillery and Captain Backhouse the Shah's, and George Broadfoot (sappers and miners) formed the Council. Though the proceedings were confidential they were not exactly secret since the door to Macgregor's room was open and his Afghan assistants came and went.

'Capt Macgregor and Gen Sale', runs Broadfoot's notes, 'informed us that they had resolved to yield and negotiate for a safe retreat. They laid before us a letter they wished our assent to. It was Persian, in reply to Shah Shujah.' The meeting was immediately in uproar. Some abused Lord Auckland (whose term of office had only a few weeks to run) and the Commander-in-Chief. Others abused Sale and Macgregor, who at one point even started an argument between themselves. Broadfoot picked up Macgregor's letter to the Shah, held it close to his inflamed eyes (his spectacles were broken) and found some of its phrases so 'submissive' that he threw it on the ground in disgust and argued hotly, with a string of oaths, that a new Governor-General was on his way out and 'a feeble war policy was impossible' and thus they should hold their ground. Havelock sat silent.

Broadfoot's vehemence, however, brought Dennie, who hated him, to argue for Sale and Macgregor, with Abbott in support. After an hour or more Broadfoot proposed adjournment. As they went out Monteith scratched his wig, told Broadfoot that he agreed they should hold out 'and quoted some not inappropriate poetry' – 'the gallant colonel's usual declamation', Havelock used to say, 'having something of the nature of prose upon stilts'.

The 'Jackdaw Parliament', as Havelock called it, stood adjourned overnight. Sale was a byword for physical courage (as also Macgregor) but Auckland's system of control by politicals, and Sale's own dislike of making a decision had reduced him from a general in military command to a wavering chairman of committee. That night, when Havelock was sitting alone in his room, Broadfoot called. Havelock said he was in full agreement with him, but, recorded Broadfoot, 'he disapproved of the warmth of my language', which was defeating its own purpose. In the morning, therefore, Broadfoot put his views on paper.

The Council assembled again in the afternoon. As they chatted before taking their seats, Monteith avoided Broadfoot and 'seemed gloomy'; Macgregor had won him over. As the meeting began Dennie and Abbott were sarcastic about Broadfoot and hinted that his hot feelings made his judgment unsound. Broadfoot read his paper and Havelock, in one of the rare interventions which were all that his position allowed, mentioned his concurrence. Broadfoot proposed a fighting retreat without a treaty but this was dismissed as impracticable. Clause by clause the letter to Shah Shujah was debated, voted on and passed, though some of the more abject phrases were altered.

Broadfoot insisted that they did not hold Jalalabad for Shah Shujah but for the Indian Government and must have express instructions to yield it. Their duty to their country came first, and to this Havelock 'expressed decided concurrence'. Broadfoot maintained that 'we could hold out till relieved by Kandahar, in fact for any time we liked; could colonise if we liked; also, we *could* retreat' – without negotiation. He urged, if they must go, a fighting retreat moving through the country, 'uniting vigour with moderation'. At this Dennie exploded in a welter of inconsistencies, 'Oh yes, moderation! Sacking! None of your moderation. Bring the whole country on us!' and Sale 'got up and walked about in agitation'.

At length one clause remained – that on exchanging hostages. Broadfoot said that hostages were worthless while the enemy held the prisoners. Macgregor offered to go himself but Sale would have none of it. Monteith said no one would go. Broadfoot said he would go if ordered at which Oldfield exclaimed, with what Havelock remembered as 'astounding vehemence', 'I for one will fight here to the last drop of my blood, but I plainly declare that I will never be a hostage, and I am surprised anyone should propose such a thing, or think that an Afghan's word is to be taken for anything'. Sale said that if they were attacked on the negotiated retreat he would execute a hostage. 'Oh yes,' asked Broadfoot, to Sale's horror, 'will you do this if the enemy before our faces hang two ladies for every man we put to death?'

After the last vote Broadfoot sarcastically congratulated the Council 'on the figure we should make if the relieving force should arrive as we were marching out'. Dennie said that in such case he would not go. 'We shall make you go,' said Broadfoot. 'faith must be kept.' 'This caused merriment as we broke up.' As the members left the room Havelock heard Dennie blurting out to a knot of enquirers that 'we are going to retire from Jalalabad and abandon the country'. Havelock rushed out and implored him to keep it secret, for the sake of morale.

The letter to Shah Shujah was despatched on January 28th. To offset rumours Broadfoot secured Sale's permission to dig an extensive and necessary ditch round the town and had as many men as possible at the work. Barracks and guard rooms were completed and everything prepared as if for a siege. No sign was yet seen of Akbar's armies, the loot of Kabul still delaying them – a providence in itself, for every day gained was vital.

Havelock and Broadfoot were determined to reverse the decision of the Council. For some days they were entirely alone in their opinions, an isolation cementing a friendship which had been steadily deepening. And a letter came in from one of the prisoners, Colin Mackenzie, a close friend of both. 'I know not how this captivity may end', he wrote, 'but my first trust is in God, who has hitherto so miraculously preserved my life. Our party bears up wonderfully.' Mackenzie who had undergone a deep conversion a few years earlier, had been one of the firmest supporters of Havelock's chapel in Kabul. Broadfoot, for all his affection for Havelock and Mackenzie, and the courageous piety of his father, a Church of Scotland minister who had resigned his living on a matter of conscience, and for all his own moral courage and what Havelock described as 'his uncompromising love of truth' would never respond to Havelock's attempts to win him to a personal faith.

On the last two days of January Captain Mayne of the cavalry who called Havelock 'my dear friend and my teacher in the art of war', cleverly captured some hundred and seventy cattle and more than seven hundred sheep, which improved the prospects of prolonged defence. Morale rose. Backhouse, having 'recovered from his anger against the Governor-General', was becoming ashamed of his vote for capitulation. A lieutenant of artillery who knew nothing of the decision of the Council of War happened to mention to Havelock and Broadfoot some incoherent mumbles and growls of Monteith's, which they recognised as signs that he also was regretting his vote.

On February 8th Shah Shujah's official answer was brought in: if the garrison were sincere in their offer to capitulate, 'let the principal gentlemen affix their seals'. A long and vague private letter to Macgregor seemed to point to the Shah being favourable but powerless. Sale and Macgregor discussed the situation for two days and on February 11th the Council of War reassembled, Havelock once more taking down the minutes of a violent debate.

Sale and Macgregor urged that seals should be fixed as requested. Broadfoot promptly read a draft he had prepared telling the Shah that since his answer to their last was evasive they should await the Governor-General's direct orders. Broadfoot's draft was rejected as violent. Backhouse, now thoroughly behind Broadfoot, scribbled a more temperate alternative. Sale told him he was facetious, and began swearing at the opponents and soon they were all shouting at each other across the table. At length, after an adjournment and more argument, only Sale and Macgregor stood for negotiating. Then Sale, Major-General and KCB, whose authority and responsibility were supreme, meekly said that he would be guided by the opinion of the council – and thus, against his own decision, became in time a national hero.

Macgregor despatched a letter to Kabul, refusing to negotiate. The next day a message arrived from General Pollock, that he had reached Peshawar, that further reinforcements were coming up to him and that the Government were determined to relieve Jalalabad. When the message was reported to the senior officers most of them avoided each other's eyes.

A LITTLE AFTER eleven o'clock on the morning of February 19th Havelock was sitting beside Sale in the office writing, in such French as they could remember, a letter to General Pollock in answer to his plea, received a day earlier, that they should hold out until he was strong enough to advance with certain success. They had detailed their dwindling resources. 'Ces circonstances me semble' wrote Havelock in Sale's name, 'de demander que votre avance a notre secours sera prompt – the only means of securing the avowed object of government, i.e. the relief of the –' At that moment the table began to shake.

The walls swayed. They rushed out, as rumbling grew louder and louder, 'as if a thousand heavy wagons were driven at speed over a rough pavement'. A column of thick dust was rising, houses, walls, and bastions rocking and reeling, the parapets crumbling like so much sand. From inside the fort came screams. As Seaton said afterwards, 'the ground heaved and set like the sea and the whole plain appeared rolling in waves towards us.

The roaring died down – and then was renewed with such fury, with houses falling like ninepins and dust blotting out the sky, that all thought that their end had come.' Suddenly the earthquake stopped. 'A dead silence succeeded... The men were absolutely green with fear. This silence was no less awful than the thunder of the rumbling, for we expected it would be succeeded by something yet more terrible.'

Someone reported that Monteith was lost in the ruins. Sale and Havelock ran round to find him and saw the carefully oiled wig, covered with dust, under a heap of timber and rubble. Sale pulled at it, and heard a cry, 'Let go my head!' Sale, overjoyed at this sign of life, pulled ten times harder, and Monteith was heard roaring, 'Who is the scoundrel tugging at my *hair*?' Monteith was dug up, none the worse; his two orderlies, both killed, miraculously proved to be the only casualties.

Havelock went on round the walls and found men of the 13th standing in groups, badly shaken. 'Now, men,' a young soldier, Edward Teer, remembered him saying, 'that is the voice of the Great "I am" telling us not to put our trust in the big guns and mud walls, but to trust in Him, our God! At the same time we must get to work to get the guns up!'

And then they looked at the damage. Thomas Seaton described what they found: 'the place presented an awful appearance of destruction and desolation. The upper stories of the houses that a few minutes before had reared themselves above the ramparts so trim and picturesque, were all gone, and beams, posts, doors, planks, windows, bits of walls, ends of roofs, earth and dust, all mingled together in one confused heap, were all that remained... A month's cannonading with a hundred pieces of heavy artillery could not have produced the damage that the earthquake had effected in a few seconds. Our walls, in which we took so much pride, and in which we had so much confidence, were in even a worse state. The hand of the Almighty had indeed humbled our pride, and taught us the wholesome lesson that He alone is a sure defence.'

7

The Crowning Mercy

Mohammed Akbar Khan was seven miles away. 'We guessed', wrote Havelock, 'that he was not in less consternation than ourselves. His camp could scarcely have escaped the shock; but it was necessary to guard against a sudden rush being made upon our walls by parties of his people who might have been concealed behind the hills. As soon as the agitation subsided the troops were assembled at their alarm-posts by sound of bugle; but after a short pause, to ascertain that no foes were near, piled their arms, resumed their entrenching tools, and set themselves with determination to the task of restoring the defences... In a few hours the walls wore a more encouraging aspect.'

In a matter of days the defences had been improved back to reasonable strength. 'The energy with which our troops of all arms laboured in restoring the defence', wrote Havelock, 'exceeds all calculation and beggars all commendation. They worked like men struggling for their existence, but with as much cheerfulness and good humour as industry and perseverance.' An additional reason for their energy was not far to seek: all the rum supplies had been lost on the march from Kabul, and once again Havelock had proof before his eyes of the truth of his contention that temperance, so seldom experienced in the ranks with the ration then normal, was one of the strongest aids to efficiency and morale. 'They had no rum to paralize their nerves, sour their tempers or predispose them to idleness and sullen discontent', he went on. 'A long course of sobriety and labour has made men of mere boys of recruits and brought the almost raw levy, which formed two-thirds of the 13th, to the firm standard of the Roman discipline.' What is more, as Sale wrote in his despatch, 'Crime has been almost unknown among them...'

So swift was the recovery from the earthquake that Akbar Khan was convinced when he saw Jalalabad that the whole affair was arranged by English witchcraft.

TWO DAYS AFTER the earthquake, foraging parties were again attacked, some miles up the valley. On February 25th Akbar planted his camp only two miles westwards from the Kabul Gate. Havelock observed 'a single poled English tent among others, which is ascertained to be the canvas abode of Mohammed Akbar Khan. Our telescopes distinctly notice three or four other tents of white canvas; the rest are of black felt.' The next day the Afghans were astride the Peshawar road to the east and communication with India was cut. The siege had begun. In the last mail which came through Havelock heard from Marshman that Hannah and the boys had sailed for England. 'She has splendid accommodation, a good captain, a strong and new ship and most agreeable company.' Their two little girls were left at Serampore. Havelock was relieved to know that the news of the Kabul massacres had missed her.

On this first day of close siege the Afghan cavalry took post on the high ground out of range of the garrison's guns. 'Their infantry', noted Captain Abbott in his journal, 'occupied the broken ground around us and fired, but to no purpose. They had four standards, two red, one white with blue stripes and another white. An old Mullah of their party, as if in derision of such vanities, displayed a dirty turban at the end of a bamboo.'

Sale would not permit the men to return the Afghans' fire lest they waste ammunition, but officers were allowed to snipe with their sporting rifles. Each evening the Afghans would draw off, Akbar preferring blockade to assault. Grass cutters would be attacked in the morning and come flying back to the gates, but later could go out again and cut as much as they needed.

Afghan musket balls were picked out of the parapet and walls for re-use, and a block of wood, carved into the figure of a man dressed in Sale's spare uniform and showed over the ramparts with a sword which waggled when a string was pulled, for several days brought a shower of bullets for collection. Communications with Pollock beyond the Khyber depended on the courage of cossids. Several were caught. One, sent out with a note hidden in a cake, was marched up into sight of the walls and choked to death with his own cake. Another was returned to the garrison with ears and nose sliced off. The plain was coloured and shadowed by Akbar's thousands, with their horses, tents, cattle and baggage, against which a bare two thousand, British and sepoy, held Jalalabad with diminishing supplies. On March 7th a formal demand for evacuation was delivered by Shah Shujah's envoy, who privately informed Macgregor that on refusal an additional army was to move from Kabul with the siege guns captured from Elphinstone. He brought also a letter from the commander of the Ghazni garrison reporting its surrender on the failure of the water supply. Among the prisoners was Henry Williams, son of Hannah Havelock's eldest sister.

Akbar's blockade grew more stringent. Sale had reckoned he could hold out till the end of March, but a message from General Pollock asked whether he could survive till mid-April. Sale ordered his camels to be destroyed, to provide more forage for the horses. All ranks were on reduced rations. There was bread but little meat, no sugar, tea or coffee; no wine or beer, but plenty of tobacco and no shortage of water.

The days were hotter. The garrison began to experience that forlorn sense of isolation of the besieged. Their lives were bounded by the unchanging scene of the river, now rapid and full, with the marshy grassland in the foreground below the walls and the distant yellow-brown hills; all around on the plain, at a respectful distance but effectively blockading, were the Afghan positions, while groups of horsemen 'perpetually insulted our walls by attacks and alerts'. Far away to the east lay the opening which led to the Khyber, from which, so they almost thought, they would never see a redcoat emerge. To complete the depression, continual mild earth tremors produced a nervous sense of insecurity. 'It savours of romance but is a sober fact', wrote Havelock in Sale's official despatch, 'that the city was thrown into alarm within the space of little more than one month by the repetition of full one hundred shocks.'

Havelock began to urge Sale to attack Akbar's camp, in order to relieve the pressure on Pollock as he entered the Khyber and to maintain morale. Sale said he must husband their scanty ammunition. Broadfoot believed that 'the poor General is tied by the fear of retaliation on the captives in Lughman', and certainly Sale would sometimes be found silent and sad on the ramparts looking across to the north, while once, in his office, he wept openly.

On March 24th the Afghans harassed the grass cutters closer under the walls and Broadfoot was badly wounded. Each day the enemy grew bolder, even occupying, until driven off, an outlying corner of the works. At the end of the week Backhouse was disgusted to see one of his own guns, captured from the Kabul force, trailed under his nose, 'a disgraceful sight', with a gleeful escort of Afghan foot and cavalry setting off for the Khyber. He asked Sale's leave to sally out and recover it – 'in less than twenty minutes the gun might have been in this fort' – but the General refused. Backhouse was furious: 'the General is worse than I have hitherto called him,' he said, and now publicly called for an offensive. 'We have only', he wrote in a letter, 'to attack Akbar with vigour to floor him and his altogether, and it is undoubtedly the General's duty to make the attempt now that an opportunity offers itself; most officers in the garrison are of this opinion, and Capt Havelock has said all he could to the General in favour of it, but in vain.'

The belief was that Pollock would not arrive in time. A full-scale assault might be launched any hour, and at night both officers and men off-duty lay down fully clothed. On March 30th Havelock wrote to Harry Smith at Simla his farewell letter, asking (should it ever reach Smith) that he should pass it on to Marshman at Serampore: 'We still hold our own, by God's blessing, but shall have grain provisions on a reduced rate for men, and corn for troops only to the 13th proximo. Existence may be supported by one contrivance and another ten days longer, but the most sanguine cannot hope to protract that term. You will see then how much depends on General Pollock's success in forcing or turning the Khyber... All is in the hands of God. I wish Marshman clearly to understand that if I fall in this struggle, which humanly speaking is so probable, my wife and children will, as regards worldly prospects, have to depend entirely on the money lodged for the purchase of my majority, and the small pension of my rank. I trust he will be able to make arrangements to prevent their experiencing want, until the question of the issue of this siege and of Havelock shall have been decided. He can write to England that I am at present in the highest health and spirits, and relying fully on the merits of the Redeemer, and will be well pleased, if it be His will, to end my days in so honourable an enterprise as the defence of Jalalabad.'

The next day the Afghans were so emboldened that they drove their flocks of sheep and goats to graze within six hundred yards of the walls, thereby destroying much of the scanty forage of the garrison and making their mouths water. Sale was asked to permit a foray to bring them in, but he was wary. Havelock jotted in his note-book, 'for a long time large flocks of sheep have been seen grazing within cannon-shot of the place and hopes were sometimes entertained of capturing them. It was, however, commonly observed that considerable bodies of horsemen were posted in some secure place', and an ambush was suspected, with the flocks as decoy. Their closer approach seemed too inviting to miss, and on April 1st a force of the 13th and 35th, with all the cavalry and sappers, rushed out of the rebuilt Kabul Gate, took shepherds and escort by surprise and brought in nearly five hundred sheep and goats.

At once the food situation was improved. The sepoys refused their share of the meat as the need of the European troops was far greater; an old Indian camp follower said years afterwards to a young officer of the 13th, 'In that war the soldier sahibs and the sepoys were as brothers – one would see them walking arm in arm'.

A message reached Sale from Pollock, hidden in a quill, to say he was advancing into the Khyber without awaiting his reinforcements though his sepoys were terrified at the thought of the Pass and he knew he was taking a risk. Havelock suggested that the obvious course was to attack Akbar to prevent his reinforcing the tribesmen in the Khyber. Sale would not agree. The sense of frustration among the officers in the garrison increased. 'We have no confidence in Sale', wrote Abbott in a letter of April 4th, 'who is a very good fellow but a very inefficient general.'

On the evening of April 5th, Havelock's forty-seventh birthday, a Kashmiri spy who had just escaped from captivity in Akbar's camp came to Havelock's room and informed him the Afghans had heard that General Pollock had been defeated the day previous in the Khyber. On the strength of a single report Havelock did nothing. Towards midnight another spy came in and told him that the Afghans were talking of guns captured and Akbar was even then gloating over some mangled heads of Pollock's soldiers. At dead of night Havelock went across to Sale, woke him, reported the news and urged him to attack at once with the entire force as the only salvation. Sale refused.

The next morning the hills reverberated to a salute fired by Akbar in honour of the victory. 'Coupled with the news of the preceding night', wrote Havelock, 'the event did at first create some feelings of gloom. It seemed as if the tide of events had set in uniformly against us and that our hopes of succour, which had been some days sanguine, had once more vanished and that we were consigned to a new succession of privations and labours, terminating in inevitable and utterly ruinous disaster.' The more imaginative saw nothing ahead but assault and capture by storm; and, for those not lucky enough to be killed in the fighting, a long line of prisoners down by the river, British and sepoy, stripped and awaiting mutilation and a slow death under Afghan knives. A few of the senior officers, since Akbar was chivalrous as he was cruel, might be led away to slavery.

Havelock felt that he and his brother officers were 'all burnt with the desire to be led against the enemy and try their mettle in the open field'. The heads of corps went to Sale and begged to be allowed to fight. 'We talked for an hour using every argument in vain,' said Abbott. At last Sale swore at them and drove them from the room. Abbott then took an unprecedented step of insubordination: 'I proposed that we should quietly parade our men at four a.m. on the 7th and go out before he was out of his bed, but of all the party only three supported me, and the plan was abandoned'.

Two hours later Sale changed his mind. The attack would take place at dawn. 'I love the old soldier', wrote Havelock afterwards, 'and rejoice that though he did not listen to my single voice he was swayed by the united opinion of some older and some younger men, since it redounded to his own reputation and to the good of his country.'

Soon Havelock was sitting by Sale's side drawing up a plan. Sale gave him the wounded Broadfoot's place in command of the right column, to lead the attack. Havelock's opportunity had come.

AKBAR'S CAMP LAY down by the river about two miles from Jalalabad, half-right from the Kabul Gate. It was protected by a dry bed where the river once ran, and between town and camp were five or six forts held by enemy picquets.

Havelock's plan, approved and issued by Sale, divided the force into three columns. The right column, Havelock's own, of one company each of the 13th and the sepoys, and the detachment of Gurkha sappers, some three hundred and sixty in all, was to advance towards the camp keeping to the left of the steep bank which led to the marsh ground near the river, and after clearing the enemy skirmishers was to penetrate the fortified dry river bed. Meanwhile the stronger columns under Dennie (centre) and Monteith (left) with the light guns and cavalry in support, would be coming up to assault the Afghan centre. Havelock would be working round to his right, to the enemy's extreme left wing where their main strength was believed to be, and would drive the Afghans back on Dennie and Monteith. 'All three assailing columns were then to work in combination towards our own left.' Sale and headquarters would be with Dennie. It was agreed that during the advance all isolated forts or picquets were to be ignored.

Before dawn on Thursday, April 7th 1842, the garrison assembled without bugle or drum in the open space close inside the Kabul Gate. Afghan agents had been spreading a report among the followers that Akbar had abandoned his camp, but this was believed a ruse. In the chilly darkness officers gave out their orders in a silence broken only by the occasional neigh of a horse or the clink of a musket. The British troops, well fed since the sheep raid, were in highest spirits. The password was 'Forward'.

The Kabul Gate creaked open and the columns moved smartly out, Havelock's in the van. The eastern sky was streaked with light, and the river glinted in the distance. A last check with Sale and they marched off behind the skirmishers, at the light infantry quick step, muskets at the trail, with Havelock on his grey Arab Feroze leading at a brisk walk. They crossed the shallow canal and as the daylight increased saw the small forts and picquet posts before them. In the distance, a mile and a half away, the Afghan army, some six thousand strong, could be discerned drawn up to receive them.

The Afghan picquets opened fire. Backhouse, with the guns on the left, watched Havelock drawing on: 'the enemy soon opened a peppering fire on the right column as it passed to the right of the "old patched-up fort" which was occupied by 200 or 300 of their best men. Havelock kept moving and took no notice of this old fort.' One or two men fell wounded but the column was soon out of the arc of fire. The day was now fully light though the sun not up, and Havelock could see clearly the Afghan host, its green and yellow banners waving, its armoured horsemen massed to the right. Puffs of smoke and the first reports from guns (once Elphinstone's guns) brought balls kicking the dust well behind on his left: Dennie must be passing the fort. The musketry increased and it sounded as if, contrary to plan, the fire was being returned. Havelock marched on, to the throb of the Afghan drums.

He was now out in the open, with a walled enclosure a little ahead on his right from which his skirmishers had ejected a few Afghan snipers. Looking back, however, he could see the other columns not as close as they should have been. Major Frazer, Sale's acting aide-de-camp, galloped up with Sale's orders to halt; Sale had thrown Dennie's column against the fort (contrary to plan) and Dennie was fatally wounded; Havelock must wait. Havelock acknowledged the order, saying, 'I will halt where I am, but I hear Akbar's drum beating and shall soon have his whole force upon me'.

Havelock was isolated, by Sale's folly. The din was now deafening. But Havelock always found that the louder the noise and the swifter the movement of battle the quicker and clearer he could think, drawing swiftly on experience and his knowledge of military lore. And, as always in action, he experienced a strong sense of the Christian's privilege: 'I felt throughout that the Lord Jesus was at my side'. He halted and ordered the company of the 13th into the walled enclosure, the sepoys to form square a little way back outside it. The Afghan cavalry moved forward from the line. They were gathering speed, half a mile away.

Havelock placed himself, unprotected, where he could command both parties; as a young soldier of the 13th remarked, 'he was as calm under fire as if he stood in a drawing room full of ladies, a man fit to live or die'. He gave strict orders that no one was to fire until he gave the word.

In front, nearer every moment, cantered the Afghan horse. They wheeled to Havelock's right and crossed his front at five hundred yards, an untidy menacing mass half hidden by dust, and swerved round to thunder in from the flank, screaming their battle cries, waving their long curved knives, levelling lances. Havelock waited. A loud report to his left as a jumpy sepoy let off his musket, and both companies, forgetting their orders, fired. Feroze, with Havelock caught unawares, threw him and cantered riderless back to the town. Stunned, Havelock lay on the ground as the Afghan charge swept down. Two men of the 13th and a sepoy rushed out and dragged him to safety in the enclosure. He recovered himself and saw the Afghans now at only fifty yards, a wild medley of colour and movement. At a second volley, the charge hesitated, men and horses falling and the ranks behind tripping over the fallen in front. The air, acrid with powder, was filled with screaming of horses, and the cries of the Afghans, wounded and unwounded. Their leader, well forward, came galloping in and his hand was on a British bayonet before he fell, but a third volley, at less than thirty yards, broke the charge. The survivors turned and fled, leaving the ground covered with dead and wounded horses and men.

No casualties in the column were reported. Havelock looked back and saw Sale at last bringing on Dennie's men. He therefore re-formed his column and continued the advance, himself on foot, through the littered battlefield and on across the plain. They covered two or three hundred yards with the enemy guns firing heavily but ineffectually and had almost reached the river, on the edge of the marshy ground, when the Afghan horse once again bore down. Havelock quietly formed the column into square and gave strictest instructions that no one was to fire until the charge was thirty yards away. This time they obeyed. The charge was less assured, and broke on one volley.

As the Afghans turned the column advanced again and Havelock saw Backhouse's guns, which Sale had sent in support, coming across to the left. The guns unlimbered and fired into the enemy camp as Havelock and his column, cheering and at the double, charged across the dry river bed and into the

Afghan line. Despite a shell or two from the Afghan guns the mass ran forward, using the bayonet. Sale's and Monteith's columns were up, and the battle became a rout, Afghans jumping into the river or flying out at the back of their camp, which was now on fire. While the Light Cavalry pursued for a short distance the victorious columns re-formed.

By the time the sun rose high, Akbar's camp was in ashes and his army in flight. Four of Elphinstone's guns were back in British hands; a large magazine of ammunition, herds of cattle, ample stores of food and much miscellaneous plunder had been taken, and the siege effectually raised. Casualties were trivial, but Dennie was dead.

The honours of the day, as no one doubted or grudged, were with Havelock. And to the end of his life he kept the anniversary of the 'crowning mercy', as he called it with a memory of Cromwell, of April 7th 1842.[1]

THE CHIEFS OF the valley hastened to submit. The villagers brought in supplies of fresh food and the victorious garrison enjoyed themselves dividing Akbar's spoil. And they could at last bathe in the river. To complete their delight they heard that Pollock, far from being defeated on April 5th, had forced the Khyber Pass by a brilliant and unexpected manoeuvre, and was marching daily nearer, though more leisurely since he had heard of their victory.

On Saturday April 16th, Pollock was on his last march up the valley, with his strong force of British and sepoy infantry and cavalry, with guns and irregulars.

A full parade was ordered to meet him. The 13th Light Infantry scraped together a band; some wit suggested an appro-

---

[1] It is a great pity, especially in view of his letters to his wife from later campaigns, that none of Havelock's private letters about this battle or the Afghan Campaign survives, except for a few scraps published by Marshman. Havelock's letters to his wife from Afghanistan appear to have been lost during his lifetime; those to Marshman, and his journal, since publication of the *Memoir*.

priate tune; and Pollock's force marched into Jalalabad (under whose walls they had expected a famous victory) to the old Jacobite air, *Oh! but ye've been long o'coming*.

THROUGHOUT THE SUMMER of 1842 the large forces, some fifteen thousand men now camped round Jalalabad, were unable to move, through lack of transport animals (which had only been hired for the relief) and the vacillations of the supreme government. The new Governor-General, Lord Ellenborough, a clever but self-important politician who had been principal figure in a famous divorce and openly displayed his mistress in Calcutta, could not decide whether he wished to evacuate or to conquer Afghanistan. 'Lord E is fond of the army', Havelock learned from Marshman whose letters he was receiving again, 'of playing at soldiers, as they have it in Calcutta', but his policies blew hot and cold. 'The fact is that he is entirely governed by passion. He flew into the most disgraceful paroxysms of rage at the Council Chamber. He insulted everyone and then wondered he was not popular.' He had, however, treated the Jalalabad garrison handsomely, dubbing it 'Illustrious', ordering a twenty-one gun salute in its honour in every station of the army and exalting Sale into a hero.

Henry Lawrence arrived from the Punjab (though the power of the politicals had gone; Pollock was plagued by no Macnaghten) to serve on the staff. 'Havelock, in great feather, showed us round the fields of battle this morning', he wrote to his wife. 'I breakfasted with him afterwards and we had lots of talk. He is a fine soldier-like fellow.'

It was through a letter from Honoria Lawrence that Hannah, arrived in England, first heard of the Jalalabad victory. Havelock had news from John Marshman of a swift voyage of one hundred and one days round the Cape, with Harry and Joshua and two young Marshmans, though 'the four boys under her charge formed an united phalanx and occasionally treated with roughness the other boys and children not admitted into their ranks.

These as may be supposed complained to their mammas who espoused their part, and thus a kind of skirmish was kept up.'

Lawrence and Havelock were much together. 'I went to Havelock's chapel in the town yesterday evening', Lawrence wrote in July. 'He had about forty soldiers and ten or twelve officers. He prayed extemporarily, read a few verses, sang two hymns, and read a sermon on faith, hope and charity. We assembled under two united tents, where I fancy, all through the siege, he had thus collected a small congregation. It was blowing a dust-storm all the evening and night, but I went home with him to his tent, and sat for a couple of hours. He is a strange person, but is acknowledged to be as good soldier as a man; the best of both probably in the Camp.' 'He reads and prays much as if on parade', wrote Lawrence a week later, 'but he is a good man and a good soldier. I have never heard either doubted.'

Havelock had accepted Pollock's offer of the post of Adjutant-General to one of the two infantry divisions, as offering more scope in wartime than the command of the 13th, which might have come to him if the next senior, absent in England, retired. By late July Pollock was ready to move in force but it was feared in the Camp that the government had decided on evacuation, to Havelock's 'grief and shame'. In early August, after a post had come, Pollock was noticed particularly grim and determined. A few days later another post arrived and he announced that they would move on Kabul. His intimates afterwards discovered that he had been carrying in his pocket an unopened letter from Ellenborough which, sure enough, as Pollock had suspected, proved to be an order for immediate evacuation. It had been countermanded by the second letter, written after receiving a stiff directive from the Duke of Wellington in England. Pollock was to deal a blow at Kabul before evacuation and General Nott from Kandahar was also to 'retire by way of Kabul'.[1]

---

[1] This little episode (one of a long dispute between Pollock and Ellenborough) is of curious interest to the present writer since Sir George Pollock was my father's great-

Havelock marched from Jalalabad with Pollock and his first division on August 20th. While the main force was closing on Gandamak they took a detachment to punish tribesmen who had been amongst the worst perpetrators of the massacre of the Kabul force. The smoke and flames of forts, villages, crops and orchards was small compensation for the discovery of about sixty skeletons, 'the officers plainly distinguishable by the long hair which still remained attached to their skulls'.

Once again Havelock and his colleagues of Sale's Brigade found themselves in the Jagdalak Pass. The Afghans put up a stiff defence at the entrance and the 13th Light Infantry which had run away here in November now covered itself with glory. The narrow winding trail was a harrowing sight, in places literally blocked with Kabul force skeletons which 'had to be removed before our guns could pass', and caves on the hillsides choked with bodies, many still in a state of preservation. A small round tower in a valley on the third day's march was found 'filled', so Thomas Seaton described, 'with skeletons and decaying bodies up to the very roof; and there was a mound of them outside, half-way up the door, extending to a distance of twenty-six or twenty-seven feet from the wall and completely covering the steps. It was a ghastly sight. These were the remains of the poor fugitives whom I mentioned as having been stripped naked by the Afghans, and left to perish in the bitter cold.'

By September 15th the victorious, infuriated Army was encamped on the Kabul race course.

---

uncle while Lord Ellenborough was a collateral relative of my mother. Sir Frederick Pollock, then Attorney-General, wrote that Sir Henry Hardinge said to him one day, 'Your brother is a very odd person – talk of retreat and he is the dullest man in the world – no resources – a thousand difficulties – and a complete incapacity to understand orders. But tell him to go on and his faculties brighten prodigiously. He thoroughly understands you – he sees no obstacles, he stumbles on resources he before never dreamt of, and sets about the work with great cheerfulness and alacrity' (*MS letter of 4 June 1843, given by the author to Cambridge University Library*).

THE PRISONERS WERE still in the wilds of Kohistan. Sir Richmond Shakespear, an intrepid explorer, was sent to rescue them with a small force, and Sir Robert Sale and the 13th were allowed to follow as reserve. On September 21st the news ran round the camp that Sale was bringing his lady and all the prisoners (though Elphinstone had died during the summer) into Kabul, a neat piece of treachery having enabled them to escape and meet their rescuers half way. Havelock and many others went out to meet them. As the group of ex-captives, sunburnt and dishevelled, stood talking and joking with officers of the force Havelock asked whether his nephew, Henry Williams, had survived. A tall figure in filthy Afghan clothes and a bedraggled beard stepped forward, called out, 'Here I am, uncle!'

Before obeying Ellenborough's order to evacuate, Pollock, now joined by Nott from Kandahar, sent the division of which Havelock was Adjutant-General, McCaskill's, to shatter the Afghan stronghold at Istaliff, a town in a luxuriant valley deep in the mountains some forty miles north of Kabul. Two days' march from Kabul found them on a road shaded by tall walnut trees, with streams running down the hills on either side, and the vineyards on the southern slopes purple with raisins spread on the ground to dry. Turning the last corner, the pass dropped down to display a wide valley, green with trees and crops and scattered with little turreted forts. Opposite, the rock and town of Istaliff, known to be heavily defended, rose, terrace on terrace, glittering in the sun, to its crown of an ornate Mohammedan tomb sheltered by plane trees. Behind were mountains lightly topped by snow, and above them in the distance under the clear blue sky the snow summits of the Hindu Kush.

General McCaskill, an odd sort of Irishman, asked Havelock to produce a plan of attack and when it was brought told him to direct the operations. Havelock was delighted at the prospect of more or less unfettered control of a division in action. Of Jalalabad men he had Broadfoot and his Gurkhas, Backhouse's mountain train and Mayne on the staff. The plan was a surprise pincer movement at first light in the morning of September 29th.

Broadfoot and his sappers, leading the right-hand column, struck a little way into the hills and took the Afghans by surprise on their flank. 'The enemy's position', Havelock wrote, 'in gardens and behind enclosures and walls, backed by a town the flat roofs of which were occupied by riflemen, and behind which rose tremendous ridges of mountains, was strong, and the levies congregated for its defence were numerous and full of audacity and excitement, but the rapid advance of one column, aided by the manoeuvres of another, quickly dislodged them. The ground would not permit the use of artillery (except the little mountain train) but the pace of the Sappers, the 26th N I, and the gallant old 9th, was so good that the Afghans could not face them in the vineyards, and, once thrown into confusion, could never be rallied. Our troops indeed behaved everywhere well, and there was far less outrage of every kind, and above all to the women, than is seen ninety-nine times out of one hundred in cases of towns and cities stormed.'

Back in the captured town from which the inhabitants were fleeing up the mountains, Eldred Pottinger, the 'hero of Herat' and Macnaghten's successor until given over to Akbar as hostage, came over to Havelock and exclaimed, 'Oh, if we had only had you with us at Kabul things would have worn a very different aspect'. 'I will not undertake to say that I could have saved Kabul,' replied Havelock, 'but I feel confident George Broadfoot could have done it.'

McCaskill sat under a tree to the rear with a basket of Kabul plums. When Havelock's aide galloped up to announce the victory McCaskill merely said, 'Indeed! Will you take a plum?'

8

War in the Punjab

On the evening of May 21st 1843 forty-eight-year-old Brevet-Major Henry Havelock, CB, commander of No 4 Company, 13th Light Infantry, set off to walk down ten miles of rocky mountain road from Kussowlie, near Simla, to meet Hannah at the foot of the hills.

Five months had passed since he had crossed back into British India in the train of Sir Robert Sale, through ranks of gaily caparisoned elephants (who regrettably refused to trumpet the salute Lord Ellenborough had ordered), while the band of the Lancers played *Lo the Conquering Hero comes*. There had been months of disappointment. The wheel had come full circle, politically and personally. After all the bloodshed, misery, disgrace and final victory, Lord Ellenborough had returned Dost Mohammed to the throne from which Lord Auckland had so airily set out to eject him, four long years before. And while Broadfoot and other East India Company's officers of the 'Illustrious Garrison' had gone to rule provinces, Havelock, on the lapse of his war-time staff posts, had reverted to the command of a mere company.

Sale had turned against him. 'The man of all others most indebted to you', Broadfoot wrote, 'I fear feels the *burden* more than the obligations of gratitude.' 'All the *contradictions*', Havelock himself once burst out, 'I have had to endure from Sales, Pollocks, Archibald Campbells, Goughs and Wy Cottons, who have picked my brains and elevated themselves on my exertions and then treated me with the basest ingratitude!' Several senior officers had tried to help him at the Horse Guards but met prejudices. Not only had he neither money nor title but 'it was believed at Horse Guards and in other quarters that I professed to fear God, as well as honour the Queen, and that Lord Hill and sundry other wise persons had made up their minds that no man could, at once, be *a saint* and a soldier.'

Moreover, he considered that it was wrong for an officer to blow his own trumpet by constant applications. Broadfoot disagreed. 'You must indeed *speak up* – they must fear, as well as find you useful, or you will drop from the place it is your duty to occupy.' Havelock's hopes of a majority with money given by Marshman were dashed when another officer heard first of the vacancy; add to this a sharp attack of fever, and his leave hopelessly overdue and Hannah, back from England, delayed for months at Serampore by the illness of the girls, and it is small wonder that he wrote her what Marshman called 'without question the most gloomy and despairing letter I have ever seen under your sign manual'. Melancholy was never far from Havelock – not because of faith, he knew well, but because of lack of enough of it. He was unable even to amuse himself by writing a history of the Jalalabad campaign, since it was impossible to tell the whole truth (carefully suppressed in the official accounts) and keep his commission, and he had no wish to give an innocuous garbled account.

Hannah's absence was the worst. And now at last she had come. Early on May 22nd she reached Barr and 'Henry was there to meet me. He was greatly overcome at the sight of me and Pussy and very delighted with Baby'. After breakfast they got into doolies, Havelock with Pussy (as little Hannah Jane was always called) in one, and in another Hannah with three-year-old baby Honoria, who was generally called Nora but sometimes No, or even for a short time, Diddly. They reached Kussowlie at eleven o'clock, finding 'all Henry's old campaigning servants standing in a line to welcome me home', though home was a couple of tents, since the cantonment was not yet built.

'Henry looks better, infinitely better', Hannah told her mother, 'than he did when I saw him last. He is as brown as an

Afghan but *younger* rather than older.' The rest of the day 'was spent in receiving visits from our friends who dropped in one after another'.

Two days later they went to Simla on prolonged leave. Except for the few months in 1840 it was nearly four and a half years since they had been together. In the fine air of Simla, with its magnificent views and pleasant company, all Havelock's depressions blew away. 'Henry himself is very much improved in appearance,' Hannah told her mother in June. 'He drinks a glass of wine daily and is looking so well and happy. We have fallen into all our old plans the same as usual, only that if possible he is more indulgent than ever to me, and thinks more than ever that what I do is right... He has vast fun with Baby.' Their little cottage, with the portraits of the boys over the drawing-room mantelpiece, resounded to the laughter of children, for Charles and Mary Havelock were only five minutes away and the cousins played together. Charles' youngest, little Mary, whose life was to be strangely intertwined with Havelock's, was reported by Hannah to 'do nothing but eat and sleep. She is the stupidest child I ever saw and will *not* speak'. Little Nora had been shy of her father at first, but now 'she is an independent little miss and talks to Henry in the most commanding manner... We have a pretty little Afghan kid which is a great favourite with both children. And they have both got little hill sticks with which they trudge along over the mountains.' The two families went for picnics and rides and Hannah rode Feroze 'the good and handsome old Arab steed', as Havelock told his mother-in-law, 'which I rode in nearly all our Afghan fights. Age has steadied him and he carries her safely and well over the broad and well fenced roads of this mountain metropolis'.

Havelock wrote that he was enjoying a 'period of rest and leisure such as I have scarcely ever known during the last twenty years. Ease with me is not stagnation. Books are a never failing resource and this delightful locality offers me to the full as much of society as is in any way necessary to my satisfaction.' 'There is much gaiety going on here', Hannah could write, 'and as Henry has no duty here he partakes in all, which I am sure is one reason of his looking so well. Mrs Harry Smith gave a ball on the 5th to which Henry went but I could not, owing to my cold being at its worst. However, she sent the children a box full of cakes the next day.'

And so the months of leave in Simla sped by, with the Havelocks 'on calling terms with everybody, on friendly terms with most, on intimate terms with the best people; having frequently new friends to dinner and yet deriving our greatest enjoyment from each other's society and never so happy as when alone!'

The *London Gazette* of June 30th reached Simla late in August, announcing that Havelock had been given a regimental majority which had become available without purchase. Despite his twenty-eight years' service the step was conceded 'as an act of grace to me, with the innuendo, I expect, that it closed the door to all further claim for the last Afghan campaign'; but at least it improved their finances. A week later he was appointed Persian Interpreter to the Commander-in-Chief; Marshman's friend Wilberforce Bird, at the head of affairs in Calcutta while Lord Ellenborough toured the upper provinces, had prevailed on Sir Hugh Gough to give Havelock an unexpected vacancy.

HAVELOCK JOINED SIR Hugh Gough at Cawnpore where an army was being assembled in consequence of an anti-British revolution in the independent Mahratta kingdom of Gwalior. The Mahratta army was large and formerly had been trained by French officers, and believing since Afghanistan that British power was on the wane the Mahrattas were spoiling for a fight.

Though a counter-revolution restored the situation, Lord Ellenborough decided to make a demonstration and hold durbar with the Maharani of Gwalior, a widow twelve years old. Gough understood from the politicals that the Mahratta army was a leaderless rabble, and not having lived through Afghanistan presumed them always right. Besides, Lord Ellenborough assured him that it would be a picnic and invited Lady Gough and her daughter and Mrs Harry Smith to share the fun.

Gough's force, some five thousand strong and predominantly sepoy, crossed the frontier river, the Chambal, on December 22nd and was soon immersed in the curious ravines and hummocks which form a natural defence to the plain of Gwalior. On Christmas Day Lord Ellenborough's grand dinner in camp was rudely interrupted by news that the little Maharani, far from coming to meet Lord Ellenborough, was sending her army to throw him out. Harry Smith later reported that the Mahrattas, ten thousand strong and evidently expecting reinforcements, were about eight miles south in an unfavourable position behind the village of Maharajpur. Gough decided to attack them the following morning.

Lord Ellenborough and the ladies were delighted at the prospect of a skirmish while General Churchill, the Quartermaster, exclaimed that the only weapon he should need would be a horsewhip. Havelock and others had read of the Mahratta Wars; moreover, the spirit of the sepoy troops had been badly shaken by Afghanistan. Before dawn Gough's army set off from the encampment, over the river, and through hummocks and ravines which the sappers blasted, thus warning the Mahrattas of the British advance. Lord Ellenborough and the ladies rode on elephants. At about seven o'clock, as the army emerged on a flat cultivated plain a mile from Maharajpur, through which Harry Smith had ridden unharmed the previous evening, a loud bellow and female screams were heard; a round shot had carried away the ear of one of the ladies' elephants.

At half past eight Gough launched his attack by sending the horse artillery to engage the Mahratta guns. Before many minutes passed it was obvious that the 'skirmish' was a highly serious battle. The Mahratta fire was hot and accurate. The enemy guns were less than four hundred yards ahead; the British foot were moving steadily, though men were falling continually, but a sepoy regiment was hanging back.

Havelock, riding once again on Feroze, kept close beside Gough through the storm of round shot. Gough was swearing. 'Will no one get that sepoy regiment on?' he roared above the din. Havelock went forward. He asked one of the British officers its name and was told 'the 56th Native Infantry'. 'I don't want its number – what is its native name?' '*Lamboorun-ke-pultan* – Lambourn's regiment.' Havelock trotted to the front, took off his cap and waved it, shouting encouragement in Hindustani and reminding the sepoys that they fought under the very eye of the Jangi Lat Sahib. Then he turned and rode at the batteries. The sepoys cheered and ran after him with such a zest that they began to get out of line. As he galloped down at the mouth of the guns the fire slackened but the gunners stood their ground and the charge ended in a hand-to-hand fight until not a gunner was left on his feet. He was to meet that sepoy regiment again.

'Now that I have leisure to look back', wrote Havelock to Hannah a few days later after 'our desperate encounter with the Mahrattas', 'I feel to my heart's core God's unspeakable mercy to me; and only desire to live all my days to His praise. Our hospitals are filled with sad spectacles. Why have I always been such a monument of mercy? Right and left brave men were struck down but neither I nor dear Feroze were touched.'

Havelock believed that direct rule of native states was the best course for their inhabitants as well as for the British. 'I was at first angry enough at the old raj not being smashed outright; and in a conversation with the great lord over the grave of General Churchill[1] I told him with a magniloquent emphasis that this ought to have been a war of subjugation; but the fact is, that he could not go farther than his ministerial friends at home would support him in advancing.' By a curious twist of history, had Havelock got his way in December 1843 it might have sealed his own fate at the moment of crisis thirteen and a half years later. Lord Ellenborough, on his return to Calcutta, having been

---

[1] So much for the horsewhip.

recalled to England by the Court of Directors, was loud in his praise of Havelock. 'I will not affront your modesty', wrote Marshman, 'or tickle your vanity by recording the fine things he said of you'; and in due course Havelock was promoted Brevet Lieutenant-Colonel for his services at Maharajpur.

Though nominally in a minor post Havelock was high in the counsels of Gough, who was glad of a man of experience and knowledge who allowed his brains to be picked without pressing for favours in return. But when Havelock refused to write a history of the China War, with especial reference to the glories of Sir Hugh Gough, Gough did not take the refusal kindly.

At Delhi the Commander-in-Chief received alarming news that sepoys of several regiments under orders for service in Sind had mutinied. The mutinies had been suppressed; and Gough's orders on the punishment of the mutineers were awaited. He asked Havelock's advice. Havelock saw the affair as primarily a matter of discipline and urged that though grievances, if justified, might be met in due course, exemplary punishment should always be inflicted without hesitation on mutinous troops – whether British or Indian. Gough at first agreed. Thirty-nine mutineers were found guilty and sentenced to death.

Gough then changed his mind and remitted the capital sentences for all but six. Havelock was convinced that no worse decision could have been made. 'Prompt and decided measures' would have killed any incipient mutinous tendencies in the Bengal Army, on which the safety and peaceful development of India's millions so much depended. Marshman said the same in the *Friend of India*. At this, or so the gossip ran, Gough 'flew into a fury, blamed Havelock for writing the article of which he was utterly innocent, and told him that when he had a literary man on his staff he expected all his measures to be defended by him'.

Headquarters moved back to Simla. 'I do not think poor Henry has been so comfortable since before the wars separated us', wrote Hannah to her mother during the summer of 1844.

Will Havelock, reinstated, the horsewhipping forgiven, had returned to India and both he and Charles and their wives came to stay. 'We are all so happy as a family', Hannah reported. 'The three brothers try so to vie with each other in pleasing me. I sometimes turn round and say, "I don't know which I love most. You are all such darlings."' Hannah wrote to Harry and Jos, 'If we could but come to England now you would indeed think it holiday time to be with your dear papa. There is a perpetual cheerful activity of mind and body about him which makes him agreeable to all ages.'

EARLY IN 1845 Hannah gave birth to another girl and was so ill that in June Havelock wrote to Mrs Marshman: 'The last six months have been to me a time of harassing anxiety such as I never endured within the walls of Jalalabad or in any other of my adventures. But I have been enabled to come in faith to a throne of mercy and to cast my care upon Jesus Christ and have found blessings of peace. I hope it will (like other means of affliction) be one of spiritual improvement to us all.'

That winter a new Governor-General came to Simla, General Sir Henry Hardinge, a brother officer of Will's in the Peninsula, where he had lost a hand, who had been sent to India to succeed his brother-in-law Ellenborough. He was bluff, good-natured and unassuming. He had hoped to take Havelock as his own Persian Interpreter but Gough perversely would not release him. The Hardinges became intimate with the Havelocks, Sir Henry spoiling 'those nice little girls' and jocularly telling Hannah that she 'had the bump of maternity very strongly marked'.

Headquarters was at Umballa when on December 11th 1845, 'dear Jos's birthday, as we were all happily encamped here', so Hannah wrote, 'an order came from the Gov. Genl. that all the troops in this station, amounting to 10,000 and the Commander-in-Chief and all his staff should without delay repair to the banks of the Sutlej'. The Sikhs had invaded, and Ferozepore was besieged.

Since the death of Ranjit Singh, a short while after Havelock had observed him during the review at the start of the Afghan War, the Sikh kingdom in the Punjab had relapsed into blood-drenched anarchy. Power had passed into the hands of the Army, highly equipped, well paid, unbelievably brave, and trained by French officers who had gone east after the fall of Napoleon. To maintain a precarious leadership the ruling family had encouraged the Army to think of sacking Delhi. The situation had slowly worsened. A Sikh invasion would not be mere frontier raiding but a conflict of armies on almost a European scale.

A week later, after days of forced marches, Hardinge, Gough and Havelock were riding through the dawn across a sandy plain broken here and there with thick scrub and ploughed fields which slowed up the battalions which had to cross them. After eighteen miles, with two more to go to Ferozepore, Gough received a note from Broadfoot, who had been agent at Lahore and was ahead with the Irregular Cavalry, that Mudki was occupied by the Sikhs (whom Havelock always called 'the Six' and the British privates 'the Sykses'). At once the staff cantered off in the noontide heat to change the column of route into column of battle, but Mudki was found abandoned – a typical Punjab village; with mud walls and houses, a well, and a ramp for the well buffaloes, a pond, and a mill where a blindfold camel would walk round and round; but now deserted. Picquets were thrown out, and in the fields and scrub across the plain the tents were going up while the men rushed to the well and pond and stragglers drifted in. No one had eaten properly since the night before and the camp fires were curling with smoke. Havelock joined Hardinge, Gough and Broadfoot and at about 3.15 pm they were at last having a meal.

An orderly rode in and handed a note to Broadfoot, who called out, 'the enemy are upon us'. He mounted and disappeared to the front. Abandoning the meal the others rushed to their horses while the 'Assembly' sounded and the men ran to arms. Away to the front a distant cloud of dust was spreading across the countryside and Broadfoot returned, panting and excited. Havelock heard him exclaim to Gough, 'There, your Excellency, is the Sikh Army!'

The British line was forming and Havelock could see divisional generals and brigadiers on their horses taking post to the front. Sir John McCaskill, his friend of Istaliff, was there to the left, Harry Smith was away on the right. Sir Robert Sale, Quarter-Master General, was close at hand near Gough, who had put on a white coat so that all should see him.

With a wave to the staff Gough trotted forward, Havelock and the others behind him, to join the guns. Breaking into a canter, staff and guns swept on towards the jungle, as the plain reverberated to the first reports of the Sikh artillery. In the first salvo Havelock fell. Feroze was crushing his leg but he disentangled himself and stood up unhurt. Feroze was dead, 'my dear old charger that has carried me thro' so many battles, shot clean under me'. The guns were returning the Sikh fire, while the scarlet and blue lines of British Infantry advanced.

Broadfoot came up with a pony and remounted Havelock. The dust and smoke of battle were already blinding, but Gough led off to the left where Sikh cavalry were charging in. Hardly had he covered a hundred yards when Havelock was down again, Havelock was unhurt and Broadfoot, 'my persevering friend', produced a third pony jovially remarking that 'it appears to be of little use to give you horses, you're sure to lose them'.

Backwards and forwards along the line Havelock rode with Gough, wherever the fire was thickest and encouragement or control was needed. Through the eddying smoke and dust he saw McCaskill fall shot through the heart. He saw Harry Smith riding forward into the thick of the Sikh infantry, carrying the colours of a battalion of British foot which had been hesitating until he took personal command. At one point Gough sent Havelock to rally a sepoy regiment which had turned its back on the Sikhs, fleeing from those fierce, bearded warriors until Havelock rode up and urged them into the fire again. As he rejoined the staff on his makeshift pony he saw Sale down, his thigh shattered. Twilight, and the battle increasingly sanguinary and confused with men and guns even firing on their friends as the British line eddied and swirled, though steadily penetrating the Sikh position.

Darkness came and the Sikhs retreated, abandoning seventeen guns. By the light of torches Gough and what was left of his staff picked their way across the scene, where the wounded and dying of both sides were lying in scores. It was midnight before the troops were back at the Camp, 'our faces and hands', as one private wrote, 'covered with blood mingled with dust and filth from all kinds of smoke, our clothes from head to foot painted all over and our once white, now sable, belts besmeared with it'.

Dismounting at last at Mudki Havelock went to see Sale whose wound was mortal.

FOR THE NEXT two days the British Army licked its wounds and buried its dead. Havelock was gratified to be told that Hardinge ('who has treated me with much confidence') had remarked on hearing that Havelock had not been killed, 'I am glad of it. Indeed I should have been grieved to have lost so good a man'. Hardinge had been in the heart of the fight and now waived his rank as Governor-General, and put himself under Gough as Second-in-Command. Reinforcements had come in and word was sent to General Littler in Ferozepore that he should slip out and join a concerted attack on the Sikh camp at Ferozeshah, half way between Ferozepore and Mudki. After his narrow escapes Havelock had little reason to expect to survive unscathed again. 'We shall have another great battle to fight', he scribbled to Hannah, 'but put your trust in God who will not forsake you. I delight to read of your firmness of mind.' He little knew that their baby, Alice, was desperately ill.

On Sunday, six hours of marching through the clogging plain, at first in darkness and cold and then under the sun, brought them within two miles of the Sikh positions. Havelock joined Hardinge and the others for a scratch breakfast. Gough came in from reconnaissance and leaning over his horse said to Hardinge, 'Sir Henry, if we attack at once I promise you a splendid victory!' Hardinge looked surprised, stood up and beckoned Gough to dismount and follow him to a clump of trees out of earshot. The staff saw them in earnest conversation and when the two generals returned Hardinge announced that on his authority as Governor-General he had stipulated that they must wait for Littler; too much was at stake to attack with insufficient strength.

Littler arrived. With scarcely two hours of daylight left on this shortest day of the year, Gough gave the order to advance.

The Sikh fire was murderous. Their entrenchment was bristling with guns, based on a cluster of low hillocks masked by jungle but with a clear field of fire. A cavalry charge broke through to the Sikh camp but was stopped by the explosion of a magazine. The infantry pressed on, and victory was in sight when night fell. Ammunition dumps blew up and tents caught fire, while in the confusion of such numbers fighting furiously and blindly in a restricted area at night it was almost impossible to know what was happening.

At about eight pm Gough withdrew the remains of his troops from the breastworks they had so nearly won. The Sikh batteries continued firing and noise from the left showed that Harry Smith and Littler were still engaged, though communications had been lost. Riding over the corpses and litter of the battlefield under torchlight, Gough and the staff found themselves with Hardinge, and Havelock learned that Broadfoot was dead.

The battle would be resumed at daylight and the confusion and casualties made the prospect a gamble. Hardinge remarked to Havelock, 'another such action will shake the Empire'. They were all hungry and in agony of thirst, for the wells were still in Sikh hands, and the night miserably cold. The two generals and the Headquarters staff (Hardinge's staff-officers had all been killed or wounded) picked their way along the lines cheering up each unit in turn, but Hardinge sent orders to Mudki that all state papers should be destroyed.

Havelock was still unscathed, though unutterably weary, thirsty, cold and hungry. The battle so far could be considered a victory – 'We fought a great fight with the Sikhs', he could write of it, 'and after tremendous efforts beat them' – but the next day might bring anything. It dawned with a thick mist and when the mist lifted, the entrenchments were seen reoccupied by the Sikhs. The action recommenced with a charge of British horse gunners who opened up at close range. Hardinge and Gough then took personal command of an infantry division and Havelock rode forward beside Gough 'under a tremendous fire of heavy guns', at the south face of the Sikh earthworks. The generals leading, the division swept in with the bayonet and with more ease than they had expected, took battery after battery. Turning to the east they carried on, with Ferozeshah on their left, emerging victorious on the opposite earthwork, at which the Sikhs fled across the plain. The division halted, and as the Governor-General and the Commander-in-Chief rode down the line they were greeted with wildest cheers.

Men were told to fetch water and Havelock and other staff officers rode to the central well at Ferozeshah. Havelock's thirst was 'unbearable'. The stench from the well was foul and the water brought up was brown and Havelock's charger refused it 'with a shudder of disgust'; dead bodies almost certainly were rotting in the well, or it had been poisoned. But men were drinking, and Havelock drank.

As he returned to Gough a cavalry officer reported a fresh Sikh army advancing – the force which had been investing Ferozepore. Disaster seemed imminent. The men were exhausted and hungry and ammunition almost spent. As Gough formed his divisions into a hollow square, roughly on the old Sikh positions, a heavy fire opened from the advancing army. How the worn troops would stand bombardment and assault no one dared predict; if they broke, the Sikhs could sweep on unchecked to Delhi.

The Sikh cavalry bore down on the left but did not press home a charge. The fire on the infantry was working havoc and Gough, in a supremely gallant action, rode off in front at an angle to draw the Sikh fire on himself. Wheeling round he ordered the cavalry brigade to charge and they could be seen urging their exhausted horses into a gallop and breaking into the mass of Sikh infantry. And then, to the dismay of all who watched, they formed line and with the horse batteries filed away off the field in the direction of Ferozepore; an officer of the Adjutant-General's staff, half-crazed by heat stroke and thirst, had given orders to retreat which the brigadier had accepted as coming from the Commander-in-Chief.

While the horrified Gough sent to discover what had occurred, the Sikh army began to draw off. Certain, as the British discovered later, that he could never defeat troops who had fought so hard, and supposing the cavalry retreat to be a movement threatening his rear, the Sikh commander had resolved to break off the action. Havelock remarked, 'India has been saved by a miracle'.

Troops and officers were dead-beat and the battlefield a grisly sight. The bearers placed the wounded in doolies and water-carriers went from shattered man to man, and tumbrils were brought on in which to pile the dead, and coolies set fire to the carcasses of horses. Tents were thrown up on the field, and long after nightfall Havelock, sick from the well water, with Colonel Birch and an ADC, Bannatyne Fraser Tytler, at last made for the headquarters tent. Gough was sound asleep on a charpoy. 'We had to lie on the ground in the tent', wrote Birch, 'and Tytler and I went out in search of pillows. He found one, a bag full of something or other which sufficed for Havelock, and himself, and I a small bag which did for me. We fetched them in the dark from some small tents near the one which Gough occupied and we thought they contained grain. Soundly we slept upon these bags. And in the morning we found they were full of powder!' Had anyone lit a match they would have all been blown to pieces.

And the legend was told in India that Havelock had knowingly slept with a bag of gunpowder for his pillow, secure in his contempt of death.

'WE HAVE TAKEN numerous standards,' Havelock told Hannah, 'and upwards of 70 pieces of cannon. Indeed, when all is collected it is probable they may amount to 100, and no popguns I assure you, but tremendous battering guns, and the rest fine brass field artillery. Sir R Sale has died of his wounds. We buried him yesterday in a soldier's grave. In all these dangers I am unhurt. For 36 hours we have not tasted food nor changed our clothes. Charles is wounded in two places but is riding about. The GG has ordered us all another medal, but you must reflect, dearest, with humble trust in God, how likely it may be that I shall never live to wear it. God may yet keep me from greater dangers. Pray for me constantly that I may be kept from greater dangers, and above all that I may be strengthened to do my duty.'

Gough and Hardinge were unable to invade the Sikh kingdom and end the war until reinforcements and a siege train should reach them. With his headquarters Gough took up position on the Sutlej north-eastward from Ferozepore. The Sikhs still had a strongly fortified position on the British side of the river at Sabraon, a bridge of boats connecting it with their own country. Havelock prepared a plan which Hardinge endorsed, involving a turning movement by bridging the Sutlej at Ferozepore, but Gough preferred (in Havelock's phrase) 'smashing combats', and rejected it in favour of frontal assault; Havelock believed his plan would have achieved the victory 'with a third of the loss on our side', and Sabraon gave him a horror of frontal attacks. He again had a horse killed under him – a hair's breadth escape, for a cannon ball struck the saddle cloth within an inch of his thigh. The battle ended in fearful carnage, the Sikhs driven into the river or fighting bravely to the last on the ruins of their bridge of boats.

The Sikhs sued for peace. Havelock was drawn by Hardinge

into the discussion of terms, and advocated annexation, as inevitable in the long run, but recognised the force of the argument that the British had been too weakened to be able to police the whole Punjab, while the Sikhs, though defeated, were strong. Hardinge allowed them conditional independence, and Henry Lawrence was nominated Resident. On March 6th Havelock was present at the durbar in the spacious fort at Lahore, where the treaty was signed in the inner court, with its black and white marble set with a myriad fragments of looking-glass.

The War had been swift but perilously near disaster. 'I entered upon this campaign', Havelock summed it up, 'fancying myself something of a soldier. I have now learnt that I know nothing. Well! I am even yet not too old to learn.'

HAVELOCK HAD NOW added to tried tactical skill and deep knowledge of military theory the experience of a major campaign, throughout which he had been close to the centre of direction. At fifty-one he was a foremost authority on Indian warfare; he could claim to have been in twenty-two fights and had written much on military affairs. Moreover, aware of wasteful mistakes of strategy and organisation he wished for an opportunity to demonstrate better ways. And his great ambition still was sole command in a successful action.

Hardinge and Gough had been made peers and a shower of lesser promotions cascaded from the Horse Guards. Lord Gough, however, had read in the *Friend of India* some comment on his recent strategy. Marshman's criticisms were 'most moderate', and represented general opinion, but Gough fell into a rage with Havelock whom again he supposed, wrongly, to be responsible and suppressed his name from the promotion list. He withdrew his promise of materials for a history of the War; and his wife, once so friendly, joined in her husband's vendetta, and retailed Simla drawing-rooms with malicious gossip.

Lord Hardinge was grieved by Gough's neglect of Havelock, and wrote to the Duke of Wellington. Havelock was gazetted

Deputy Adjutant-General of Queen's Troops in Bombay – the head of the Adjutant-General's department in the presidency, a minor post for a man of such experience, but promotion.

On January 1st 1847 Hardinge came to Fort William Ghat at Calcutta to see the Havelocks sail for Bombay. And it may have been then, as he turned away after waving farewell to the erect grey-haired little Colonel who stood by the steamship's rail with his wife and girls beside him, that Hardinge uttered his famous phrase, 'Every inch a soldier, and every inch a Christian'.

HAVELOCK ATTENDED WITH the staff to salute the retiring Commander-in-Chief of the Presidency, Sir T McMahon, as he boarded ship. Bombay was already unpleasantly hot and the Apollo Bundar waterfront the stickiest spot of the city. Havelock felt decidedly faint with sunstroke. The doctors ordered him up at once to Mahabaleshwar, the hill station deep in the hills above Poona in which the government took refuge for the hottest weather. In the second week of April he fell so ill at Mahabaleshwar that Hannah was 'seriously alarmed'. And, she wrote to the boys in England, 'the house is so dull and sad without him that his being confined to his room for even a day casts a gloom over all else'.

By April 16th he was sufficiently recovered to write his funeral directions and an epitaph which, after detailing his career, he closed with a graphic epitome of his faith: 'Twenty-four years he strove to serve his God according to the rule of the Gospel. Contrite and humbled under a sense of his innumerable sins, and trusting for pardon in the blood of Jesus Christ, he died at this place... 1847, aged... years and... days, calmly trusting for acceptance in his Redeemer's name'.

The sharp illness was a warning that, at fifty-three, English leave should not be long delayed.

In April 1848 the second Sikh War broke out. The Bombay Army was not involved and Havelock chafed at his absence from the field. In November William Havelock was killed in a wild cavalry charge at Ramnagar, to Henry's great grief. In the same skirmish the Adjutant-General fell, and Hardinge in England went to the Horse Guards to secure the post for Havelock. He was unsuccessful, though 'Lord Fitzroy Somerset', he told him, 'admitted your strong claims and distinguished services in India and I closed the conversation by expressing what I had previously written, that in my opinion your appointment would be the most advantageous for the public service considering your experience in Indian affairs and your acknowledged talents and that I regretted your having been set aside on public as well as personal grounds'.

With the battle of Chilianwala in January 1849 the war moved towards its climax and Havelock was more than ever impatient with his routine peace-time duties in Bombay. On February 5th he heard that among the reinforcements being sent to the Punjab to replace the heavy casualties of Chilianwala was the 53rd Foot, the regiment to which he had exchanged. For a week he brooded on the thought of the regiment going into action without him and then went to Sir Willoughby Cotton, now Commander-in-Chief at Bombay, and persuaded him to grant leave of absence from the staff. Once at the front he could get a Brigade, or serve humbly as a major.

Leaving Hannah, the girls and the infant George Broadfoot Havelock, he set off at once by carriage dawk and was out of the Presidency and had reached Indore in the Mahratta states, far up on the Delhi road, when he heard news of Gough's victory of Gujerat. Havelock pressed on, each day bringing him nearer what was left of the war. On March 12th, at a staging bungalow half way between Indore and Agra, he found a letter from Gough's Headquarters – a peremptory order to return forthwith to Bombay. He would be punished by an official reprimand for quitting his post without the supreme Commander-in-Chief's orders, as Cotton also for allowing him to do so.

Havelock had played into Gough's hands. Before Gujerat Gough had learned that a successor was on the way out and he ascribed his supersession to critics of his slashing, costly Irish-man's strategy; of the critics Harry Smith (now in South Africa) and the *Friend of India* were the strongest. To hit at Havelock was to hit at both.

Havelock sadly retraced his steps. 'They would not have me for fear I should command a brigade contrary to the principles of the Tipperary tactics.' 'To an ardent soldier like him', wrote Hardinge to Hannah, 'this is no doubt a great annoyance but I scarcely think he could have been in time... and really if there is an officer of the army who on his own account could dispense with the glory of seeking further opportunities of leaving you a widow, your husband is the man – for he has done more, seen more, and been shot at oftener than any man of his rank.'

9

Harry

Shortly before Havelock had hurried north on his abortive Punjab adventure, his eighteen-year-old son Harry had spent a brief, extraordinary period at Poona before being packed off home again.

When Hannah took the boys home in 1841 she had placed them at the school of a Reverend Dr Cuthbert in St John's Wood, and there they stayed, the Havelocks sharing the contemporary evangelical distaste for public schools, still scarcely touched by the influence of Arnold. Holidays were spent with Havelock's sister Jane, married to the Commissioner of Plymouth Dockyard. Jos was a somewhat untidy boy, and a great mimic, but willing and affectionate; Havelock hoped to get him an East India Company's cadetship but assured him that he could choose his own profession. For Harry, already a 'beautiful horseman', a commission in the royal army was planned, an exchange in due course to bring him out to India. Harry too was urged not to 'imagine that we will force you unwillingly to anything'.

Dr Cuthbert reported Harry 'idle and rebellious'. His rages were notorious. He was 'obstinate and neglectful of his duties'. In 1846, at Hardinge's request, the Duke of Wellington gave him a commission at sixteen, though Dr Cuthbert 'from the most sordid motives' tried to keep him longer by refusing a certificate. After a period at Sandhurst, Harry joined the 39th Foot. He soon proved as extravagant, casual, and thoughtlessly generous as any Havelock or Marshman before him (Joshua Marshman, Hannah's youngest brother, was as spendthrift as William and Charles Havelock, and Hannah herself when let loose had tendencies in the same direction). He received an adequate allowance (double what his father had got) but at the end of 1847, when Havelock already had heavy commitments, one of Harry's rare letters arrived with a plea for more. He had 'fallen into the hands of a pack of rascally Jews who cheated me in all directions'. And there was 'a man in the 16th Lancers who called himself my cousin. Well, this fellow keeps on bothering me for money. I have assisted him several times but now I find it necessary to leave off unless I wish to appear in the London Gazette as a bankrupt.'

Havelock sent £60 extra, which Harry spent on 'a lot of new clothes and books', on furnishings for his quarters and on an 'immense cub of a retriever whom I am trying to teach to fetch and carry and other tricks of the same kind'. He had a carefree idea of his father's position: 'I can fancy you riding about in great state at Bombay with your carriage and Arab horses and heaps of syces running before you'.

For long they heard no more. Then, early in 1848, a 'very distressing letter' reached them, humbly pleading for yet more help. 'The fear of those abominable Jews together with the weather, FitzBingo's[1] bullying and two or three other things have made this the most miserable Christmas I have ever spent... I am ashamed to ask for the money I mentioned in my last letter but if you could by any means send it it would be of the greatest use in paying these horrid Jews.'

Hannah undertook to answer the letter. 'You now appear to be in great distress for more money. And have done, at the eleventh hour, what you should have done at first, that is, laid your case before your good kind father, who is ever ready (far more than I am) to make allowance for the faults of his children... He begs me to tell you with his love that he is too much grieved by your negligence to sit down to write to you himself, but as you are pleased to make your distresses known to him now, he sends you at sight an order for £30.'

The sooner Harry was under his parents' eye the better.

---

[1]Lord Frederick FitzClarence, his commanding officer.

Havelock therefore purchased a lieutenancy in the 86th Foot serving in the Bombay Presidency and in June 1848 Harry left for India by the overland route, through France and the Mediterranean, across from Alexandria to Suez, and down the Red Sea. Passing through Egypt he had sunstroke. He did not warn his parents and they were scarcely prepared for the result.

He reached Bombay late in August to find joyful notes urging him to come up to Poona at once, where his parents and sisters were awaiting the merry times he would bring them. Havelock had last seen him as a boy of ten in 1840, now he was a lanky youth of eighteen, of good height and with the dark hair of the Marshmans. But his behaviour was extraordinary. He was alternately morose and boisterous, and when in a temper could be positively alarming. Much could be put down to the sunstroke, but the sunstroke had made chronic weaknesses acute. He seemed especially set against his mother; the Havelocks feared his mind had been poisoned against her in England by her ne'er-do-well youngest brother. Once Harry insulted her in front of her friends and continually he hurt her, as his father told him to his face, 'with your rudeness and want of affection'. His regiment at Poona proved him a keen and efficient soldier, if rather partial to champagne tiffins, until fits of wildness and eccentricity became so serious that the Havelocks consulted the doctors. Harry was ordered back on sick leave to England by the route round the Cape of Good Hope.

The voyage and leave would restore health but the trouble went deeper. 'I well know', his father wrote after him, 'how vain it is to expect much as regards any moral requirement until the heart is changed. Therefore, in a word, turn to God, trust in the Saviour'. It was not a morbid anxiety to impose parental beliefs; and they had not the slightest desire to make him a Baptist as such. They wanted to meet his spiritual need, and felt a natural, heartfelt desire to give him the best that life could offer – the friendship of Christ. Without that, they were certain, Harry could never be consistently happy.

On Harry's ship from Bombay to the Cape sailed a certain Captain Young whom Havelock had known at the Scottish Church – 'a *brick* in his own invaluable way and looks to truth only', but excessively earnest and speaking a sort of Cromwellian mixture of piety and military metaphor. Young wrote 'in his own peculiar way' that 'It has been one of the most difficult tasks I ever had, to do my duty to that soul... He has been much shaken and I believe he would have been saved. He was hit and I saw him melted more than once. But this Dr Austin (the ship's surgeon) has been the ruin of all that. He is the essence of worldliness and is at the poor lad all day long.'

Entering Simon's Bay the ship was 'in great danger of shipwreck, and I had then an opportunity of speaking to young Havelock. I saw he was in fear', (Havelock could scarcely believe this, from what he knew of Harry, but remarked 'I suppose we none of us feel quite comfortable either under a shower of grapeshot or when likely to bump ashore'), 'and would listen. So I said a few things which I hope fell into his heart by God's hand'. After a safe landing they stayed at the same hotel and when Harry left to continue the voyage he accepted a religious book 'which he would never do before. Also at the hotel here when parting', concluded Young, 'I was enabled with a burning love to press home to him the great Word and he took it well' – or so it seemed to the insensitive Captain Young.

Before Harry reached home, Puss fell seriously ill (and lost all her hair) and Hannah was obliged to take her and the others at once to England, leaving Havelock alone at Poona, to be cheered by a visit from the thriftless Charles. 'I never saw him looking better', Havelock wrote to Hannah. 'Alas! his affairs are in a state of greater desperation than ever... there seems to be no resource but selling his commission which is destitution'.

With so many extra calls through the family's return Havelock was 'making every effort to reduce my expenses. Books are my only amusement. My meals are on the most economical scale'. He wrote to Hannah by every mail. 'You never saw such a crop of roses as I have had,' he told her at the end of July, 'I have three plants of the flowering cactus with high flowery stalks and I call them Puss, No and Georgie. Two of them are planted one on each side of the entrance and the third is in the circular partia in front. The house and ground are kept very clean and neat; I make the mali bring me six splendid bouquets for your little porcelain stands every morning.'

On August 27th 1849 a Dr Ross, surgeon of the 20th Hussars, came to the house on official business and after a long discussion Havelock 'went out into the verandah to see him to his carriage. The heat was very great and I had been dining out the evening before and felt it unusually. As we continued the conversation my limbs seemed to fail under me and I leant against the wall for support; and then feeling confused about the head went into the house and sat down on a chair. Ross perceiving me turn pale came to the rescue and made me lie down on my bed and drink a little wine and water and I quickly revived.' But on August 30th the doctors declared that there was heart trouble which 'will become organic if I remain working in this climate'.

Some months later Padre Fraser of the Scottish Church drove Havelock from the hotel to the Apollo Bundar 'in his little carriage drawn by the old office horse'. Havelock was so weak that he was glad to lean on Fraser's arm as they walked up the gangway of the *Akbar* paddle steamer which would take him to Aden and Suez. The white-sailed dhows tossed in the harbour. The islands in the Bay and the hills beyond shimmered in the heat. Coolies shouted as they handled the baggage. Tongas trotted back and forth to the ghat and the inevitable beggars cried to the sahibs for *bakshish*. India was as it had ever been.

And Havelock left, after twenty-six years' continuous service, a broken, feeble old man.

AT PLYMOUTH, HANNAH had been staying near Jane Creak. Jane found her long-absent brother 'mild, gentle and forbearing', and decided with satisfaction that 'no remnant of the irritability of his boyhood was left, but that to everybody and in everything he was kind, considerate and Christian-like'. Havelock occupied himself with slum-visiting. The spare erect figure of the diminutive colonel with grey hair and whiskers quickly became familiar and beloved in the grimy streets and lanes of the city. About Jos, now eighteen and as small as his father though chubby and with a shock of untidy fair hair, Havelock had news 'cordial to my heart', and could now see for himself that Jos's conversion to a personal faith was deep and genuine.

In London Havelock called on Lord Hardinge who 'urged me to plunge into histories. I could only reply that I could not afford to part with my bread'. He began canvassing East India directors for Joshua's cadetship, was presented at a Levée, where he met Lord Gough who shook hands with him, 'old quarrels forgotten', and attended a banquet at which the Duke of Wellington made a speech, a most affecting spectacle of 'mouldering greatness. He is so deaf that he seemed to me to utter prolonged inarticulate sounds without being aware of it. He begins, but rarely concludes a sentence, and where he breaks off in a period the spectator doubts from his manner whether he will commence another or fall down apoplectic in the next effort to begin one.'

Harry, now at his regimental depot, was still the same lovable wild incorrigible, too frequently reducing his mother to tears and gripped by hero-worship of the dissolute Uncle Joshua. Captain Young's godly salvos had missed their target, but Harry hoped soon to be off East again. 'I wish you', wrote his father after further experience of his eldest, 'every success; but you are not upon the true path of success in anything so long as you impinge that solemn commandment which inculcates dutiful and respectful and deferential conduct to mothers, in your case to the best of mothers.'

When Harry was on leave at the little house they had taken in London, an incident, shrouded in mystery, led to a painful interview between father and son and a tear-stained letter from his mother, delivered to Harry sulking in his room by hand of the housemaid: 'Your father tells me that he has desired you to seek another home for yourself. Let me say in a word that it is not *my* wish that you should leave the paternal roof as long as you can be happy and make others happy also. I would not adopt this formal mode of communication (with one who, in spite of all his efforts to have it otherwise, I shall always love) were it possible that I might speak freely to you... We don't *send* you away. But you leave us, with your eyes open to the dangers and temptations that may assail you and from which I, even I, am ever ready and willing to shelter you. Once more I ask, are you content to live with those who love you? ...I pray God may direct you to do what is most for your own good, and I hope you will forgive yourself as readily as I forgive you.'

This sobered him. Harry was not vicious; merely intolerant and impulsive. The family lived more or less harmoniously until he left in the second week of August 1850 to join the troopship *Aboukir* for India. Havelock, enclosing a letter of introduction to Sir Harry Smith at the Cape, wrote a warm farewell. '...I continue to hope that if you avoid unnecessary exposure to the sun, you will regain and keep your health. But my great concern is, my beloved boy, that your eyes should be opened to see the Saviour whom you deny, ever stretching out arms of mercy to you and willing to lead you into ways of wisdom, righteousness and peace.'

In December Jos left for India by the overland route. Havelock was already embarrassed by a loan raised in Calcutta, and by help to William's widow, and after equipping and despatching him he was 'almost drained to the dregs' and could give no allowance. He wrote to Harry, 'I trust I need not prompt you to give him every aid in your power', and added, 'I have only to ask that whatever your own opinions may unfortunately be, you will, as a gentleman, respect his pious character and habits and if you cannot help him on in the right way, at least not strive to drive him from it by scoffing or evil example'.

Soon after Jos reached India Harry wrote apologising to his mother for 'the grief and pain I have so often caused you', and at his twenty-first birthday in August 1851 he declared 'if the power be granted me you shall never again have reason to complain of act or word of mine'.

OCTOBER 27TH 1851 dawned cold and clear at Bonn in the Rhineland where the Havelocks had spent most of the past year. The final farewell at the quay was 'heart-wringing bitterness' – for Colonel Havelock was returning to India without Hannah. 'He grieves so much that the low state of his finances prevented his taking me out with him', wrote Hannah to Harry. 'His health is wonderfully improved and his spirits when he is not alone are quite buoyant but he should never be entirely alone – gladly indeed would I have gone with him but we both considered that my presence was most required here. The living and education is so moderate and within our means until your father has paid his debt to your uncle John, which he has so nobly waited for until he could return to India. But with you and dear Jossy to comfort him I hope and know he will do well.'

The paddle-boat chugged smokily out into the river and round the bend. Hannah and the girls and Georgey ran back to the house and frantically waved white handkerchiefs as it passed by in mid-stream, and they saw a small figure on the deck wave back.

Havelock's first day was not too dismal. Two English military acquaintances were on board; they saw only a quiet, courteous Colonel with a remarkable knowledge of the history of the places they steamed past.

They reached Coblenz in the afternoon. He had promised Hannah to distract his mind by sightseeing and obediently climbed to the castle which overlooked the town. On his return to the hotel, at half-past five, he immediately wrote a line to Hannah. 'My very dear Hannah', he began, 'Heaven's best earthly gift to me.' He described his day briefly and ended, 'God bless you – kiss for me the darlings in private who I would not kiss in public, and pardon all my faults'.

The next day the full force of his desolation nearly submerged him. He left by steamer at nine, transferring to another at Mainz and so to Frankfurt, where he arrived 'more harassed than I ever felt in my life. In fact my troubles are perpetual or seem so, with baggage and one thing and another.' The weather was warmer and rainy and the wooded hills beyond the banks were beautiful with shrouds of mist, and now and again a famous castle or church was in sight. But Havelock had 'really lost all desire to see anything or enquire about anything; for I have no one to whom I can communicate my feelings of pleasure or pain'.

At Frankfurt officious Germans charged him excessively for his numerous boxes, and the railway made him pay as heavily for its registration. At every turn he needed Hannah. 'If only I had your aid, I should do well.'

At the hotel he ate a poor dinner, had his wine and biscuits, went to his room and wrote to Hannah. After detailing his miseries he continued: 'However, I ought not to write thus, as it may grieve you. I trust I have commenced this journey under God's guidance, and not an effort on my part shall be spared to do something for you and my little ones. Aid me by your prayers, and by practising the strictest economy while I am absent from you. I trust God will preserve your health and mine until these little ones are provided for; and that in His mercy through Jesus Christ He will receive us to Himself. If you knew what I have endured since I left you – I fear it would give you pain. But God will support me – I trust.' His mind, typical of a man's, was wrapped in his own sorrow almost to the exclusion of hers; on the other hand it was for her and the children only that he had accepted the separation.

He signed the letter and began to read a book. A knock on the door brought in the hotel-keeper, with demands for more money for baggage-dues. Havelock was immediately fussed lest he would have enough cash in hand for the whole journey. He decided that he had planned wrong; he should never have agreed to stay a day here and there to sightsee. He wrote a postscript to Hannah to tell her this, with a few more expressions of woe. He added, 'Mind, I am not the only one that sinks thus, when separated from those who are dear to him. Read the account of the great Marlborough under such circumstances. But I have Jesus Christ to trust to and His presence to comfort me. Yet in this mortal state we do feel keenly. Pray for me.'

That night was 'the worst I have had since Ferozeshah'. 'A totally sleepless night', he told Hannah in his next letter, 'a thing, as you know, most unusual with me.' When called at six he was certain that he 'had not once closed his eyes, not even dozed or slumbered'. 'Oh how hardly I desired to turn back and rejoin you at Bonn as I lay on my bed', he wrote. 'The bitterness of parting, my poverty after so many years of labour, which renders this unavoidable, and I fear not a few doubts about the worldly future, passed in rapid succession through my brain, which without being in the least fevered was so wrought upon that I never slept a single second.'

Yet all was not utterly desolate. 'I did indeed find sweet relief in the thought of meeting you in that better kingdom, for all earthly meetings are uncertain, and terminate in longer or shorter separations. Join with me in prayer; that we through faith in the blood of the Lamb may be held worthy to partake in His resurrection; and be together with Him and our children in glory. I know not what lies before me; but I *do* feel that we are both in the path of sacred duty. Let us do His will and leave the rest to God! May He give us grace to perform it well! Perhaps He may be merciful to us and grant that we may soon meet again, though we see not how.'

The next day he took the train towards Leipzig. He had to spend a night at Eisenach, and when well away again found he had lost his warm gloves, so that cold added to his misery since the railway was not yet completed and they had to proceed in 'omnibuses, a whole drove of them', for some ten miles before meeting the next line.

A letter from Hannah was at Leipzig. The next morning he went over the battlefield, and on returning to the city found another of her letters. By Dresden, after a short and comfortable journey, he was a little brighter: 'I feel for the present a sad houseless wanderer. But I must not repine; God is with me. That ought to be enough.'

He toured the picture galleries, as he had planned, and on the Sunday went to church, walking back with a German military acquaintance he met there, who 'talked two or three hours with me'. Monday's journey up the Elbe strengthened his spirits, and the behaviour of an Austrian customs official at the frontier set him really laughing for the first time since Bonn.

On November 6th, after almost a surfeit of sightseeing, and picture galleries at Vienna he set off for Trieste – a freezing journey through the mountains. He had not expected such weather; his warm clothes were at the bottom of the trunks, and his gloves were lost, and when they reached Trieste he had a chill.

The Adriatic brought forty-eight hours of seasickness, but after coaling at Corfu they met better weather in the Mediterranean and he was already feeling fitter for the sea air. On board, among others returning east, was an old comrade-in-arms, Colonel Franks of the 10th Foot and his wife. With Franks, a peppery but efficient soldier, Havelock spent happy hours 'fighting our battles over again to the great edification of all the listening company'. Franks shared Havelock's opinion of Lord Gough: 'he too undervalues Lord G and detests his clique, blames their treatment of me and complains of their conduct to himself'.

Slowly Havelock was becoming again his placid self. 'My Redeemer's comforts have been very sweet to me', he wrote to Hannah on board ship, 'for during a part of my late journey my nervous excitement has been such that to use poor Colonel King's phrase before he destroyed himself I have for many hours been "scarcely a responsible being". ' To such a state have care and sickness reduced one, to whom in former days men were wont to point as a pattern of hope in time of public danger. But we are poor inconstant creatures at the best. The cross of Christ is my support!'

From Alexandria, after a wait of 'three weary days and nights', and further delay through fog on the lower Nile, the party reached Cairo on the morning of November 20th. As he was eating breakfast at Shepheard's, Havelock was accosted by Colonel Hale of the Company's service at Bombay, with news that Harry and Jos had passed their language examinations. On the camel journey across the desert Colonel Franks offered to recommend Harry for the adjutancy of his regiment, the 10th. 'You had better have a look at him first,' said Havelock. Franks replied that the report he had heard of him and the family name were enough. Though Havelock could have no idea what he was letting Harry in for, he was pleased: 'it might be the boy's making'.

At Suez as the lighter steamed close to the Indiaman *Feroze* a voice hailed him from the deck asking if Colonel Havelock was there. 'The First Lieutenant forthwith gave strict orders for the carriage and disposal of my baggage; and I have since been so be-Coloneled and looked after that I am afraid after being kicked about in England and the Continent that it will spoil me altogether.'

And so, as he approached Bombay, the horror of the journey in Europe was a fading memory. The wound of separation was healing, and the boys would be with him, at times, in India. Professionally, Havelock could see nothing ahead but a few years more of dull routine service before obscure retirement.

He would have been amazed to know that in less than six years he would be world-famous.

HARRY CAME DOWN from Poona to be inspected by Colonel Franks, and found his father 'looking very well and in excellent spirits and in no way inconvenienced by his rapid journey'. As they drove along Harry 'looked up in my face and clapping me on the thigh, said in his yet husky voice of adolescence, "Oh, sir, is it not jolly to be going along with you again?"'

Jos, some months earlier, had been thrown from his horse at night near Poona. The syce had woken Harry up bemoaning that 'somewhere on the road the small gentleman from his horse has fallen and is not found. The small gentleman's whip is found but the small gentleman is not found.' They searched without success. Colonel Hancock, the Company's Adjutant-General, had been trotting home in his carriage when the lamps shone on a scarlet jacket. 'When Jos recovered from his long swoon', so Havelock related the story as it was told him, 'he found himself on a sofa in the Adjutant-General's bungalow with the ladies of the house busy over him with smelling bottles, etc, etc. He rubbed his eyes and what should the fellow's first exclamation be, but, "Why I declare there is old mother Hancock!" Conceive the horror and indignation of the lady of the A G of the army. Of course the story was in the mouth not only of every subaltern but of everyone from the General downwards in Poona the next morning and then travelled to Bombay, and has been repeated to me in forms somewhat varied and made me laugh many times. This is one way of getting an appointment... He received no damage whatever.'

Havelock's days slipped into 'the invariable life of India'. 'Remarkably light work hitherto', he wrote in January 1852, 'and so have continued to visit some of the persons who it was most desirable I should visit and have dined out twice or three times a week besides attending one public breakfast and one reception'. At Mahabaleshwar, in the hot weather, Harry and Jos joined him and made their father happy in that place of happy memories, which 'is beautiful beyond description this year'. 'I never saw two young men so full of affection towards each other, towards their parents, and all whom they ought to love.' They had morning and evening prayers together and 'Harry seemed always to take a great interest in our worship'. When the time came to see him off to join H M's 10th Foot in the Punjab, Havelock, though saving every penny to pay off his debts, gave him an extra £100 towards travelling expenses. And thus Harry departed for his adjutancy, getting at twenty-two what his father had been glad to have at forty.

Havelock, though now fifty-seven, kept himself as fit as on a campaign. The sensual life of luxury which ruined the constitutions of so many of his contemporaries was not for him. 'Thus I live', he wrote at Poona after the rains of 1852, 'as the gun fires, the ramoosy from without calls out to me, but old soldier like I have been sometime awake, and answer his cry with another. Then after short prayers I arise, dress in very light clothing and a solar hat; and walk round the camp about four miles and a half. Then the Indian cup of tea, cold bathing and breakfast, then business until three – dine – and then *siesta*, tea – never go out for exercise in the evening; then reading and retire at eleven. This varied only by occasionally dining out and the meeting at Candy's and the worship of the Sabbath.'

There were several other thoroughgoing Christians of varying denominations in the cantonment and Jos and his father attended weekly Bible studies and informal meetings where, as with his family, the slightly severe, silent exterior which normally protected Havelock's acute sensitiveness gave place to a relaxed geniality. The other Christians were drawn with affectionate admiration to the little Colonel whose outstanding professional reputation ensured them the respect of the cantonment; who could lead them in devotions or expound Scripture; and who at the tea drinking before or after the meeting seemed always to have a twinkle in his eye. Moreover he was adept at intimate personal conversation on spiritual matters, though he could be brusque enough with the insincere; several officers joined the circle through his influence.

JOS WAS POSTED to Sind. Harry in the Punjab was finding Colonel Franks almost more than he could stomach. Franks constantly flew into tempestuous rages, and tended to spy on his adjutant, which infuriated Harry. The spirit of the regiment was rebellious and young Major Wellesley, in command when Franks temporarily took the station, 'is such an intense idiot', said Harry, 'that I cannot stand it, and as I never had any great skill in dissimulation he could not possibly help seeing that I consider him an arrant ass. And though he has never had any opportunity of finding fault with anything, he has yet taken every means of annoying me in little trifles.' The heat in summer had been intense; the 10th was one of the earliest British regiments to wear tropical kit, but 'as a point of military etiquette the Adjutant is closely buttoned up in red broadcloth during the whole of the hot season while every other man in the regiment is comfortably clothed literally from head to foot in white linen'. Harry was also, of course, overspending; and his longsuffering father nobly sent more funds though it meant more sacrifice for himself. He urged Harry to persevere and remarked, 'I always prided myself on showing that I could serve under the devil himself, if it pleased her Majesty to give the commission of Lt Col to that respectable personage, in the regiment to which I belonged'.

A new Commander-in-Chief, Lord Frederick FitzClarence, son of William IV and Mrs Jordan, reached Bombay, with his wife and daughter ('a cross looking girl with a bad cough'), a niece, a service of plate which had belonged to Queen Adelaide, and 'five ladies' maids, a French cook, a butler and a groom'.

Lord Frederick (Harry's 'Fitzbingo' of the regiment at Gosport) was four years younger than Havelock but one year his senior in service. They took to each other at once. 'Though he has some strange whimsies', wrote Havelock, 'he is a more likely man to improve our army than any who has sat in the same saddle for many long years... He has given me the most flattering tokens of his consideration and confidence.' Not only was Lord Frederick a soldier after Havelock's heart, 'as particu-

lar about small things as I used to be when adjutant of the 13th',
but he showed an interest in welfare unusual for men of his
rank, and established a school for soldiers' children. Soon, however, he was having attacks of gout and fever: 'He not only works
too hard but lives so imprudently that even Lord Falkland says
"it is frightful to see him eat"'.

In May 1854, after more than one further disappointment,
Havelock was promoted to Quartermaster-General, Queen's
Troops in India, almost a sinecure but well paid.

He said farewell to FitzClarence and to Lord Elphinstone
who in the short time since succeeding Falkland as Governor
had become a firm friend, and came down the steep twisting
road from Mahabaleshwar for the last time, through the Western Ghats to join the new railway for the final section of the
journey to Bombay. He heard 'quite by accident' that Jos had
arrived on his way to a posting at Poona and was staying with a
friend. Havelock found out the bungalow 'and no sooner approached it than the dear fellow rushed out and threw his arms
round me as he would have done when he was five'.

Havelock sailed for Calcutta, to continue by carriage dawk
to Simla, on June 1st 1854. Lord Frederick FitzClarence issued
an Order of the Day, 'to express how highly he appreciates Colonel Havelock's ability as a staff officer, and to tender his most
sincere thanks for the zeal and punctuality with which all the
important duties of the department of Queen's Troops have been
invariably discharged by him... His Lordship is convinced that
the regret he feels in parting with Colonel Havelock will be
fully shared in by every officer of the Bombay Army who has
enjoyed the happiness of his acquaintance'.

WHEN IN SEPTEMBER 1854 Harry, on leave, joined his father at
Simla in the one house obtainable ('a very gloomy house, not at
all to my fancy', Havelock had said) a long report went back to
Hannah. '...He is fond of society', wrote his father, 'rides well
without the stiffness of an adjutant and is very upright and easy

in all his movements, well and exceptionally neatly dressed. Now come the defects. He is irritable, somewhat self-willed, in fact at times his temper is frightful, though Franks who praises him to the skies as an officer and a gentleman assures me that he has no vice or extravagance. But his ambition is to be the best dressed and mounted adjutant in the service and thus all his pay and allowances, what fed all our family at Agra and Karnal has scarcely kept him.'

A year later, almost broke, Harry spent a long sick leave at Simla before being invalided home. His father loved his company, but was distressed because though 'his conduct is moral, his tastes and habits gentlemanlike, he is not only indifferent to religion but does not scruple to state that he has no proof of the truth of Christianity and that he only goes to church as a matter of decent observance'.

To Havelock, conscious that all the best in life was owed to personal trust in a 'heavenly Father and powerful Friend' Harry's attitude seemed strange and grievous. 'Turn to Him', he wrote once more, as a dejected Harry sailed down the Sutlej for Karachi and home, 'and He will give you peace; and the witness of the truth and power of his gospel within yourself.'

'How sad', he commented in a letter to Puss, 'to think that he has no love to God, no knowledge of him, but seems entirely wrapt up in this world's cares, hopes and crosses. The prayer of faith will however bring him to God and the Saviour at last, at least so I fervently hope and trust. Let not that prayer be restrained, but let all of us unite in it.' And when Harry, back at the Sandhurst Senior Branch, the embryo Staff College, wrote despondently of his failure to reach the Crimea, of his ill-health and his customary lack of funds and said, 'something invisible seems to thwart me at every turn', Havelock wrote back that he was not surprised, though he did not 'quite take the gloomy view that you entertain of your earthly prospects... Often as I have entreated you, in vain, once more I would entreat you to take God for your father, and Christ for your counsellor and friend. Both are ready and willing to stand in these relations to you.'

When Harry read this further appeal, devoted as he was to his father and admiring him as a soldier, he wrote a remark which rejoiced Havelock's heart when he read it up country on the banks of the Ganges: 'I feel all you say about matters of religion to be true and hope that at the appointed time I shall come to give them the attention they deserve but we cannot anticipate the course of events'. That was good as far as it went.

10

Before the Storm

In January 1855 the Commander-in-Chief and his staff were touring the Punjab, in bitter cold. On January 15th, as Havelock rode in towards the site of the battle of Gujerat, he saw the Adjutant-General, Colonel Markham, riding out from camp to meet him; who, 'pulling off his hat with mock gravity said, "I come to salute the rising sun. Behold the Adjutant-General, Her Majesty's Forces"'. The Gazette had come in, announcing Markham's promotion to major-general and Havelock's nomination to the vacancy. 'So now I must prepare for hard work again. I think', he concluded to Hannah, 'you ought to write a line to Lord Hardinge.'

Next senior on the General Staff to the Commander-in-Chief, the Adjutant-General was responsible for the discipline and efficiency of the royal regiments scattered all too thinly across the length and breadth of India. On him depended their readiness for war. But in 1855 the prospect of war in India was so remote, except for small isolated expeditions, that many of the regiments were slack and their officers suffering from the malaise of the tropics, as Havelock had noticed during the tour. He set himself immediately with the utmost energy to imprint on the European troops his high conception of discipline. 'It was part of his creed', wrote a contemporary, 'that the discipline of a regiment depended mainly upon the example set by the officers, and that where these were careless the men would be negligent also. Convinced likewise of the importance of impressing a rigid sense of individual responsibility upon all officers, it was his especial care to inform the commandants of royal regiments that he held them personally and individually responsible for every breach of discipline that might be committed under their orders. On this point he insisted with a pertinacity that caused him to be regarded in some quarters as a martinet. He was nothing of the sort...' And thus a fresh, bracing wind began to blow from Simla, though none realised how timely.

For great dangers were growing, which few discerned. Since the Afghanistan disasters Indian belief in Western supremacy had waned. The sepoys, men of good caste and proud background, outnumbered the white troops by five to one and were beginning to be aware of their power. There had been mutinies in the past; in 1806 and 1824 mutinous regiments had suffered such prompt and exemplary punishment that the trouble had stopped where it began. Gough in 1844 had been weak. This was not forgotten.

The character of the Company's regiments had changed. Their British officers had lost the paternal torch which had made each unit a family. Political posts took the best, the Broadfoots, Lawrences, Nicholsons, Edwardes; for the mediocre remainder the rigid promotion system, similar to that under which Havelock suffered in the royal army, brought too many inefficient men to commands, thus increasing the incipient indiscipline generated by caste. To the Hindu soldiers caste meant more than rank; off parade a Brahman sepoy could lord it over his lower caste seniors.

Lord Dalhousie's westernising, the telegraphs and railways spreading across India, unsettled the countryside, giving rise to rumours of enforced conversion to Christianity. His annexations increased discontent and the Bengal sepoys especially felt it. The annexation in 1856 of the Kingdom of Oudh, chief recruiting ground of Moslem soldiers, however desirable on humanitarian grounds, not only had political repercussions but an adverse effect on the sepoys' conditions of service, increasing their grievances, though the placid surface of India appeared to remain unruffled.

1857, centenary year of the Battle of Plassey, and long prophesied as a year of doom for the British, was drawing near. It would need only a spark to set Bengal ablaze.

HAVELOCK'S NEW POST of Adjutant-General brought considerable increase of salary. Hannah in Europe thought good times had come and began a spending spree, submitting an inflated account including £30 for a Cashmere shawl. 'I fear,' Havelock replied, 'that after Indian fashion you reckon on my present salary as if it were the rental of a landed property of which I had the fee simple, or a sum in the funds, forgetting that an accident or six hours' illness might put me out of possession.'

With retirement not far off, economy now dominated Havelock's mind. The horror of debt – now cleared – the awful example of his brother William's widow and younger children in penury through William's extravagance, made him scrape and save. He continued to give to his denomination; he answered generously his sister Jane's pleas for help. But at Simla where he had now obtained a 'very comfortable cottage', more modest than ever any Adjutant-General had lived in, he had few visitors and kept no table. His parsimony was a source of merriment to his colleagues. Yet unwittingly, while they lived softly, Havelock was preparing himself for the desperate, unimaginable tasks ahead.

Hannah would have preferred to be at her husband's side while he lived, leaving widowhood to take care of itself. But again and again her return had to be postponed. 'God knows, my heart yearns to see you all again', he wrote, yet neither the health of the girls nor of his pocket seemed to offer a way. Perhaps it would have been better had Hannah sponged from brother John (now retired to England) and arrived unannounced with Puss. Havelock was too gripped by his fear of future poverty. 'I hold to my purpose', he wrote when the staff were on the Ganges, 'as strongly as ever, I trust, of drawing on the Bank of Faith; but have learnt in my old age that there is another establishment too much before neglected to which God's Spirit as strongly invites attention, viz, the Bank of Prudence. I should be as worse as if I threw myself from one of the funnels of the vessel if I did not now provide for the probability of finding myself a battered and shattered old man with unprovided for belongings and only the half pay of a Lt Colonel to supply the wants of all'. He was wrong. Larger drafts from the Bank of Faith would have saved him much worry, for his exertions in circumstances which could not be foreseen were to give Hannah and the girls an ample income after his death. From the same source even Harry had more than enough, while in middle age a windfall which none of them could have expected made him a wealthy landowner.

The final decision was that Hannah and Puss should come out early in 1858, when Headquarters returned from a prolonged tour in the North-West. It was as if an inner urge drove Havelock, without knowing the real reason, to prevent his family being in India in 1857.

EARLY IN 1856 Headquarters left Simla for Calcutta to meet a new Commander-in-Chief, the ill-starred George Anson. 'Our new chief is a man of fashion, and a clever fellow without much military experience, and he is at present so hardly worked with Legislature and Supreme Council work that I can hardly get him to attend much to H M's regiments; but he seems likely to do all I require about discipline... His wife calls him George from the next room whilst I am reading papers with him, and I start and turn round, expecting to see my boy with his dog.' Dalhousie handed over to Lord Canning on March 1st; Havelock attended Anson at the swearing-in ceremony on the steps of Government House and was touched when 'Lord Dalhousie, who is very ill and lame, left his chair and hobbled down the steps to shake hands with me before all the assembled thousands'.

Havelock worked hard at his measures for disciplinary improvement, often in the teeth of idle commanding officers who could see no reason to take life so seriously. 'Pray for me', he asked Hannah in June, 'for I have trouble enough, believe me.'

On September 22nd 1856 Headquarters set off by steamer for the great tour of inspection. Anson planned to spend part of the hot weather of 1857 in the hills but not to return to Calcutta until March 1858. The best part, so Havelock felt, would be in the later months of 1857 when they would reach Peshawar, for Jos was now serving there with Herbert Edwardes after a term at Kohat on the North-West frontier, where as Adjutant to Punjab Irregulars he had been one of the first British officers to wear khaki.[1]

Before the departure Havelock learned that 'an expedition is to go at once from Bombay to the Persian Gulf, and it is to be reinforced from Bengal if the Persians do not give in. This I have from the very highest authority.' Anson consulted Havelock as Adjutant-General on the question of the command, favouring General Stalker. Havelock deprecated Stalker (who in the event, as a subordinate commander, committed suicide soon after arrival in Persia) and recommended Sir James Outram, who had been Chief Commissioner of the newly annexed state of Oudh until forced early in 1856 to return to England on sick leave.

The weeks which followed were spent either 'toiling up against stream with weak steam' or inspecting, reviewing and socially gallivanting in sticky oppressive heat. Station after station was visited, each much as the others: spacious, with compounds and gardens, wide roads and dusty parade grounds; self-contained, and away from the noisy, dirty native cities; with respectful efficient house-servants, and an array of sweepers and coolies scarcely seen or noticed by their masters. The sepoy regiments, the larger and on many stations, the only force of the garrison, marched past Anson and his staff with customary smartness, their devoted British officers proudly at the head,

---

[1]Jos had been horrified when his father obtained him the adjutancy. 'I foresee too well the result – failure, utter failure,' he told Havelock, adding the information that though 'a Governor-General may make a man an adjutant, the qualities which can alone assure him success are not in the gift of a Governor-General, they are bestowed *once for all* by the Sovereign of the Universe, and any attempt to reverse His decree must ever be futile.' But father promptly wrote off to Harry, 'If the lad has come up to you tell him to give up dreaming and repining and in a spirit of common sense to set himself to his work.' Jos made an excellent adjutant. 'Jos is the best of boys,' Havelock commented to Hannah, 'but has inherited from me the evil habit of letting his cogitations and anticipations too often assume a gloomy aspect.'

and in the evenings Havelock found the usual brittle social round. Anglo-India moved serenely forward, undisturbed by the stirrings far out of sight below.

Havelock was glad he was independent. It was not merely the constant steamer travelling, though he told Hannah, 'I do not know how I should have disposed of you and the girls in this cabin of ten feet by six'; but his whole life was absorbed by the thankless task of bringing the royal regiments to efficiency, stirring up complacency, overcoming the prejudice of those who resented his insistence on an intense application to duty, and shaking commanding officers out of satisfaction with second-rate discipline, as if he knew their very lives depended on it.

Early in November they were at Benares, not yet the railhead. John Marshman had been urging the building of a Bengal railway for years before it had been undertaken; had he been listened to, Havelock's task a few months later would have been far easier. At Allahabad a great march-past took place in the Fort, none knowing the circumstances in which Havelock would next be on that parade ground. Cawnpore was reached on November 17th where they met the divisional commander, Sir Hugh Wheelers, whose past distinction appeared to make up for his advanced years, and whose friendship for the natives was such that he had married an Indian. The staff gossiped lightly with the crinolined ladies of the station; no thought was given to a dirty little house not far from the Assembly Rooms, or a well near by.

On November 19th Anson, Havelock, and the staff took the road to Lucknow rattling through Mungalwar, Unao and Busseratgunj, names which then meant nothing to Havelock, and over the Char Bagh Bridge through the city and out of the Baillie Guard Gate into the Residency compound. Havelock's niece Mary (daughter of Charles, now a Turkish pasha) was in Lucknow to be married; and her future husband, John Bensley Thornhill of the Company's civil service, came to call, 'a shocking ugly fellow, but gentlemanlike, clever, and a good public servant and I should say a kind heart'. Havelock could not stay for the wedding and his next meeting with them was to be very different.

Early in January 1857 Headquarters were at Agra, and there, utterly unexpected, an official telegram from the Governor of Bombay was shown to Havelock. 'Lord Elphinstone has telegraphed General Anson offering me, at Sir James Outram's recommendation, a divisional command in the Persian expedition.'

'Old as I am', Havelock wrote delightedly to Hannah, 'I did not hesitate a moment. The wires carried back my unconditional and immediate acceptance.'

THE PERSIAN WAR had arisen from the old quarrels over Herat and a new one concerning a Persian princess who had married an Englishman. The Royal Navy had already captured Bushire and Outram's larger forces were to proceed there and penetrate to Teheran.

Havelock, his commission as Brigadier-General in his pocket, set off from Agra on January 12th 1857 at such a pace that the official arrangements for his comfort were always one stage behind. He sat in a springless mail cart which rattled and shook and careered through Gwalior and the Mahratta states, even the necessary night stops being too long for his liking. Past Indore the mail cart caught in a hole and overturned at speed, pitching him into a corn field, 'but being a small, spare man', as another officer recorded who passed six hours later, 'he fell light and is none the worse for it', though his long nose and one of his arms were bruised.

After galloping through Nasik and down the Ghats – missing the sedate palanquin and bearers which Lord Elphinstone had arranged – he reached the railhead and arrived at Bombay railway station on the afternoon of Wednesday January 21st. Lord Elphinstone had at last caught up with him, sending Harry (who had landed in time for the campaign) to meet him, with an amused letter describing the unwanted arrangements and remarking, 'you must have been terribly jolted. I hope you are none the worse for your journey.'

Outram, having reached Bombay from England, had sailed for Persia two days before. He had left a letter saying, 'I am indeed exceedingly rejoiced at your having accepted the 2nd Division and happy at the prospect of being again with you in the field. It is not likely anything further will be done till you join. Goodbye until we meet at Bushire.'

Lord Elphinstone, having understood from Outram that there was no hurry in Persia, hoped that Havelock would stay a week or more at Government House at Parell, Bombay, but Havelock itched to embark. He was in the highest spirits. Persia was a large country and the war would probably be long. He would have two brigades under him and Harry, who did not want to be ADC, on his staff in the Quartermaster-General's department. 'Lieut-General Sir James Outram commands the whole force', he wrote breathlessly to Hannah on January 23rd, 'to his and Lord Elphinstone's good opinion I owe my nomination. The command is responsible but my trust is in God. It is a rare thing for an officer in the Bengal Presidency to be summoned to command Bombay troops. I am to get the same pay as when AGQT. How many kind old faces have I recognised here! And all give me a hearty welcome which for a *Bengali* is much!! Ladies do not come to Persia so you are left now in concert with your brother John to consult about a residence. I have done my part in securing here for you regularly receiving your £600 p.a. John and Harry both agree in the propriety of your pressing on George in the duty of *mathematics*, this is our duty. A merciful God will dispose the rest but I advise you to live in England but *within* your income.'

Before he had finished writing the post brought a letter from Harry redirected from Agra, and when he read it his cup ran over. He added to Hannah: 'I have just received a letter from Harry come back from Agra containing expressions of the most pure and humble piety!!! – we embark in two days'.

Havelock went on board the steamer *Punjaub* at the Apollo Bundar on the night of January 26th. The next morning he heard the shore battery fire a salute and trotted up on deck to discover it was in his honour, 'as I was supposed then to have gone on board, the first expense of the kind to which I have ever put the Indian government'. To his chagrin he was told the ship's engines had broken down. Elphinstone invited him to return to Parell but he refused, though it was not until January 29th that the *Punjaub* sailed off into the Arabian Sea.

A fortnight later Havelock and Harry reached Bushire to find that Outram had penetrated inland and inflicted an easy defeat on the Persians. His force had just arrived back at the coast since it was clearly impossible to reach Teheran by the immense, sparsely populated southern plateau. An alternative was to leave one division at Bushire and land the other at the head of the Persian Gulf to capture the heavily fortified position of Mohumra near Abadan, then a name of no significance, and afterwards work north-east by tributary rivers to the capital. Havelock wrote home on February 14th, 'it seems determined that I shall go with the force to Mohumra at the mouth of the Tigris and Euphrates'.

Four days later, in the midst of preparations for the expedition, which promised heavy action and responsibility, Havelock wrote again to Hannah, 'I have good troops and cannon under my command, but my trust is in the Lord Jesus, my tried and merciful friend, to whom all power is entrusted in Heaven and on earth. Him daily seek for me, as I seek Him without shadow of doubting... If I fall in the discharge of my duty, the Queen will provide for your wants, and Lord Panmure who may remember me as a boy at Charterhouse is the Minister at War, to whom you must apply.'

Havelock had been received with open arms by Outram, whom he had admired and liked since Afghan days when he had described him as 'one of the most resolute, intelligent and active officers in the army'. Though the younger, Outram as a Company's officer had risen more quickly and had already undertaken wide political responsibilities. Their paths had not often crossed since Afghanistan but each respected the other. Havelock knew also that Outram was a man of deep Christian faith, though shy and reticent in such matters. 'I am most happy in being under the orders of Sir James Outram', Havelock told Hannah from Bushire, 'who is as kind as he is brave, skilful and enterprizing.'

Reinforcements from Bombay for Havelock's division were delayed by adverse winds and on March 1st he was still at Bushire. The climate was cool and bracing and the camp 'on a sandy plain surrounded with entrenchments, in front of a small asiatic town with its grey stone curtains and round towers, and a horizon of date trees'. The officers had all grown beards and Havelock, who had always disliked the peace-time regulation which allowed him mutton-chop whiskers but forbade a beard, now had a white fisherman's fringe. Father and son slept in a small tent on iron camp-beds, and Harry 'tells me stories of Bonn and his adventures in France, Germany and England'. Harry was well but hard-worked. 'His value is already felt as a staff officer', Havelock wrote home on March 7th, 'indeed his activity and intelligence are first rate, and I have every hope that his mind and heart have undergone a change. May God make him wholly his own.'

ON MARCH 15TH HAVELOCK was anchored at the mouth of the Shatt-el-Arab below Mohumra. With him, in an array of transports escorted by men of war, were the 78th Highlanders which he had known and admired at Poona, the 64th Foot, two sepoy regiments and gunners, and a small detachment of the Scinde Horse. Several days were spent reconnoitring the strong Persian position and preparing rafts while awaiting Outram who was delayed when General Stalker committed suicide, followed shortly by the naval commander. Outram was obliged to stay at Bushire and ordered Havelock to plan the assault, arriving himself only shortly before the day, leaving the landing troops under Havelock's immediate orders.

March 26th 1857 broke bright and clear as the warships of the Indian Navy sailed up river to bombard the forts and the batteries hidden in the groves of date-palms protecting the Persian Army, commanded by a son of the Shah. Behind the men-of-war were the paddle-steamer transports which anchored while the Navy did its work; Havelock, as happy as a sandboy but as calm as at Jalalabad, was in the *Berenice*, crowded with Highlanders, leading the line.

The men-of-war, each covering a battery or fort, opened fire, joined by some mortars carefully positioned on land. The enemy batteries replied. There was just enough breeze to disperse the smoke and to the men watching from the transports the scene was entrancing. As one of them wrote, 'the ships with ensigns flying from every masthead seemed decked for a holiday; the river glittering in the early sunlight, its dark-fringed banks contrasting most effectively with the white canvas of the *Falkland* which had loosened sails to get into closer action; the sulky looking batteries just visible through the grey fleecy cloud which enveloped them; and groups of brightly-dressed horsemen flitting at intervals between trees where they had their encampment.'

After enduring three and a half hours' bombardment the Persian batteries began to slacken and Havelock ordered the transports to advance. On the *Berenice* he took post on one of the paddle boxes. The *Berenice* sailed close under a fort which was still firing and he ordered the Highlanders to lie down though remaining in position himself, bullets whistling overhead and shot from the batteries splashing closer as the ship chugged and belched unhesitatingly forward. She passed through without a casualty, such was the shooting, and in Harry's steamer, next in line, 'the only man killed was his head servant who was smashed by a cannon ball that had traversed the vessel from stem to stern, where the poor nigger met his fate'. The *Berenice* steamed on and reached the landing place.

Then came the anticlimax. The Highlanders disembarked and

formed up 'in good order and the highest spirits', but before Havelock could lead them through the date groves the battered Persians had fled. The Highlanders had no time to fire a shot and the enemy were already too far for the handful of cavalry to catch them. It was not a rout but a parade, and not one of Havelock's soldiers was lost. Visions of promotion to major-general faded: 'I had hoped my troops would have won great laurels, but Providence decreed it otherwise'. Great quantities of stores, guns and booty were taken.

Thus the affair of Mohumra which Havelock hoped would be his hard-fought victorious Toulon, fizzled out in laughable ease. Indeed the only reminder of his tough battles with Afghans and Sikhs was 'the whiz of bullets passing over my crowded steamer and the sense of the same protecting and guiding Providence'.

To men thirsting for action Mohumra was a bitter disappointment. Worse was to come, as Havelock and his army then saw it. A detachment sent a hundred miles inland had trounced a greatly superior force with the same ease as at Mohumra. On April 4th news of this victory had reached the encampment, where officers and men were enjoying luxuries such as chickens and fresh milk, paid for at exorbitant prices in the Arab bazaar, and where Harry, though working perpetually in the sun, was looking remarkably well and his father had never felt fitter in his life. The next day, Sunday, was Havelock's sixty-second birthday and he woke feeling ten years younger. He organised his troops for Church parade 'and then returned to worship God in private, as a dissenter may' (there were two Church of England chaplains but one was a 'terrific Puseyite' and Havelock after trying him had been obliged 'to give him up'). As his private devotions concluded he heard the Church parade dismiss. A few moments later Sir James Outram dismounted at the door of the tent and walked in to announce that the war was over, peace with Persia having been signed in Paris as far back as March 4th.

It was a bleak birthday present. 'So ends my hope of advantage from this war', he wrote that afternoon to Hannah; adding bravely, 'but the intelligence, which elevates some and depresses others, finds me calm in my reliance on that dear Redeemer who has watched and cared for me, even when I knew Him not, these three score and two years.'

The Peace Treaty had deprived them all of 'a glorious opportunity of annexing the southern provinces of Persia', which Havelock was convinced would be 'an accession to the happiness of millions thus brought under our rule'. It seemed also the end of Havelock's personal hopes. His commission as Brigadier-General would lapse and on April 6th he wrote his dearest Hannah 'a few most serious words' on the consequences: 'by the new arrangements I may wait my natural life in vain for the rank of Major-General by seniority. The only way to get it is by selection. It was to improve my claim that I faced every risk and promptly answered the invitation of the Bombay government to come on this service. It has ended in smoke. I must return to my post of A G, H M's Forces after having all my establishment twice broken up and been put to a fearful expense. Therefore it is that I call upon you solemnly to aid me with your best endeavours to economise in every way. If I can save a little during the two remaining years it will be well, if not you and my children will be left absolutely or nearly penniless. Lay all this to heart and practise the most rigid economy as I will. This peace is a sad blow to poor Harry's prospects.'

As APRIL WORE on, the weather in the Gulf getting unpleasantly hot, Havelock cast in his mind what the future could be. He half hoped the Shah would refuse to ratify the Treaty and 'force our government to prolong the war until it can terminate in conquest, without which the word peace is an illusion'. War with China was blowing up and he wrote to Anson to ask if he could be given a command. A letter from Anson, dated March 15th, had mentioned some trouble with the sepoys at Barrackpore.

'We have been', he wrote, 'and still are in trouble here with disaffection in regiments on account of the cartridge question. The 19th Native Infantry are in open mutiny, a stronger case than any I know on record in India; the Government will deal with it, I hope, judiciously. I only know the facts, but very few particulars as to who or what is to be blamed. There are generally in these matters faults everywhere; but open mutiny cannot be passed over or even partially excused.' Havelock regretted the extra burden to Anson but saw in the news no personal significance.

Meanwhile, Harry had gone to make a survey 'in an island called Abadan' and Havelock wrote home on May 1st that 'his work will occupy him ten days at least, which I reckon a gloomy period, his presence being the earthly accident of my existence most cheering to me. From all the rest of you I am separated by considerations of stern duty. I am most thankful when at intervals his employments enable me to see *him* twice a day'. Yet Harry was still a grief: 'Alas! I cannot say anything positive about his change of heart. He wrote me from London in a style most hopeful. But has since appeared to swerve to perverse and faithless notions and given way to frowardness and discontent'.

A day or two later the *Berenice* brought mails from India. Havelock had a long congratulatory letter from Anson dated April 20th, giving him high hopes of a command in the China war. At the end of the letter Anson remarked, 'we are in an uncomfortable state here with our sepoys, but I hope the worst is over. A jemadar of the 24th N I is sentenced to *death*. It is satisfactory to find that a court of native officers have done their duty and I trust that this example and that of the sepoy who was hung will have a beneficent effect upon the whole of the army'. Lord Elphinstone also wrote, congratulating Havelock on Mohumra and condoling with him on the '*premature* conclusion of peace'. He added, 'I hope that we shall get back nearly all the European troops before the Rains... When the treaty of peace is ratified I suppose that you will not wish to remain in

Persia. I trust therefore that I shall have the pleasure of seeing you again before very long, and that you will not be quite so impatient to get away as you were in January.'

On May 6th the Shah's ratification of the Peace Treaty was announced. 'The breeze is all over', wrote Havelock, 'the British troops are to return to Bombay, only some natives to be left at Bushire until Herat is given up. So I return to Bombay and thence to my ordinary avocations.' Havelock was most displeased with the Shah – not aware that unwittingly the Shah had saved British India.

ON MAY 15th Havelock sailed from Mohumra in the steamer *Berenice*, the battalion transport *Ocean Monarch* in tow, both ships laden with Highlanders.

The Gulf and the Arabian Sea were hot and dazzlingly blue and for a fortnight Havelock, his officers and men were isolated from news.

On Friday May 29th 1857 they sailed into Bombay Harbour. 'I arrived here the day before yesterday', Havelock wrote on May 31st, 'in time to receive the astounding intelligence that the Native regiments had mutinied at Meerut, and that the fortress of Delhi was in the hands of the mutineers, whilst disaffection seemed everywhere spreading in the Upper Provinces.'

PART THREE

Man of the Hour

11

Mutiny

Through most of May 30th and 31st 1857 Havelock was closeted with Lord Elphinstone and Sir Henry Somerset, who had succeeded as Commander-in-Chief at Bombay on FitzClarence's death in office.

The news they gave him he summed up in a memorandum: 'It is evident that there has been mutiny and devastation at Ferozepore, where the native regiments doubtfully contended for the mastery with H M's 61st regiment, and that there has been a bloody massacre at Meerut. The perpetrators of this infernal outrage marched upon Delhi in the night, where the same scene of lawless violence and murder was repeated by the garrison who, in conjunction with the Meerut mutineers, have taken possession of the fortress and arsenal after destroying the bridge of boats and attempting to seize the powder magazine, which was blown up to save it from their hands. A detachment at Muttra has possessed itself of the treasure. The same has been done at Bulandshahr by some body of the mutineers. The native troops at Agra have been disarmed; those at Mhow are distrusted. The mingled vigour and moderation of Sir Henry Lawrence have hitherto kept tranquil the province of Oudh. The Nusseri battalion, charged with the duty of escorting the siege train from Phillaur marched to Syree, and then mutinously returned to Jutog, where it remained moody and suspected within a few miles of Simla'.

The mutiny at Meerut had been touched off by the same cause as that at Barrackpore which Anson had mentioned in his letter in March – the belief that the cartridges of the powerful new breech-loading Enfield rifle were greased with animal fat and that both caste Hindus and Mohammedans would thus be defiled, when biting off the ends before loading. This was the spark which set ablaze the Bengal Army, primed by the deeper causes of the mutiny. Misjudgment, indecision and downright folly on the part of commanders on the spot had led to a conflagration which, as the Electric Telegraph messages showed, was spreading almost every hour.

Havelock, as Adjutant-General of Queen's Troops, saw that his place was beside Anson in the Upper Provinces and that he must set off at once. 'But after a full consultation with Lord Elphinstone and Colonel Melvill, I came to the conclusions that the route by Indore was in no sense safe; that I could not get through without an escort, and that none could be spared me'. It was therefore settled that with Harry he should go round to Calcutta by sea and thence hope to get through up the Ganges Plain. The 78th Highlanders and the 64th had been sent straight on without landing. 'This is the most tremendous convulsion I have ever witnessed', Havelock wrote to Hannah from Bombay on May 31st, 'though I was in the thick of the Kabul affairs. But the same kind Providence will watch over me now. Calcutta is in alarm, and we are here almost denuded of British troops, so I know not what to expect to hear if I get round to Calcutta. General Anson is marching on Delhi, but waits for a battering-train from Phillaur. This morning they telegraph us from Agra that they have been compelled to disarm the native regiments. The crisis is eventful; for General Anson cannot be before Delhi until the 9th proximo, and meanwhile, the military insurrection, for such it is, gains strength. The Jigur Nawab alone has joined the mutineers, all the other Native powers around have ordered their troops to *aid us*.'

The Havelocks sailed from Bombay on June 1st in the passenger steamer *Erin*, one of the P&O's fine new steam and sail ships, bound for Ceylon and Shanghai with £150,000 worth of opium. It was comfortable, except for the tea which appeared to be mixed with coffee, and the servants were Chinese with pigtails down to the calves of their legs.

On the night of June 5th the *Erin* was approaching Ceylon where they would call at Pointe de Galle to coal and to make the connection for Calcutta. She was steaming at eleven knots, the moon was bright and the night fair. Havelock turned in. 'I was awoken a little before one in the morning by rain coming in at the port. I rose and shut it. In a few minutes I felt a shock, which induced me to think the vessel on shore. Another followed, which convinced me it was even so; but my mind rejected the idea as I confided in the good look-out kept by the officers of the great P&O Company. The next moment Harry, who had been sleeping on deck, came very calmly into my cabin and said, "Sir, Sir, get up, the ship has struck"'. Havelock hurriedly dressed and went on deck, to find 'an awful scene'. The captain, half-dressed was running around utterly distraught and 'the crew had lost their wits and obeyed no orders. Indeed few were given'. It was pouring with rain and blowing a gale. There was much shouting but nothing being done and the European sailors were as useless as the lascars. Havelock stalked across and said in his parade ground voice, 'Now, my men, if you will obey orders and keep from the spirit cask we shall be saved'.

They lit distress rockets and burned blue flames, with no answer from the shore, and then fired a gun, when an answering signal came at last. The English district judge came to the shore with a crowd of Singalis carrying torches and a native swam through the surf with a line by which the women and children at least might be saved. Four long wet hours of suspense passed, with the *Erin* repeatedly shuddering as she worked harder on to the sandspit, until at last dawn broke and canoes were seen paddling swiftly from shore.

Passengers and crew were taken off without loss and they then realised that had the ship struck a mile or so to the north, where it was rocky, she would undoubtedly have sunk with all hands. As soon as they were ashore Havelock made his boatload gather round and kneel down while he led them briefly in thanksgiving. For, as he put it succinctly to Hannah, 'the madness of man threw us on shore, the mercy of God found us a soft place near Kalutai'. The specie and mails were saved, and some of the baggage, though both Havelocks lost several of their trunks and their two horses.

The Havelocks were taken down to Galle as soon as possible. They found the P&O ship gone but obtained passages on an E I Company's steamer, the *Fire Queen*, which had been sent to Ceylon to take north any European troops still left. Harry did not help matters by assuming 'an air of sulky despondency most painful to behold'. As usual everything seemed against him. His regiment was in Dinapore and probably in action and he not there and he had lost his baggage.

On June 13th they steamed into Madras to find the flag on the white walls of Fort St George at half mast because, they were told, General Anson had died of cholera at Umballa on May 26th. 'Thus my friends are snatched from me', was Havelock's reaction in a letter to Hannah, 'for I think he was as kindly disposed towards me as poor Lord Frederick'. Havelock was driven at once to the house in Mount Road of the Commander-in-Chief of the Madras Presidency, Sir Patrick Grant, an old friend and colleague. 'He received me in the kindest manner and insisted on my writing at once to Harry, who came with the worst grace possible'.

Havelock said that if Anson was dead, his own place was back at Bombay with Sir Henry Somerset who as next senior must be acting Commander-in-Chief. But Canning had telegraphed ordering Grant to come to Bengal to quell the mutiny. He might be appointed acting Commander-in-Chief and told Havelock that he must come with him and held out hopes of a command. If not, he could always go to Bombay later.

The *Fire Queen* left Madras on June 14th. Havelock now had as fellow passengers Sir Patrick Grant and his staff. Harry was moodier than ever, though Havelock assured him that the acting-adjutant of the 10th would resign when he rejoined, or there might be something on his own staff if he got a command.

Besides, after the *Erin* 'we should be thankful for our lives so mercifully spared'. But Harry 'will listen to nothing but the dictates of despair and childishly rails at his ill luck'.

During the two days' passage up the Bay of Bengal Grant and Havelock were much in conference. Havelock produced a memorandum on the Bengal Mutinies which he had written on the *Erin*, intended for Anson and based on such facts as had been available when he left Bombay. He recommended the most stringent measures: 'It is clear that no regular Native Infantry regiment can now be trusted. All are in heart implicated in the treason, if not in act. All must henceforth be jealously watched by the British troops. Every other act must be visited with prompt attack and bloody overthrow... No piece of cannon must be henceforth entrusted to a native... The whole of the Enfield rifles must be given over to the British troops... But there must be no more disbandments for mutiny. Mutineers must be attacked and annihilated; and if they are few in any regiment, and not immediately denounced to be shot or hanged, the whole regiment must be deemed guilty and given up to prompt military execution'. This was the sort of advice he had given Gough in 1844 and had been kicked for his pains; had it been accepted there would probably have been no Indian Mutiny.

As for military operations, he emphasised the value of movable columns. Two in effect were already formed, since Barnard, once he had retaken Delhi, could operate from the Sutlej and Allahabad while John Lawrence had one in the Punjab; 'it might perhaps be desirable to form a third to overawe the lower provinces'.

Sir Patrick Grant studied the memorandum and though demurring from Havelock's statement that no regular native regiments could now be trusted – he had served nearly all his life with sepoys and like many others was convinced that most regiments would stand firm – he fully approved the recommendation of a third movable column and expressed the hope that Havelock would be put in command. He remembered Havelock

173

at Maharajpur and the battles of the first Sikh War; and he recalled the saying of their old chief, Lord Hardinge, 'if ever India should be in danger the Government have only to place Havelock at the head of an army, and it will be saved'.

The conversations on board ship strengthened his conviction. When the *Fire Queen* tied up at the Fort William Ghat on the night of June 17th and Lord Canning walked up the gangway to meet them, Grant led Havelock forward and said, 'My lord, I have brought you the man!'.

HAVELOCK WENT TO his old room at the United Services Club on Chowringhee. Three days earlier, on Sunday June 14th, the city had been thrown in panic by a report that mutineers were marching down from Barrackpore: English officials and Indian merchants were seen racing across the Maidan in their carriages to seek refuge in Fort William. The panic had subsided but bad news continued. 'There has been a dreadful massacre at Allahabad', Havelock wrote to Hannah on June 18th, 'and here things do not look bright. At Nasseerabad and Benares there has been mutiny. The troops here are so harassed that they could not afford Sir P Grant a guard of honour'. The grim reality of the revolt had already come close home to the *Fire Queen* party: at Kedgeree at the mouth of the Hooghly, Grant had learned that one of his sons had been killed at Lucknow. He took it well, but as they sat in the saloon steaming up to Calcutta Havelock saw Grant's other son's eyes 'suffused with tears all yesterday evening with a cheroot in his mouth and a novel before him'.

A wing of the Madras European (Fusiliers) Regiment which had arrived in Calcutta on May 24th had been sent up country under the vigorous command of Colonel Neill, and the 78th Highlanders and the 64th were in from Persia. Neill had apparently restored the situation at Benares and Allahabad; Delhi was believed, falsely, to be recovered, while the sepoy regiments at Dinapore astride the line of communications from Calcutta being quiescent, Canning would not disarm them. But the situation as seen from Calcutta remained serious, for Wheeler at Cawnpore and Lawrence at Lucknow, with all the women and children of their stations, were not yet secure.

On Saturday June 20th, Grant having been made acting Commander-in-Chief, Havelock was appointed to command the Movable Column. 'I have barely time to tell you', he wrote to Hannah the next day in time to catch the home mail, 'that I was yesterday reappointed Brigadier-General, and leave by dawk as soon as possible for Allahabad... Sir Patrick Grant lost no time in recommending me for this important command, the object of which is to relieve Cawnpore, where Sir Hugh Wheeler is threatened, and support Lucknow, where Sir Henry Lawrence is somewhat pressed. May God give me wisdom and strength to fulfil the expectations of Government, and restore tranquillity in the disturbed provinces! I do not know whether there is any virtue in my beard, but you may be sure I shall carry it with me on my journey, which I hope Nora will approve'.[1]

Havelock's orders were clear: that 'after quelling all disturbances at Allahabad, he should not lose a moment in supporting Sir Henry Lawrence at Lucknow, and Sir Hugh Wheeler at Cawnpore; and that he should take prompt measures for dispersing and utterly destroying all mutineers and insurgents... It was not possible at the moment to give him any more precise or definite instructions, but he must necessarily be guided by circumstances; and the Commander-in-Chief had entire confidence in his well-known and often-proved high ability, vigour and judgment.'

The appointment was not well received by the Calcutta public. 'An old fossil', Havelock was called, 'dug up and only fit to be turned into pipe clay'. He was attacked as too friendly to natives because of his connection with the *Friend of India* which championed their rights; he certainly believed, with Herbert

---

[1]Nora (now aged 17) loved thoroughly bewhiskered men. When a child of nine returning to England she had met Sir Charles Napier whose beard and whiskers were so terrible that they had helped to conquer Sind. Nora thought him wonderful.

Edwardes and Henry Lawrence, that had the Government not forbidden the teaching of the Bible to such sepoys as were interested, the absurd belief would never have arisen that the greased cartridges were an attempt to defile Hindus and Mohammedans as a prelude to forced conversion. 'General Havelock is not in fashion', wrote Lady Canning, 'but all the same we believe he will do well. No doubt he is fussy and tiresome, but his little, old, stiff figure looks as active and fit for use as if he were made of steel'.

On the Sunday morning Havelock attended the Baptist church, but most of the day and the three following were taken up with preparations for his command. He was promised four European regiments, about 2,800 British infantry; part were already assembling at Allahabad, part would leave Calcutta immediately and the rest would follow as soon as possible. This force seemed just adequate – if all came up in time.

Since large numbers of commissariat transport animals had been slaughtered by the mutineers at Allahabad, Havelock pointed out that his column might be delayed at a critical moment unless every draught animal on the Grand Trunk Road were made available. He also asked for and received permission to make liberal use of secret service money in order to ensure that intelligence would be brought in by natives.

He was busy forming his staff. 'I have three staff appointments in my gift', he had written on the Sunday to Hannah, 'which is the usual source of perplexity. Harry though anxious for staff employ has adopted a notion that he ought not to come with me and at present declares his determination of rather rejoining his regiment where he will be reappointed adjutant if he wishes it. But his wish is to go to China which expedition is however postponed in consequence of all the troops being required here. I think he ought to go with me as he could be more useful to me as aide than one not of my own kith and kin but I suppose he will not; neither does he wish to be *my* QMG, which is hard lines, I think. I trust God will be with me'. After persuasion Harry condescended to become his father's ADC. For AQMG Havelock chose Lieutenant-Colonel Bannatyne Fraser Tytler, who had been with him at Ferozepore, and for DAAG Captain Stuart Beatson whom he had not known previously. Both were Scotsmen.

On Thursday June 25th Havelock with his staff crossed the Hooghly by steam ferry to Howrah railway terminus and set out to join his command and hasten to the relief of Cawnpore.

As HAVELOCK SAT in the shaking, smoky, dusty railway carriage for the first all too short leg of his journey to the railhead at Raniganj, he was able to collect his thoughts.

His ambition for an independent command was at last realised, but there could be little elation at the circumstances. This was no professional war but a grim race to save women and children from mutilation and death. It seemed extraordinary to think of those familiar cantonments with their spacious bungalows now derelict, their trim gardens already covered with fast growing weeds, and hatred, fear and death stalking unchecked in the steaming heat. At Cawnpore, General Wheeler was holding out in a small entrenchment against superior forces led by the Nana Sahib of Bithoor, adopted son of the last Mahratta Peishwar. At Lucknow Sir Henry Lawrence, Havelock's best friend since Broadfoot's death, might soon be fighting for survival; and in the garrison was Havelock's niece, Mary Thornhill, and her husband.

On Havelock depended the restoration of British authority in the lower provinces. If he failed all Bengal might be lost. As the train rattled onward he looked out at the ryots toiling patiently in the paddy fields, their brown bodies glistening in the sun, caring nothing who ruled in Delhi or Calcutta. On him depended whether they could till their soil in peace or be exposed once again to anarchy. And it was not only success that mattered, but how that success was achieved. This convulsion would affect India for years to come; his would be the first full scale strike back, except for Barnard's force stationary at Delhi. On his manner of striking might depend how quickly the wounds healed.

The task ahead was appalling. His troops would be fighting at the worst season of the year, when normally no campaigning or manoeuvres were ever undertaken and every European who could do so made for the hills, while the few left on the plains sweated and gasped through the days, moving as little as possible and living in rooms specially scooped out of the earth under their bungalows, with the punkahs working ceaselessly, while outside the rain cascaded down or the sun burnt its way into the very vitals of a man. Yet since the essential factor was time, there could be no waiting on the climate, no marching only in the dawn hours. Furthermore, he would have barely sufficient troops even if every man promised reached him; and unless Canning and Grant disarmed every sepoy in lower Bengal – and they had said that they would not – Havelock feared that his force would be smaller than he was told. And, not least, he would be operating, in effect, in enemy country, a small force surrounded by actual or potential foes.

THE TRAIN STEAMED into Raniganj, one hundred and twenty miles from Calcutta, and Havelock and his party transferred to dawk-garries and set off briskly, a couple of Highlanders sitting on the roof of each carriage as escort, along the Grand Trunk Road beside the unfinished railway.

On the third day, June 27th, Havelock overtook Captain Maude, who was to command the guns, with his few artillery-men and a company of the 78th Highlanders, travelling in a ponderous bullock train. He ordered Maude to take his artillerymen, impress the first dawks he could find and gallop after him to Benares and Allahabad; till Maude came up Havelock could serve no guns.

Staff and general swept across the bridge of boats and into the cantonment of the sacred city of Benares on the morning of

June 28th, having dozed in the dawks on the road, and heard from Mr Tucker the magistrate the story of Neill's timely though bloodthirsty smashing of incipient mutiny three weeks before.

Havelock formally assumed command of the Movable Column and inspected such troops as were at Benares on their way to form part of his force. His only cavalry would be undependable Native Irregulars. He now saw a number of English officers who having lost their men had nothing to do, and he telegraphed Grant asking permission to form a corps of volunteer cavalry of 'officers of regiments which had mutinied, or had been disbanded; of indigo planters, of patrols, of burnt-out shopkeepers; in short, of all who were willing to join him'.

Havelock set out by dawk from Benares to cover the eighty miles to Allahabad, on the evening of June 29th. He travelled all night (the staff were to follow the next day) and at about seven in the morning entered the great red Fort, sited strategically by the Moghuls at the junction of the Jumna and the Ganges, a little distance from the city. A few minutes later Havelock was breakfasting with Neill, who sat in his uniform of still unusual khaki with a turbaned helmet placed on the chair beside him.

Lieutenant-Colonel J G Neill, Madras Fusiliers, was an energetic and decisive soldier who had saved Benares and had recovered Allahabad before the rising got out of hand. He was enthusiastic and impatient, and believed that unhesitant action in itself won campaigns, whatever the odds or the lack of supplies. He was a Godfearing Scot, but like Cromwell, inclined to consider himself the Arm of the Lord and the Scourge of God, pretensions which, on the part of any man, Havelock dismissed as unChristian. Neill was addicted to much swearing while Havelock, as Captain Maude said, 'never used expletives'. Neill was the idol of his regiment, he had been much praised to his face for his actions and in the Press and the Calcutta clubs was loudly acclaimed as the one strong man thrown up by the crisis. He was disappointed at not being given command of the Movable Column and behind Havelock's back did not hesitate to say so.

From Neill Havelock heard the latest position. Allahabad was quiet, Neill having destroyed the mutineers, burnt part of the native city and executed anyone who might have taken part in the massacre early in June. To north and west the country was in enemy hands. Nothing had been heard from Cawnpore, one hundred and twenty miles on, but a force of four hundred Madras Fusiliers, three hundred Sikhs, a detachment of irregular (sepoy) cavalry and two small guns was leaving that very afternoon, June 30th, in command of Major Renaud to make contact with Wheeler if possible, having been held up over a week by an outbreak of cholera and by lack of transport. This force, said Neill, had orders to hang every mutinous sepoy they caught and burn the villages. As Renaud advanced, another officer of Madras Fusiliers, Lieutenant Spurgin, was to take the one and only river steamer and move up the Ganges in support.

Renaud marched out as planned, taking every available cart and animal. Havelock inspected the Fort and the defences of the Allahabad cantonment, which on two sides was protected by the bend of the wide river, and then set himself to requisition any camel or bullock which could be found in the surrounding districts. He also ordered an unstinting effort to clothe the European troops in thin linen to make the heat more bearable. With his secret service money he sent out spies in all directions.

That evening a letter for Havelock was brought in from Sir Henry Lawrence at Lucknow, dated three days earlier, June 27th. 'Once we have a thousand more Europeans here', Lawrence wrote, 'we shall be all right... we are snug enough in the city and still hold the cantonment with 200 Europeans and about 150 sepoys. This enables us to get supplies... I am very glad to hear you are coming up; 400 Europeans with four guns, 300 Sikhs, with 100 cavalry, will easily beat everything at Cawnpore, *as long as Wheeler holds his ground*; but if he is destroyed, your game will be difficult. I have a long letter from him of the 24th; he had then provisions for *eight or ten days*. I am offering large bribes to parties to supply him, but am not sanguine of success.

It is therefore *most important* that your detachment should not lose an hour. This is important on your own account and of vital importance on Wheeler's. We are threatened by about ten regiments, which are concentrating about eighteen miles off. The talookdars and zemindars are feeding them but few have openly joined them. They have two of our nine-pounder batteries and many native guns. Our position is safe enough, though they may knock the houses about our ears. If the irregulars and police are staunch, we will save the city from plunder. On your approach to Cawnpore, I will endeavour to co-operate with you; but as long as so strong a force of mutineers is close by, it will be impossible, as I have two positions to hold, and am unable to concentrate into one...' In a memorandum for forwarding to the Commander-in-Chief Lawrence wrote that what was left of Wheeler's nine hundred, which had included four hundred women and children, were holding out desperately against some four thousand of the enemy led by the Nana Sahib, self-styled Rajah of Bithoor.

The first three days of July were spent collecting supply transport. Though prepared to march now without the further European regiments which Grant had promised, Havelock (however impatient to be moving) would not fling his men forward with no commissariat, to die of starvation half way to Cawnpore. The delay caused criticism in the force. J W Sherer, the refugee magistrate of Fatehpur who had just reached Allahabad, heard officers saying that Neill would not have bothered about carts and bearers. 'We were all talking without special knowledge', he wrote in his memoirs, 'and as people do talk who are not behind the scenes, freely and critically, and it may perhaps be added, foolishly. But the general feeling was one of regret that Neill should have been superseded'. Even Beatson, Havelock's staff officer, was writing letters of complaint to friends in Calcutta.

In the early hours of July 3rd Havelock was wakened in his tent in the Fort compound by a subaltern who had just ridden in from the forward detachment now forty miles on, with a horrifying report from Renaud. Intelligence had been received in camp 'of the fall of Cawnpore and the massacre of the whole of the Europeans there. A Rajah told Sir Hugh Wheeler that if he would quit the place at once they might do so without molestation by boats. He, being very short of food, listened to the fiend, who got 120 boats for the party who embarked, and pushed off; no sooner were they in the river than he opened fire on them from his heavy guns and killed large numbers. Many jumped from the boats and reached the opposite shore, but were immediately cut to pieces, by a body of 2,000 cavalry, who have been patrolling the road to keep out all communication between Cawnpore and Lucknow'.

Havelock sent the subaltern back to Renaud with orders to halt where he was, keeping a strong look-out but burning no more villages unless occupied by insurgents. Havelock had already planned to start the next day and Spurgin's steamer was sent up stream at once.

The two native spies who had brought Renaud the news of the massacre came into Allahabad during the afternoon and Havelock examined them separately, making his staff do the same afterwards. The interrogations convinced him that their report was accurate. He telegraphed Calcutta accordingly: 'If the report be correct, which there is too much reason to believe, we have lost Cawnpore, an important point on the great line of communication and the place from which alone Lucknow can be succoured, for it would hardly be possible at this season of the year to operate on the cross roads. My duty is therefore to endeavour to retake Cawnpore, to the accomplishment of which I will bend every effort. I advance along the trunk road as soon as I can unite 1,400 British infantry to a battery of six well-equipped guns. Lawrence is confident of holding out for a month. Lieut-Col Neill, whose high qualities I cannot sufficiently praise, will follow with another column as soon as it can be organised, and this fort left in proper hands. I should have preferred to move the whole of the troops together, but the relief of Lucknow is an affair of time, and I cannot hazard its fall by waiting for the organisation of Neill's column...'

The report of the massacre caused consternation in the Allahabad camp. Neill refused to believe it, said it was an artifice of the enemy and after Havelock was gone took on himself to telegraph to Grant criticising his superior officer's decision to halt Renaud.

That night, July 3rd, Havelock found time to write to Hannah: '...Mutiny and treachery have been gaining ground every day since I last wrote, and you must expect to hear of great calamities. Lawrence still holds Lucknow triumphantly, but has great odds against him. It is believed that the force at Cawnpore has been entirely destroyed by treachery; having unfortunately been seduced into a treaty with its foes'. He was in great spirits and enclosed a copy of the only photograph ever done of him, by 'a native amateur' at Lucknow the previous December. 'You may send it to the *Illustrated Times* (*sic*) as the portrait of the general who commanded the 2nd Division at Mohumra – and did nothing because his foes ran away'.

Havelock had ended his letter, 'I march tomorrow to endeavour to retake Cawnpore and rescue Lucknow', but hopes of setting off on July 4th were dashed by lack of transport for his ammunition, food and equipment. Despite the lengthening line of elephants, camels, water buffalo and bullocks there were still too few, and too little provisions, though the column would travel lighter than any army which had marched in India.

On the Sunday, July 5th, a report from Renaud stated that 'a man has just arrived from Cawnpore and has stated that seven days ago the Rajah withdrew his men, and that Sir H Wheeler immediately left his entrenchments, hoisted the English flag in the bazaar, and is now in full possession of the place'. 'I think that this story is more likely than the horrible account brought in two days ago', a young officer of the Madras Fusiliers wrote to his wife, but Havelock was not deceived. He now had no doubt that while he was still on the road to Benares, Wheeler had been destroyed.

On Monday rain poured in torrents all day, turning the glacis of Allahabad Fort into a steamy quagmire. But at last, on the morning of Tuesday July 7th, Havelock was able to issue the order: 'the force will march this afternoon'.

12

The Road to Cawnpore

At half past three on the afternoon of July 7th, attended by his staff, Havelock rode on to the parade ground of Allahabad Fort to inspect his force, lined up in marching order. He was wearing a General's undress blue frock coat, a forage cap with a large white cover which draped down to shelter his neck, and drab-coloured waterproof leggings which also covered his feet. 'His figure was slight and small', recalled Captain Maude of the Gunners in after years, 'but neat and erect... His face was older than his years and much tanned by the Indian sun; his moustache, whiskers and beard being rather long and perfectly white'.

As the command to present arms rang out the General could survey his little army. On the right of the line was Maude, his six guns and a scratch force of gunners – the thirty Royal Artillerymen brought from Ceylon, fifty-four infantry men of H M's 64th who had a smattering of gun training, twenty-two veterans from the Invalid Depot at Chunar, and a few loyal native gunners. Next were the few cavalry – the twenty assorted officers and civilians forming the new Volunteer Cavalry under Captain Lousada Barrow, and a detachment of Native Irregulars. The infantry, drawn up to the left of the cavalry, were more numerous. The 64th Foot[1] were in strength (435 men) and fresh from Persia; next to them four companies of the 78th Highlanders,[2] the Rosshire Buffs with whom Havelock had worshipped at Poona and had led at Mumra. All came from the Highlands and nearly every man carried a Bible in his knapsack, as Havelock knew.

---

[1] Afterwards the North Staffordshire Regiment.
[2] Afterwards the Seaforth Highlanders.

On the Highlanders' left were two companies of the 84th Foot[3] which had been brought hurriedly from Burma; fifty of their comrades were at Lucknow and fifty had been in Wheeler's entrenchment. Next were a detachment of the Madras Fusiliers, 'Neill's Blue Caps', a regiment of wild, hard drinking, hard swearing Europeans which included a proportion of gentleman-rankers, 'the legion of the lost ones, the cohort of the damned'. On the left of the line were one hundred and fifty Sikhs, tall, bearded and turbaned; three hundred more with the bulk of the Blue Caps being forward with Renaud.

The parade of a thousand Europeans and two hundred natives was a motley colour. Most of the European officers and men wore white cotton or linen; all forage caps were draped and curtained with white like the General's, except for the Madras Fusiliers whose caps were curtained and covered with their customary blue. Despite Havelock's efforts the native contractors had not produced sufficient hot-weather clothing for the whole force and the Highlanders were perspiring in their red woollen highland jackets, though they had discarded their Mackenzie kilts. The Madras Fusiliers and the flank companies of the 64th carried Enfield rifles. The rest, the old Brown Bess musket.

Havelock took up position facing the centre. The hot sun disappeared behind threatening masses of fiercely coloured storm clouds and the heat became even more oppressive. Havelock's great moment had come. But before he inspected the ranks and gave the order to march he had, as a disciple of Napoleon, a distinct duty to perform: he must make a brief oration to his army. His voice rang out across the parade ground in fine Napoleonic style: 'Soldiers! There is work before us. We are bound on an expedition whose object is to restore the supremacy of British rule and avenge the fate of British men and women. Some of you I know – others are yet strangers to

---

[3]Afterwards the York and Lancaster Regiment.

me; but we have a common aspiration which knits us together as one man. 78th and 64th, I have commanded you in Persia, and I know the stuff you are made of; I know you will give me no cause to waver in the implicit confidence I have in you...' At his close the 64th and the Blue Caps cheered lustily. The Commanding Officer of the 78th, Colonel Hamilton, half-turned in his saddle and shouted 'Hurrah!' but only a grim mutter came from behind him. Havelock rode down the line and as he reached the Highlanders he said with a smile to Colonel Hamilton, 'Your men like better to cheer when the Bugle sounds "Charge" than when it sounds "General Parade". We'll try their throats by and by'. The centre company heard his words and broke into a roar of cheering, the flank companies taking it up. Havelock smiled radiantly, and passed on without a word.

At four o'clock the force moved off in column of route for the first march towards Cawnpore, the little body of Volunteer Cavalry acting as advance guard and the left of the line leading. The Blue Caps band played them out and when the Highlanders marched their five bagpipes astonished the natives lining the parade ground. As the force passed through the native city, with its tall Mohammedan houses, its mosques and Hindu temples, the inhabitants crowded scowling to the doors and on the roof tops, 'in gloomy silence', as one of the column wrote shortly afterwards, 'curious to behold the first really offensive demonstration of their Feringhi masters since the commencement of the outbreak'. 'Although the number of fighting men was small,' said Maude, 'the cavalcade made an imposing appearance.' Though marching as light as they could the column was followed by an array of elephants carrying the camp equipment, by 'long strings of cross-looking camels', and countless bullock carts 'besides the peripatetic meal for the morrow, which consisted of minute and skinny sheep. Lastly there were the suggestive "doolies", or covered stretchers, each carried by four bearers; empty that afternoon, but very soon to be filled to repletion with their ghastly load of sick, wounded and dying'.

Before the column had marched for a quarter of a mile a deluge of rain cascaded down, drenching men and ammunition and forming almost a wall of water in front and behind and bouncing with great splashes off the road. For three hours of solid rain the march continued, night falling swiftly before the end of the second hour. Thirteen miles had been scheduled but after eight miles the miserable baggage animals had dropped so far behind that at seven o'clock Havelock gave the order to camp. The men huddled in the shelter of a mango grove waiting for the tents to come up. After an issue of rum they made shift for the night in a sea of mud with the earth steaming up, even those whose tents had arrived being drenched 'as if in a vapour bath'. 'Insects of all sorts were attracted by our light and either dashed into the flame or singed their wings and fell on the table. All the noises of the rains were present – frogs and earth-crickets with, at intervals, the splashing of showers and bubbling of water-courses'.

The bugle sounded at four a.m. and the march began at five. The rain had stopped and as the sun dried them out the spirits of the force rose. That day they marched eight miles, camping before the heat became too intense, and on July 9th and 10th they did some twelve miles a day. Havelock was deliberately moving by easy stages. The 64th and the Highlanders were out of training after their voyage, and the Blue Caps had three hundred recruits; the road on these first days was littered with fallen-out young Madras Fusiliers, envious of the artillery veterans, none under fifty, who were taken along in tumbrils. Havelock knew that Cawnpore was past relief, and by latest reports Lucknow would be well able to hold its own. The primary task was to get his men fit.

They marched on through the flat pleasant countryside sweetened by rain, the numerous trees and the growing paddy-field making a landscape reminiscent of English parkland, but scarred by wanton destruction. 'All the little police stations were unroofed, the telegraph posts cut down, the mile-stones broken, the staging bungalows gutted and burnt.' Now and again they passed bodies hanging from the shade trees on the road – souvenirs of Renaud's column and probably not all guilty since Renaud was reported to be 'rather inclined to hang all black creation'. The lower limbs had been eaten by pigs – wild or belonging to the villagers – and the stench was disgusting.

The march was proceeding well. The railway line, which ran the first forty miles, had been utilised as a supply tramway, the trucks manhandled by gangs of coolies since the locomotives had been smashed in the June riots. The commissary-general had so organised the baggage train, which now kept up, that each camp was pitched swiftly and efficiently, with a bazaar for the camp followers. (Harry's syce tried to loot a sweet-meat seller and Sherer the magistrate had him tied to a tree and caned him with his own hands.) Except for lobbing a few shells into a village believed to be harbouring rebels there was as yet no action, though Spurgin from his steamer reported an attack by a rebel body; he had landed, routed them and spiked their gun.

On July 9th Havelock received peremptory instructions from the Commander-in-Chief that Renaud was not to be halted because of rumours of the fall of Cawnpore. Havelock realised that this order originated with Neill, but was forced to comply with it and therefore sent Renaud instructions to proceed cautiously forward. Harry was furious at the 'evil influence' at work to oust his father in favour of Neill.

Late on July 10th at the fourth camp from Allahabad Renaud sent back alarming news, confirmed by Havelock's native spies: the Nana Sahib was advancing rapidly in great force down the Great Trunk Road from Cawnpore to crush Renaud's detachment; and Sir Henry Lawrence had fought a battle outside Lucknow, had been defeated, and was now closely shut up in the Residency. The Nana was believed to have three thousand five hundred regular sepoys, supported by cavalry, twelve guns and innumerable native levies. Renaud had four hundred Madras Fusiliers, many of them mere boys fresh from England,

and two hundred Sikhs whose loyalty was not yet assured. If these uneven forces collided Renaud would be annihilated. Havelock realised that to order him to retire would have a devastating moral effect; the only answer was to push on and catch up before the collision.

As for Sir Henry Lawrence, the native runners brought an urgent message dated late on June 30th that all would be over if he was not relieved by July 20th – ten days ahead; Havelock commented later to Hannah, 'Sir Henry Lawrence, the most amiable of men, pressed the worst military measures. He ought to have united his small force to that of Sir Hugh Wheeler here and both would have been saved. Instead of this he took up an untenable position at Lucknow and left Wheeler to be crushed. His own small garrison is now in extreme peril'.

Havelock determined to press on at once by forced marches. The bugle went at midnight and at one a.m. on July 11th the Column set off to cover sixteen miles to Khaga, five miles further than originally planned. Although the march was over by ten a.m., during the last hours the heat of the sun had been intense and the hospital doolies were full. When camp was pitched the medical officers reported such fatigue and exposure that they urgently recommended a longer halt. Havelock said the men must march at midnight, a shorter rest than usual. The doctors, joined by Beatson the DAAG, prophesied dire results.

'After our awful walk we were not a little astonished to find that we were to march again that night', wrote Lieutenant Groom of the Blue Caps to his wife. 'We groaned when our bugles sounded the rouse and the pipes of the Highlanders began *Hey Johnnie Cope*'. The men fell in and marched for about an hour under a bright moon. Soon after one a.m. on Sunday July 12th the advance guard made contact with Renaud. The pipes struck up *The Campbells are coming* and the Column marched past Renaud's detachment who stood by the roadside cheering, their weapons and the two guns glinting in the moonlight.

The complete force marched on into the dawn. The sun swept

up high in the sky and at about seven a.m. they reached the scheduled camping ground at Belanda, five miles short of the town of Fatehpur. Havelock planned to halt for the day to recover strength, before attacking Fatehpur the next morning. 'Arms were piled in line', wrote one of Renaud's men, 'ground was taken up for each corps and the weary, wayworn men, overcome by the oppressive heat and brilliant sunshine lay down in groups, anxiously expecting the arrival of the tents and baggage which were close behind'.

While breakfast was cooked and the camp laid out, with the guns in the centre under a group of tall mangoes, reminiscent of oak trees in England, Havelock sent forward Colonel Fraser Tytler with a hundred infantrymen and the hundred native cavalry to reconnoitre Fatehpur. It was expected that the rebel force would arrive there later that day and take up defensive positions. He then rode on towards the Headquarters tent. Sherer the magistrate was talking to a friend when 'General Havelock went by – the erect, slight figure, handsome features, grey hair, with the white covered and curtained cap, and the easy seat on the natty Arab – a vignette very familiar to us all afterwards'.

As he reached the tent and dismounted two native spies from Sir Henry Lawrence were brought in, having made contact with Tytler. Havelock began examining them as the bugles sounded for breakfast. Suddenly in the distance a gun fired, and a 24-pounder ball bounced in, two hundred yards from the General. Tytler came cantering back to report. The enemy were advancing rapidly and obviously supposed that they had nothing in front but Renaud.

The enemy were now firing two guns at an impossible range and throwing forward infantry and cavalry. 'I wished earnestly', wrote Havelock in his despatch, 'to give our harassed soldiers rest, and so waited until this ebullition should expend itself, making no counter-disposition beyond posting a hundred Enfield riflemen of the 64th in an advanced copse. But the enemy maintained his attack with the audacity which his first supposition had inspired, and my inertness fostered. It would have injured the morale of my troops to permit them thus to be bearded; so I determined at once to bring on an action'.

The alarm sounded 'and the troops', wrote a Volunteer Cavalryman, 'all fell out so quickly and steadily it was quite charming to see them'. The breakfast was left untouched. Maude disposed his eight guns and checked the range as the hordes of white-uniformed sepoys emerged in the distance half a mile away across the plain. They were in good order and advancing confidently; they had swept all before them for six weeks, had annihilated a divisional general and proved that they were masters. Now they would hurry on to Allahabad and all lower Bengal would rise and drive the English into the sea.

Maude gave an order and the battery opened an accurate fire at 800 yards. A moment later a smart fusillade crackled from the Enfield riflemen, ahead and to the left. The white mass shook, hesitated and began to draw back. The sepoys expecting musket or muzzle-loading rifle fire, had thought they were still out of range, and the withering hail of bullets shattered their self-confidence, Maude's second salvo having already disabled two of the forward guns which were hurriedly abandoned. Maude limbered up and advanced as fast as his skinny bullocks allowed, his own sub-division on the road and those to left and right pushing through the swampy fields. The sepoys seemed to be reforming and cavalry were coming down the road at a trot. 'So we came into action again at 650 yards', records Maude, 'and at the first shot the cavalry turned about and bolted, leaving in view two elephants, two heavy guns and a large body of infantry. We peppered into these so smartly that they could not stand to their guns; which latter when we came up to them we found to be loaded and turned them upon the retreating masses'.

The 64th were advancing on the left and Renaud had cleared a hillock on the right, the Highlanders with their short-range muskets keeping the line between centre and right. Each moment increased the confusion in the sepoy ranks and raised the spirits of Havelock's force. Beatson and Fraser Tytler, coming up to Maude, saw that one of the retreating elephants carried a leader, believed afterwards to be Tantia Topi the Nana's general. 'Knock over that chap on the elephant!' they called to Maude, who dismounted and himself laid a gun at line of metal; the ball went in under the elephant's tail and bowled him over, Tantia Topi flying through the air. He was seen to stagger away badly shaken.

Havelock ordered a general advance. Only ten minutes had elapsed from the start of the action but, he wrote afterwards, 'I may say that in ten minutes the affair was decided. For in that short time our Enfield rifles and cannon had taken all conceit of fight out of the mutineers'.

As the line moved forward gun after gun, fine brass and iron guns looted from the Cawnpore arsenal, fell into Havelock's hands. The road was strewn with dead and dying sepoys, and bullocks and wounded horses screaming from pain and fright, and smashed carts and tumbrils. Here and there a British soldier reeled and fell dead, struck down by the sun, but not a man had been killed by enemy fire. Havelock was smiling broadly, riding ahead of the advancing infantry. He identified one of the enemy regiments retiring as the 56th (Lambourn's) which he had led up to the Mahratta guns at Maharajpur in '43. He shouted across at them delightedly, 'there's some of you that have beheld me fighting. Now try upon yourselves what you have seen in me'.

The battle moved steadily across the plain and Fatehpur came into view, which as Havelock wrote in his despatch, 'constitutes a position of no small strength. The hard and dry Grand Trunk Road subdivides it, and is the only means of conventional access, for the plains on both sides are covered at this season by heavy lodgments of water to the depth of two, three and four feet. It is surrounded by garden enclosures of great strength, with high walls, and has within it many houses of good masonry. In front of the swamps are hillocks, villages, and mango-groves, which the enemy already occupied in force'. The

British advance was unchecked, though they now had been fighting over two hours in the sun on empty stomachs. 'As we moved forward the enemy's guns continued to fall into our hands, and then in succession they were driven from the garden enclosures, from a strong barricade on the road, from the town wall, into, and through, out of, and beyond the town.' The straggling old town could have been held for hours by determined men but only isolated pickets resisted. In the outer suburbs Havelock sent for Sherer who had been magistrate of Fatehpur and began questioning him about it. 'The General was apparently recognised for some people behind the walls were plainly taking shots at him.' Havelock talked on as if unaware of it, to the discomfiture of Sherer and his escorting sowar.

About a mile beyond the town, from which the inhabitants had fled, the enemy made a last stand. 'My troops were in such a state of exhaustion that I almost despaired of driving them further.' A mass of enemy cavalry moved down on Havelock's small force of Native Irregulars riding forward on the right flank. The mutineer 2nd Cavalry waved their swords making signs that the Irregulars should come over and the Irregulars hesitated, refusing the order to charge. The two bodies of horse thus met at a gentle trot. Palisser, the Irregulars' commander, thrown by a sudden swerve, was saved only by the devotion of his native officers, three of them losing their lives, the only casualties of the day. From his position in the centre Havelock saw the mêlée and, a moment later, the Irregular cavalry galloping back in near-mutinous confusion, their English subalterns and Palisser, remounted, forced to retreat with them. 'I never rode so hard in my life,' said one of the subalterns afterwards, 'it was a regular run for our necks, for the whole of the fellows were behind our small party thirsting for our blood... They had an immense number of regulars and irregulars. For the moment I fully believed that our men were about to join the 2nd Cavalry and leave us to their mercy. You may imagine how jolly I felt.'

The guns, squelching and straining through the mud, had

again been pushed to the front and with the riflemen now poured a devastating fire into the 2nd Cavalry, which broke and turned back as they had come. This was the end. The enemy was in 'final and irretrievable flight'.

A mile beyond the site of the enemy's last stand Havelock gave the order to halt, four hours after the first roundshot had come rolling into the camp. Fatehpur was his and since it would have been folly to push his weary starving men further, picquets were set; and when the men were dismissed they dropped down where they were, many of them falling asleep without waiting for food. Havelock, Harry and the staff made merry on scraggy chickens.

The next morning, having ordered a day's rest for the troops to recover, Havelock took a fly sheet and drafted his famous Field Force Order of 13th July 1857. He wrote many corrections and insertions before he was satisfied and Harry misread some of the words when he copied it into the Order Book so that the published version lacked some of the punch of the original. 'B Gen'l Havelock' scrawled the General, 'thanks his soldiers for their arduous exertions of yesterday, which produced in four hours the strange result of a rebel army driven from a strong position, eleven guns captured and their whole force scattered to the winds without the loss of a single British soldier. To what is this magical effect to be attributed? To the fire of the British artillery, exceeding in rapidity and precision all that the Br General has ever witnessed in his not short career; to the power of the Enfield rifle in British hands, to the British *pluck* which grand quality has survived the strange changes (?) of this hour and gained intensity from the occasion – and to the blessing of Providence' – but here he paused and crossed the word out. 'Providence' was too formal and impersonal; heathenish generals readily dragged in Providence for their public despatches. Havelock inserted 'Almighty God'. '...the blessing of Almighty God on a most righteous cause, the cause of justice, humanity, truth and good government in India'.

He next drafted his despatch and then wrote triumphantly to Hannah: 'My dear Hannah – One of the prayers oft repeated throughout my life since my school days has been answered, and I have lived to command in a successful action. I must refer you for the particulars to my despatch. I will here only say that I marched down upon this place yesterday morning, Sunday the 12th (battle of the Boyne[1]) with harassed troops intending to attack the insurgents next day, but their fate led them on. Out they sallied and insulted my camp...' He described the action briefly and ended, 'but away with vain glory! Thanks to Almighty God, who gave me the victory! I captured in four hours eleven guns, and scattered the enemy's whole force to the winds. I now march to retake Cawnpore, where, alas! our troops have been treacherously destroyed, and to succour Lawrence at Lucknow. Harry was in the thickest of the fight, but God be praised, escaped unhurt'.

THE EFFECT OF Havelock's victory of Fatehpur, when announced in Calcutta, was electric. His small column had trounced a rebel army over twice its size. For the first time the mutineers had been beaten in the open field and the long catalogue of disgraces brought to an end. His Field Force Order rang round British India and, as John Marshman afterwards commented from his long experience, 'it was a novelty in India to see an Order of the Day ascribing victory to "the blessing of Almighty God"'.

During July 13th the captured guns and ammunition were organised, several lighter pieces brought from Allahabad being now abandoned and burst, together with any for which there was no transport. The bullock drivers, none of whom was a regular employee, were rewarded for their good service by gratuities.

In the force, Havelock allowed no slackening of discipline.

---

[1] Maude told him this during the action. A few days later Havelock recollected that it had not been the anniversary of the Boyne but of the battle of Aughrim the following year. Maude was most impressed.

All Government property, looted back from the mutineers, was to be handed in. No officer or soldier was to leave Camp without permission and any firing within three miles of it forbidden; officers disobeying the order (snipe were plentiful in the marshy fields) were to be placed under arrest and any soldier or follower given a dozen lashes. The staff were kept rigidly to the mark. Stuart Beatson received a peremptory note: 'I wish to have within an hour a return of killed and wounded according to established form of the force in the action of yesterday. Also a general return of your force now in camp. If I cannot have these without further reference I shall not form a favourable opinion of things in your department. These reports should be ready at any moment they are required'. Havelock's strictness was galling to some. 'He was always as sour as if he had swallowed a pint of vinegar,' one officer grumbled afterwards, 'except when he was being shot at, and then he was as blithe as a schoolboy out for a holiday.' But Havelock knew that discipline was the secret of victory.

Neill, fearful of renewed attack, had been clamouring from Allahabad for the return of the Sikhs and the veteran artillerymen. Havelock considered that Fatehpur should relieve any pressure. He consented to return a hundred Sikhs but the ancient artillerymen carried along in their tumbrils to be fresh for action were more than ever needed, since the captured guns were now to be served, including one 24-pounder. He urged Neill to send up the European reinforcements promised by Grant, with utmost despatch. The Sikhs were ordered to punish Fatehpur by setting it on fire before returning towards Allahabad, but Havelock would have no indiscriminate slaughter.

The column marched at midnight, with forty-six miles and a hostile army between them and Cawnpore. The usual fiery sunrise of the rains found them tramping on the Grand Trunk Road which stretched ahead straight and narrow, shaded by trees and skirted by muddy fields flecked green with blades of grass or swamped with shallow water. The countryside was slightly less flat, though no rise of ground more than a few feet. Now and again they passed a Mohammedan tomb, or a small shrine beside the road, the god ungarlanded because travellers were scarce in time of war; two or three deserted, blackened villages, their mud walls crumbled, were seen across the fields, and trees covered the distance and stood scattered to left and right in the fields, with bases banked up against flooding. Black and white storks flew away at the sound of tramping feet, though large black crows and hideous vultures ('turkeys', the men called them) tore at the bodies of men and animals left by the retreating sepoys. 'A more desolate scene than the country we passed through can scarcely be imagined.'

After some hours marching in the sun the column became certain that they could see the glint of enemy horse watching and retiring in the trees in front and on the flanks. At last Havelock called a halt to investigate. 'Before the halt there had been the tramp of feet, the rattle of the gun-carriages, the creaking of cart wheels, the hum of human voices, and the sudden pause was very striking. For as the guns were unlimbered and field-glasses sedulously applied to the distant trees, expectation arrested speech and there was a dead silence. At this rather interesting moment there sounded from a neighbouring copse the cry of *Cuckoo*! A soldier was heard to exclaim, "I say, Bill, who'd ha' thought o' the likes o' that? Blest – if it was not a damned old cuckoo!" – a bird seldom heard as far south in India.'

Shortly before the march ended, the Irregular Cavalry who had been set to guard the baggage train in view of their doubtful loyalty raised a false alarm, which brought the column again to a halt. Havelock decided to disarm them and when, after a full march of fifteen miles, camp was pitched at about ten a.m. at Kallaypore, he superintended the operation himself. The loyal native officers remained with Palisser. The fine horses of the sowars were handed over to the twenty gentlemen of the Voluntary Cavalry to replace their hacks.

That day a spy brought urgent news to Havelock and a

rumour about Cawnpore ran round the Camp: 'We have heard that the head of the rebels there is a Mahratta chief, and that all the women and children are safe in his palace at Bithoor. If so, please God, we shall be able to save them. He, of course, has been keeping them as hostages in case of his capture at Cawnpore'.

At three a.m. on July 15th the bugles and pipes again roused the weary men. There were still thirty-three miles to Cawnpore; Havelock hoped to cover seventeen that day, a maximum march. Soon after four a.m. the column was on the road again, the General nettled by 'unnecessary delays' on the part of some of the units.

As day broke native scouts brought word that the village of Aong ahead, in thickly wooded country, was fortified; an entrenchment had been thrown across the road, an enemy battery was in position and his cavalry were in strength – the first stand since Fatehpur. Sending part of the force ahead under Tytler, with Beatson and Harry, Havelock took personal command of the vital baggage train which in the absence of sufficient cavalry would be vulnerable. A stiff fight developed and two hours passed before the enemy were thrown out of Aong, with Renaud badly wounded and several men killed. More than once the sepoy cavalry charged down on the baggage train. 'These attacks were very persevering', wrote Havelock in his despatch, 'it is gratifying to have to report that the enemy was unable to capture a single baggage animal or follower'.

At length the enemy turned and fled, but having only twenty horse Havelock was unable to follow them up. He called a halt for breakfast a mile beyond the burning village, close to a pond surrounded by trees. 'Most grateful was their shade', wrote one officer rather frothily, 'inviting to repose after recent exposure to the fiery sunbeams, which seemed literally to pierce and seethe the brain. The relief was unimaginable'.

It was not for long. Havelock's mind was on the Panda Nudi river some miles ahead, which in the rains constituted the only serious natural obstacle before Cawnpore. Since he had no pontoons and could not expect boats from a hostile population, much depended on seizing intact the fine new stone bridge which carried the Grand Trunk Road. Native scouts had now brought word that the bridge stood but that the enemy were busy mining it. Havelock determined to get there before the retreating sepoys could detonate their mine. He ordered breakfast to be abandoned and the men fallen in at once.

Exhausted as they were the men cheered him to the echo and moved forward briskly. As Harry wrote, 'when every man to the youngest drummer in our force knew that he was striking for the *existence* of the British empire and for the lives of our country-women and children – heat and fatigue and exposure were alike disregarded'. The sun beat down, the reflection from rifles and muskets adding a painful dazzle to the glare which the peaked forage caps did little to offset. Footsore and hungry the column pushed forward, each milestone reminding them of Cawnpore and the women and children they were determined to save. The road 'was strewed for miles with abandoned tents, ammunition and other materials of war'.

After two hours the advance guard came round a bend of the road, saw the bridge intact half a mile ahead, and received several 24-pounder shot which killed or wounded two or three. Havelock galloped up to reconnoitre. The bridge crossed the river, some seventy yards wide and in spate, where it curved outward towards them. The banks were steep, making the bridge easy to defend, and the enemy were well dug in on the further bank with horse in reserve and two guns sited on the bridge and its approach. Maude suggested enveloping the rebel battery with cannon fire from right, left and centre. Havelock agreed and ordered the Fusiliers, as the best riflemen, to deploy along the banks above and below. The Highlanders were to wait under cover of a slight drop of ground until the assault.

As the artillery duel warmed up Havelock was standing with the grenadier company of the Highlanders, steaming in their muddy scarlet wool, who were lying down as ordered, the enemy round shot whizzing and whistling overhead. One fell and smashed a grenadier's head to red pulp. Havelock turned and took a long look. Then he said, 'His was a happy death, grenadiers. He died in the service of his country.' 'For masel', sir,' piped up a voice down the line, 'gin ye've nae objections, I wad suner bide alive i' the service o' ma cantra!'

The next moment a loud roar was heard from the bridge above the noise of rifle and gun fire. 'There goes the bridge!' cried the soldiers and Havelock mounted and cantered forward. As the smoke cleared away, the bridge was still there, the mine having only crumbled part of the parapet and roadway. Maude himself, on the road, was right up to it, pumping shrapnel at point-blank range into the battery beyond. With a cheer the right wing of the Madras Fusiliers rose from their places and 'with rare gallantry' swept forward, a compact mass, across the bridge to give the rebel gunners the bayonet, the Highlanders following. The enemy horse turned and fled leaving the gunners to be cut to death or flung into the stream by the furious Blue Caps.

At two in the afternoon, one mile beyond the bridge, Havelock halted the column. The men threw themselves down, dead to the world. The two actions had cost only twenty-five killed and wounded.

Owing to the damage to the bridge the commissariat could not get the ration bullocks across and slaughtered, skinned and cut up before night. By then most of the men were fast asleep or too weary to get up and cook. And so hot was the night that by reveille much of the meat had rotted and was thrown away, the force having to march again on nothing but biscuits and a drink of porter from hogsheads captured in Aong. Nor could tents be erected in time and the men had to do as best they could against the hordes of flies.

Havelock at once wrote a despatch for the Commander-in-Chief detailing the two successful actions. He also wrote to Neill ordering him to hasten reinforcements, ammunition and the rum which, since he had not opportunity to train them out of it, was vital to his soldiers under such arduous conditions. '...In conclusion I recapitulate my immediate and pressing wants. They are, 1. Enfield ammunition. 2. Gun ammunition. 3. European soldiers. 4. Field artillery. 5. Commissariat stores.'

A restless night followed, broken by an alarm of fire. Many of the men were too tired to sleep properly; for some time before the bugle sounded in the early hours they saw a light at the General's bivouac. The Highlanders at least knew what he was doing, though they had no light to open their own worn Bibles.. The moon was bright when the men fell in again. There could be no day's rest as at Fatehpur, much as it was needed. Twenty-one miles to Cawnpore, and the Nana's army lay in strength before the city. Havelock's troops had fought under the most exhausting conditions two skirmishes the day previous; this day they would have to march over sixteen miles and fight a full scale battle. When all were in line Havelock addressed them. He told them categorically what previously they had known incorrectly as rumour, that more than two hundred British women and children were alive, in Cawnpore, prisoners of the Nana. With head bared and hand on his sword he cried, 'By God's help, men, we shall save them, or every man of us die in the attempt. I am trying you sorely, men, but I know the stuff you are made of. Think of our women and the tender infants in the power of those devils incarnate!'

Three wild cheers from a thousand men rent the night air. And the leading company, without waiting for word of command, turned as one man and stepped off in the moonlight towards Cawnpore.

13

Cawnpore

Havelock's force reached the village of Maharajpore, seven miles from Cawnpore, at about half-past ten on the morning of July 16th 1857. They had marched sixteen miles – more than full day's work for the cold weather campaigning season – but Havelock proposed to fling them that very day under a broiling sun, after a brief rest, at the whole might of the Nana Sahib. Only then might the women and children be saved.

While the men breakfasted from their haversacks, Barrow's Volunteer Cavalry reconnoitred in front. They brought in two travellers who proved to be loyal sepoys, two of the many scattered throughout the mutineer regiments who were risking certain torture and death by loyalty to their salt. The sepoys, who were down from Delhi, courageously had accompanied the Nana's army as it advanced from Cawnpore, had noted carefully their defensive positions and now came to give detailed intelligence to Havelock.

He spent an unhurried season interrogating them under the shade of a clump of mango. He then drew up his plan and at noon called for commanding officers. He 'explained to us his proposed plan of attack', wrote Maude, 'the spies at the same time drawing in the dust of the road a clever sketch of the enemy's position. He invited any suggestions or improvements we might have to offer, but his dispositions appeared to be admirable'.

The Nana's position, three miles ahead, formed a crescent of a mile and a quarter, its centre some eight hundred yards behind the fork where the road to Cawnpore Cantonment left the Grand Trunk Road. The roads were cut and heavy guns sited on the junction. His right (which would be on Havelock's left) rested on the mud-walled hamlet of Tuttea, protected by a mango grove in which were two 9-pounder guns, and beyond this hamlet, still further to the Nana's right, lay the railway embankment, an effective screen. His centre, between the roads, was a close packed mud village, in which were entrenched a 24-pounder howitzer and a light-horse gun. His left, beyond swampy ground, rested on another hamlet, called Beebiapore, with a garden enclosure and pond, round which were earthworks in which he had positioned four 24-pounders. The right flank was further protected by broken ground and a slight rise of contour before the land fell away to the Ganges, a mile and a quarter distant. Between and around the gun emplacements was the Nana's massed infantry, much of it well armed and with all the advantage of British training. In the rear waited his cavalry.

It was a formidable position and Havelock estimated that a frontal attack would cost him three hundred men – it would be worse than Ferozeshah, without Gough's strength. He had therefore decided to make a flank march under cover of a line of tall mango trees round the Nana's left, and remarked to his officers that this was what Frederick the Great did at Leuthen exactly one hundred years before. The baggage and line of communications would be uncovered by such a move; if the Nana got wind of the flank march in time he could sweep forward, break through the weak Volunteer Cavalry which was all that could be left in front, destroy Havelock's base and then deal with him at leisure. This was a risk to be taken.

At half-past one the column once more set off, 'dreadfully tired and with the sun fearfully bright', the Volunteer Cavalry scouting ahead and the Blue Caps leading the march cheering wildly, some of the younger being decidedly merry with too much porter on empty stomachs. The advance of three miles to the turning point for the flank movement was, in the opinion of a gunner officer writing a few days later, 'one of the most severe marches ever made in India. In the full midday heat of the worst season in the year did our troops start, each man fully armed and accoutred with his sixty rounds of ball ammunition on him. The sun struck down with frightful force. At every step a man reeled out of the ranks and threw himself fainting by the side of the road – the calls for water incessant all along the line'.

At the agreed point, half a mile from where the road forked, the rifle skirmishes of the Blue Caps moved to left and right, Barrow's cavalry riding on towards the enemy's centre to draw his fire and deceive him as to the general's intentions while Havelock rode off into the fields to the right at the head of the main column and the guns, shrouded by mango trees. As he heard the first gun fire on Barrow, Havelock took out his watch and handed it to Drummer Pearson of the 78th, his personal bugler riding close to him, and told him to note the time.

A quarter of the distance had been passed when a gap in the trees uncovered the column and brought down enemy artillery fire. They marched on, no return of fire permitted though each company suffered casualties in passing the gap, 'rather unpleasant, progressing slowly as we did, through very heavy marsh and ploughed land'. The men's gorge was rising as they heard the sepoy bands in the distance playing parodies of *Auld Lang Syne* and other tunes learned in the cantonments. The Nana made no forward movement and evidently was puzzled as to Havelock's intentions.

After a mile of marching through the plough Havelock wheeled his men into line. He was almost opposite the sepoy left flank in the village of Beebiapore which he could see through the gun smoke about nine hundred yards away across the plain, its guns firing rapidly, canister and roundshot coming over, though the guns on the Nana's centre and right were effectively masked. Through his glasses Havelock could detect white-clothed infantry hurrying across to the threatened front and more guns being brought up; the enemy had at last awoken to his meaning. Havelock hoped to clear the village by gunfire. The enemy 'were pelting into us all this time' with cannon and musket fire; Havelock ordered the infantry to lie down while Maude tried to silence the sepoy guns in the village. But a few rounds at different ranges showed that they were too well sheltered by mud houses and walls, and Maude's pieces were too light to deal with heavy guns well served by mutineer Bengal Artillerymen.

Every moment increased the enemy strength and jeopardised the initiative which Havelock had gained. He ordered an immediate advance. Sending the 64th with the Sikhs towards a less heavily fortified village on his left Havelock launched the Highlanders against the gun emplacements in Beebiapore. 'Never have I witnessed conduct more admirable,' he said in his despatch. He saw them rise, fire one volley and march steadily forward 'with sloped arms and measured tread like a wall, the rear rank locked as if on parade', through the storm of grape and musket fire. At the 'Charge!' they broke into a wild yell, the pipes skirling a pibroch, and 'burst forward', said an eyewitness, 'like an eager pack of hounds racing into the kill, and in an instant they were over the mound and into the village'. It was all done with the bayonet: 'the men were very fierce and the slaughter was proportionate'. 'Well done, 78th,' cried Havelock, cantering up close behind them, 'you shall be my own regiment! Another charge like that wins the day.'

The sepoys scattered in two groups, the larger falling back on the Nana's centre from which a howitzer now had a clear field of fire on the Highlanders. The 78th reformed in the shelter of the causeway which carried the cantonment road up to a small bridge across the marshy stream. Havelock placed himself at the head, waved his sword at the howitzer and shouted again above the roar, 'Now, Highlanders, another charge like that wins the day!'

The Highlanders followed Havelock as he threw himself into the thick of the enemy fire; the momentum of the charge took them into the gun emplacement and out on to the Grand Trunk Road beyond. Further on, the 64th and the Sikhs had cleared the hamlet of Tuttea, the Nana's original right flank, and the whole sepoy line was retiring covered by their cavalry, the greater part to another hamlet in the rear between the roads, and some towards the railway embankment. Barrow's eighteen Volunteer Cavalry cantered up the Grand Trunk Road and Barrow besought Havelock to let him charge the mass of native horse, but Havelock shook his head and rode off towards the 64th. A few minutes later Beatson, lying on a tumbril, dying of cholera, saw a chance for Barrow and gave him leave to charge. The sheer audacity of the charge ensured its success and it ended only when a third of their little number were killed or unhorsed. The infantry re-forming between the villages cheered them loudly and Havelock, trotting up, said with a broad smile, 'Well done, gentlemen volunteers, you have done well. I am proud to command you.'

Havelock had now reached a point opposite his original line of advance from Maharajpore, having worked his way round in a wide arc. For a few minutes the battle slackened. But it was not over, for the enemy had rallied in the village of Suktipore half a mile back between the roads, well protected by deep plough partially flooded. Maude's weak gun bullocks were exhausted after being urged and flogged through two miles of heavy country and refused to move further; he was forced to rest them. The infantry line re-formed and the men, already desperately weary, were ordered to advance half right, Blue Caps on the right, Highlanders in the centre, 64th, Sikhs and the detachment of the 84th on the left. No sooner were they sludging through the mud towards Suktipore when heavy fire again opened from the enemy's rallying position. It was an unpleasant advance, and half way across there was a distinct waver. 'But', wrote Major North of the 60th, attached to the Highlanders, 'our noble general seemed gifted with ubiquity as, scornful of danger, confronting death burning with the lust of victory, he was present wherever most needed. Again the clear tone of his peculiar voice raised to the highest pitch the courage of his men, as he hurried towards the Highlanders and said, "Come, who'll take this village, the

Highlanders or the 64th?" looking to the latter as he addressed them, with the utmost coolness. There was no pause to answer...'.

Both regiments swept forward, the ranks closing over their comrades' bodies as they fell; the line surged into the village, driving the sepoys out and away, while the Blue Caps cleared copses to right and left. A bullet struck Havelock's horse which fell dead under him. Once again he picked himself up unwounded.

The battle seemed over, the enemy in full retreat. It had been a stiff yet not impossible fight. But the men had been marching and fighting since midnight on scanty rations. The sun was dropping to the horizon as the tired British line once more crossed the road to the cantonment and moved towards a small mud village intending to consolidate on a slight rise of ground in front. The skirmishers walked over the skyline. A heavy fire suddenly opened from a reserve howitzer three-quarters of a mile in front, and the skirmishers were appalled to see a massive array of sepoy infantry in line to left and right of the gun.

The 64th under Major Stirling were on the left of the line behind the skirmishers, the Highlanders in the centre. Harry Havelock and Moorsom, another of Havelock's staff, were about eighty yards behind the 64th. 'When first the line halted', wrote Harry not long after, 'at and behind a little ridge, to enable our guns to come up (which were more than a mile in the rear, and we had scarcely 800 men in line) the 64th had got a little in advance of the general line – when a shrapnel shell from the 24-pounder in their front struck their No 5 Company, burst, and knocked over six men, one of whom was killed and the other five awfully mutilated. At this some one shouted out they were to halt and lie down. They got into confusion. Many broke their ranks and ran into the village for shelter and it looked as if they were going to break into a general rout.

'Moorsom shouted out, "Shame, men, shame!" and I rode up, dismounted and got the men out of the village by abuse and entreaties (I bet the survivors will never print what I said to them) and got them to lie down in the general line. There the wounded men were left, groaning a few paces in front of the line. And Stirling, instead of sending a few men to remove them quietly, kept calling to me in presence of his Regiment, "For God's sake get a doolie for these poor fellows", and lamenting what had happened in a way that was in itself enough to cause discouragement. I at last spoke to him about it quietly and he left off and the men were removed.'

Harry had noticed earlier in the day that Major Stirling's nerve was badly shaken, and now 'the thing was critical enough in itself without his making it worse. And I confess that I thought it was all up with us. There were barely 800 men in line, lying down behind the ridge, no cavalry, our guns a mile in rear and apparently inextricably stuck, while the enemy, about 1,200 yards off and therefore secure out of Enfield range, was pounding us desperately with his reserve 24-pounder and a 6-pounder beside it. His infantry *swarmed* in our front. His cavalry hovered on both flanks and was at that moment hacking to pieces the wounded in our rear. Our men had been marching 15 hours and actually fighting three under a blazing July sun. Some swell on an elephant (they said it was the Nana but no one knows) was riding about amongst them trying to screw them up to come on; their drums and trumpets were making a fearful row with the same idea and our men were dispirited by being compelled to lie still under tremendous fire, for the 24-pounder had just the right range.

'It was the turning-point of the day and of our campaign. If we had receded one inch not a hundred of us would ever have got back to the shelter of the walls of Allahabad. I must confess that I felt absolutely *sick* with apprehension, and if I looked calm, I never was before and hope never to be again in such a funk in my life. The enemy thought we were lying down from fear.

'Just then the dear old Governor rode bareheaded to the front, spoke half a dozen words – and at the magic of his example up sprang the line, and advanced. And that advance *saved India*.'

Havelock had seen the waver. He had sent an urgent message to the guns but realised that he could not wait. He rode round, as Harry said, to the front of the prostrate Highlanders, calmly smiling while bullets and shells whizzed and whined within an inch of his face. 'With increasing darkness, shadows lengthened', wrote Major North, 'which added to the imposing effect of the rebel line, seeming yet more dense and numerous; drums and trumpets insolently sounding the advance in quick repetition. General Havelock, who had just had his horse shot under him, now appeared boldly riding a hack, the only man who dared raise his head - so close and thick was the fire that rained upon us.' He reined up with his back to the fire, facing the line and spoke clearly, firmly and without a trace of excitement, and still smiling: 'The longer you look at it, men, the less you will like it. Rise up. The brigade will advance, left battalion leading'.

'Hardly were the words spoken', wrote North, 'when a feeling of confidence inspired every breast and displaced the overwhelming weight and uncertainty and doubt engendered by inaction. Up sprang our thinned line... the odds being fearfully against us. But to this act of intrepidity in our general his troops worthily responded'.

Havelock turned and at walk march rode forward at the head of the Highlanders, the 64th as ordered leading on the left, right opposite the heavy gun, and taking the full brunt of its fire. As he rode onward Havelock noticed that its field-officers were walking dismounted, hardly visible to the men. And then, to his joy, he saw Harry – calmly riding, fully exposed, in front, straight in line of the gun. 'When', runs Harry's own private account, 'the dear old Father called upon his little band to carry the guns that were decimating them, and the line sprang up and advanced, I led the men of this Regiment, shamed and ridiculed into steadiness up to the gun, which they carried. In this advance over 1,200 yards of level ground with the enemy blazing grape and shrapnel into us the whole day, all the field officers of the regiment dismounted and advanced on foot so as to be less exposed. They were consequently lost in the ranks as far as example or leadership was concerned'. After a hundred yards the 64th began to charge, at 1,100 yards, which would have blown and disorganised them before they had covered half the distance. Harry 'stopped that and persuaded them to advance steadily. Then when they got to 400 yards from the gun, the fire getting awfully galling they stopped dead short bodily – and began firing. This would have settled the whole business as the enemy immediately took courage, howled and shouted and redoubled their fire, and there is no knowing what the result might have been. But I rode along the front knocking up the rifles with my sword, stopped the fire and got them on again, and from that moment it was all right'.

And thus the weak British line advanced in the semi-darkness led by the Havelocks, father and son. 'It was irresistible', said Havelock in his official despatch, 'the enemy sent round shot into our ranks until we were within three hundred yards and then poured in grape with such precision and determination as I have seldom witnessed. But the 64th, led by Major Stirling and by my aide-de-camp, who had placed himself in their front, were not to be denied. Their rear showed the ground strewed with wounded; but on they steadily and silently came, then with a cheer charged and captured the unwieldy trophy of their valour. The enemy lost all heart, and after a hurried fire of musketry gave way in total rout. Four of my guns came up and completed their discomfiture by a heavy cannonade; and as it grew dark the roofless barracks of our artillery were dimly descried in advance, and it was evident that Cawnpore was once more in our possession'. 'I never saw so brave a youth as the boy Harry', he wrote to Hannah, 'he placed himself opposite the gun that was scattering death into the ranks of the 64th Queen's and led on the regiment under a shower of grape to its capture. This finished the fight. The grape was deadly but he calm as if telling

George stories about India'. And, Havelock might have added, so also was he, as he led the Highlanders in their 'most determined onslaught' right into the enemy line.

Thus the battle ended. After the last shot Drummer Pearson handed back Havelock's watch, remarking, 'Two hours, forty-five minutes, sir!' The line advanced a short distance and was halted on a rise of ground in the darkness, 'and the General', wrote Groom of the Blue Caps, 'rode down the ground of the 78th and Fusiliers. You never heard anything like the cheering'.

To continue further in hope of rescuing the women and children would throw away all that had been gained, since the troops would have been lost and trapped in the darkened streets of the city. And though battle casualties had not been excessive, sunstroke had increased them, and the troops had reached the limit of endurance. Havelock could do nothing but despatch two native spies into the city to discover the position.

Major Stirling, his nerve recovered, was abusing and swearing at Harry whom officers and men were congratulating on his courage. Havelock, dismounted, was standing a little behind the Highlanders. By some error a bugler sounded the 'Officers' call and the Highland officers gathered round him. At this Havelock said in fact he had not sent for them, but, he added, 'I am glad to have this opportunity of saying a few words to you which you may repeat to your men. I am now upwards of sixty years old. I have been forty years in the service; I have been engaged in action about seven and twenty times; but in the whole of my career I have never seen any regiment behave better, nay more, I have never seen anyone behave so well, as the 78th Highlanders this day. I am proud of you, and if ever I have the good luck to be made a Major-General, the first thing I shall do will be to go to the Duke of Cambridge and request that when my turn comes for the colonelcy of a regiment, I may have the 78th. And this, gentlemen, you hear from a man who is not in the habit of saying more than he means. I am not a Highlander, but I wish I was one'.

One of the officers, writing home the day after the battle, commented on this speech: 'Like all lofty natures superior to egotism he seemed to forget the greatness of his own example whilst recognising our prowess. Well is such a leader calculated to inspire confidence, secure esteem and lead us on to victory; or if need be, to death'.

Harry came up and the Havelocks shared the only biscuit Harry could find in his haversack. Colonel Tytler produced some porter. And Havelock lay down beside his pony ready saddled, the bridle over his arm, 'in good spirits though without dinner, my waterproof coat serving me for a couch on the damp ground'.

THE NIGHT WAS disturbed. Enemy cavalry were reported and the troops stood to arms, only to find loose horses careering over the battlefield.

At daybreak the spies returned bringing Havelock the awful news that the women and children had been massacred two days earlier after the Nana's defeat at Panda Nudi. The Nana was himself withdrawing from Cawnpore; lest there should be a trap Havelock sent a reconnaissance forward. Hardly had they gone when there was a roar and a flash from beyond the city, the ground shook and a cloud of smoke and dust 'having the appearance of a great plume of ostrich feathers' showed that the enemy had fired the magazine. Shortly afterwards Cawnpore was reported free.

Havelock moved his troops to the half-ruined cantonment and put them out of the sun in the cavalry stables until their tents should come up. Nearby was Wheeler's pathetic entrenchment, 'that scene of matchless desolation'; all marvelled that Wheeler should have held out so long.

That afternoon Sherer, riding in from Maharajpore exhausted by the heat, lay down in an empty room of a deserted bungalow. 'When I awoke I looked up, and beheld the General entirely by himself, sitting down close by. I scrambled up, and begged pardon for having intruded into the house, which I had no idea had

213

been selected for him. But he was in a most gracious mood, begged me not to go, and said he had read accounts of the war in the Peninsula, and a life of Wellington, by an officer of my name; and then, when I told him it was an uncle of mine, Moyle Sherer, he asked me if he was still alive, and so on. Then he launched a little into the events of the last few days, and spoke with great satisfaction of what had occurred... Though exceedingly interested in what he was saying, I took an early opportunity of making my bow, as I was clearly an unbidden though a politely-treated guest'.

Havelock had come in from a round of the field hospital where in stench and filth battle casualties were lying beside cholera and dysentery cases, and the few overworked surgeons were amputating limbs without anaesthetics, still unused in war. Havelock had encouraged the wounded with those magnificent phrases which still in the eighteen-fifties could thrill the British soldier: 'He will recover, doctor,' the general had said in a deliberately loud voice as he stood beside the cot of a private of the 64th who on the battlefield, lying with a shattered thigh, had shot down three enemy cavalrymen as they attempted to cut him up, 'he will recover; he has a heart in that chest as big as a cart wheel. That will yet carry him through.'

In the afternoon he entered the city. Sherer, representing the civil power, had been received with protestations of joy. Fraser Tytler had already discovered the house, with its harrowing relics, where the Nana had foully sullied the name of his country, and the well nearby with its ghastly rubble of human limbs. Havelock was shown these places, and later rode down to the ghat where Wheeler's men had been massacred on June 27th; a quiet place among trees in which monkeys played, with a small Hindu temple jutting out a little into the Ganges, over a mile wide, full and swift from the rains.

The troops had been maddened and enraged by the discovery of the house and well; men were shouting that in revenge they would rip the stomach of any native they should catch. Havelock would have none of it. Criminals should be brought to swift and merciless justice, but barbarism must not be met with barbarism. Only the strictest control would prevent sack and rapine and he gave immediate orders against reprisals on the civil population and to stop the looting which already had begun. He discovered also that Cawnpore was full of liquor 'from champagne to bottled beer', and promptly ordered the commissariat to buy up all that could be found. 'It will thus be guarded by a few men,' he told the Commander-in-Chief, 'if it remained in Cawnpore it would require half my force to keep it from being drunk by the other half, and I should scarcely have a sober soldier in camp. When I was winning a victory on the 16th some of my men were pillaging the commissariat on the line of march.'

The river steamer *Burrampootra* under command of Lieutenant Spurgin had tied up at the Artillery Ghat and the river could now be crossed. 'The General says', wrote young Groom to his wife that afternoon, 'he intends going to Lucknow in two days (fifty miles)! He seems quite unconscious that any soldier can ever get fatigued, and accordingly punishes us very unmercifully'.

That evening, the stimulation of the excitement of battle ebbing away, depression spread through the Camp. The men were worn out. Their hopes of a triumphant rescue of their countrywomen had ended in the appalling discovery of the house and well. The lament of the bagpipes as burial parties marched to the cemetery seemed to emphasise the horror of Cawnpore and their sense of isolation. In his tent, at dinner with Harry, Havelock sat silent. He now knew that his dear friend Sir Henry Lawrence had died of wounds at Lucknow. He must press on to its relief with his woefully inadequate force, yet leave a garrison in Cawnpore. The Nana was reported to be massing at Bithoor, eighteen miles away, for counter-attack. Delhi was still in mutineer hands; Agra was in danger. Havelock was in the heart of enemy country, and cholera had broken out in the Column, weak as it was. For the first time on the Campaign Harry saw his father gloomy. They sat long in silence. At last Havelock raised his head, looked at Harry and smiled. 'If the worst comes to the worst,' he said, 'we can but die with our swords in our hands.'

The next morning, July 18th, Havelock moved his force to the Civil Station on the further outskirts of Cawnpore where he could protect the city from attack and prepare to cross into Oudh. He then selected a good position back nearer the city on a slight plateau overlooking the river, opposite two or three partly submerged islands, and ordered the construction of a considerable entrenchment which could cover his crossing and protect the small holding force in the event of attack after he had left.

He took forty infantrymen who had some knowledge of riding and joined them to his Volunteer Cavalry. He also went down to the ghat with Maude to choose twenty of Spurgin's Invalid veteran gunners, to their dismay as they had liked the easy river life. 'As soon as the men had been selected', wrote Maude, 'Havelock ordered them to parade, and proceeded, with the necessary pomp and circumstance, to deliver to them a Napoleonic oration. "My men," he said, "I have come to thank you for so nobly volunteering to assist your country in the hour of her great peril." The poor fellows did not appear to realise the situation, and looked rather puzzled as to the precise meaning of the language addressed to them, when one of them stepped forward and, saluting in a slouching sort of manner, interrupted the General by saying: "Beg pardon Sir we ain't no volunteers at all; we only come 'cos we was forced to come!" Ready-witted as the General was, this interruption took him so completely aback that he utterly collapsed and brought the parade suddenly to an end'.

In the evening Havelock settled to drafting more telegrams and Field Orders and his despatch. He had already promised the 78th and the Blue Caps a Victoria Cross each for whom they would select. He now handed across to Harry for copying and forwarding a long telegram for the Commander-in-Chief. Harry was horrified to read, after a paragraph concerning the Nana Sahib, Agra, Spurgin's arrival, and 'troops in highest spirits', the following words: 'I recommend for the Victoria Cross Lieutenant Havelock, 10th Foot, who in the last action placed himself in front of the 64th Regt. right opposite the muzzle of a 24 pr. gun which scattered grape into our ranks leaving a trail of killed and wounded behind us. This young officer an Ensign of 1836 (*sic*) captured that gun the last of six'.

Harry said at once, 'You cannot send that! I cannot possibly receive it at your hands.' 'I told him', Harry wrote to his uncle John Marshman the next year, 'that it would make him ridiculous. People at a distance would never have believed that the recommendation was impartial; and last, though not least, I could not be brought forward in this matter without casting reflection on the 64th Regiment'. Reluctantly Havelock crossed out the words before sending the telegram. Some weeks later, having occasion to recommend a Highland officer for the Cross, he forwarded Harry's name also, without telling him, and Harry never knew during his father's lifetime. The Victoria Cross was awarded him in March 1858 on this recommendation, to the intense annoyance of the surviving officers of the 64th. A long dispute rumbled and echoed through officers' messes and the Horse Guards, with Harry unable to tell the truth without compromising a regiment 'who have since nobly redeemed any momentary weakness they may have displayed on that occasion'.

ON SUNDAY MORNING, July 19th, after the whole force had attended Divine Service at daybreak, Havelock, as at Jalalabad, reading the service since there was no chaplain, a detachment of Fusiliers marched for Bithoor; reliable intelligence had been received during the night that the Nana, far from massing for counter-attack was disorganised. The detachment found Bithoor deserted and after some destruction and looting returned the next day to Cawnpore with sixteen captured guns.

On July 19th rain set in again with full force, continuing with scarce a pause for three days. 'No words can describe the state of mud and filth the camp is in.' A plague of flies, and frogs, 'large, black, streaked and fretted with dun', or 'dingy yellow, variegated with black', made life a misery. Beatson died of cholera and in his place Havelock appointed Harry as Deputy Assistant Adjutant-General.

Havelock issued his Order of the Day congratulating the troops on the Battle of Cawnpore. 'Soldiers! Your general is satisfied, and more than satisfied with you', it ran in part. 'He has never seen steadier or more devoted troops; but your labours are only beginning. Between the 7th and the 16th you have, under the Indian sun of July, marched 126 miles and fought four actions. But your comrades at Lucknow are in peril; Agra is besieged; Delhi is still the focus of mutiny and rebellion. You must make great sacrifices if you would obtain great results. Three cities have to be saved; two strong places to be deblockaded. Your General is confident that he can effect all these things, and restore this part of India to tranquillity, if you only second him with your efforts, and if your discipline is equal to your valour'.

This last phrase was no empty sentiment. Troops were breaking out of Camp to loot the shops and derelict bungalows, and stripping innocent townsfolk in revenge for the massacre. The General issued a stringent order: 'The marauding in the Camp exceeds the disorders that supervened on the short lived triumph of the miscreant Nana Sahib. A Provost-Marshal has been appointed with special instructions to hang up in their uniforms all British soldiers that plunder. This shall not be an empty threat. Commanding Officers have received the most distinct warning on the subject'.[1] Any soldier caught outside Camp without leave was to be summarily flogged.

---

[1] Despite this, Havelock refused to use lightly his powers of capital punishment. Only when the Provost-Marshal, asking permission to hang a native gunner for looting, assured the General that the man had been caught red-handed in his uniform, did

Neill, now a brigadier-general, arrived on July 20th after a brisk march from Allahabad. 'General looks well and in good spirits', he telegraphed Grant. Havelock was glad of his coming for he brought two hundred and twenty-seven men, a paltry reinforcement but enough to enable Cawnpore to be garrisoned, with Neill sufficiently senior to leave in command. But Havelock now had a knowledge of Neill's character; he received him, in the pouring rain, with a salute of eleven guns and as soon as they were in shelter and alone, he said, courteously but firmly, 'Now, General Neill, let us understand one another. You have no power or authority here whilst I am here, and you are not to issue a single order'.

That night, at midnight, Havelock rode down in the wet to the partly completed entrenchment and superintended the ferrying of his forward troops, the Highlanders, across the swollen Ganges.

Havelock give leave saying, 'then that shall be my justification before God'. In Oudh two mutineers, caught spying, were blown from guns by Maude, who wrote that 'these were the only two occasions on which this truly fearful punishment was inflicted by Havelock'. 'I have had for two months', Havelock wrote to Hannah on August 27th, 'the power of life and death in my hands, for all the Provinces are under martial law. I trust God has enabled me to use it discreetly'.

14

The Impossible Task

By July 28th Havelock's Movable Column – a bare twelve hundred Britons and three hundred Sikhs – were in position at Mungalwar, a group of mud villages six miles beyond the Ganges into Oudh.

The crossing, 'of a swollen, broad and rapid river, with only one small steamer and a few boats', was slow and harassing. The rain poured in torrents; the *Burrampootra* continually went wrong and Colonel Tytler of the QMG, who had some knowledge of machinery, spent most of his time, soaking wet and covered in oil, wrestling with its engine. To speed the crossing and to ensure that every cart, elephant and camel was free for ammunition and the transport of sick and wounded, no tents were taken, 'only a change of clothes and some food and drink'. General Neill was left behind 'to hold Cawnpore, and organise everything. He will complain of this', Havelock said in his telegram to Calcutta, 'but I have not another officer to whom I could entrust the duty for an hour'. Neill began immediately to flog and hang any native remotely suspected of complicity in the massacre, delighting in first forcing Hindus to break caste so that they should die convinced that they were eternally damned. He sent a stream of blustering messages to Grant – 'all well here; I will hold my own against any odds' – and among his subordinates laughed at Havelock, whom he called 'the old gentleman', and hinted that he had been left behind from jealousy.

Havelock gave his officers orders for marching at daybreak. The task ahead was enough to appal the stoutest. As Major North wrote, 'the enterprise is a desperate one, and it will be seen whether a force so weak as ours can do more than make the attempt'. Forty-three miles to Lucknow through a hostile countryside, fanatically Mohammedan, which until recently had been part of an independent state, whereas Cawnpore had been British for nearly forty years; a large and well-armed army across the path and the heavy besieging force to meet at Lucknow; the Nana with three thousand men on the left flank 'with the avowed intention of cutting in upon our rear when we advance'; cholera already gripping the force – such obstacles might well have dictated a wait in the safety of Cawnpore until promised reinforcements arrived, even if Lucknow fell.

'The chances of relieving that place are hourly multiplying against us', Havelock telegraphed Grant, 'the difficulties of an advance to that capital are excessive. The enemy has intrenched and covered with guns the bridge across the Sai at Bunni and has made preparations for destroying it if the bridge is forced. I have no means of crossing the canal near Lucknow, even if successful at Bunni. A direct attack at Bunni might cost me a third of my force. I might turn it by Mohan, unless the bridge there also were destroyed. I have this morning received a plan of Lucknow from Major Anderson, engineer in that garrison, and much valuable information in two memoranda which escaped the enemy's outpost troops and were partly written in Greek character. These communications and much information orally derived from spies, convince me of the extreme delicacy and difficulty of any operation to relieve Colonel Inglis, now commanding in Lucknow. It shall be attempted, however, at every risk, and the result faithfully reported. Our losses from cholera are becoming serious, and extend to General Neill's force as well as my own. I earnestly hope that the 5th and the 90th can be pushed on to me entire, and with all despatch, and every disposable detachment of the regiments now under my command be sent for. My whole force only amounts to 1,500 men, of whom 1,200 are British, and ten guns imperfectly equipped and manned. I am very thankful for your Excellency's kind interposition at the Horse Guards regarding my promotion to Major General'.

They marched from Mungalwar on July 29th. 'There was an all pervading sense', wrote Maude, 'that we were, humanly speaking, carrying our lives in our hands, and that there was nearly as much danger in the rear as in the front of the day's work'. The morale of the troops was good – they knew nothing of the odds and were determined to avenge Cawnpore. They were Havelock's men, devoted to the little General with the big voice, who drove them to the limit but cared for them as individuals; who was stern but fair; who commanded instant obedience and yet never swore. They believed he was invincible and also, knowing of his twenty-seven actions without a scratch, personally indestructible. Havelock as he rode forward was quiet and thoughtful. Every ounce of his military skill would be needed in what lay ahead. But, as always, his plans had been a matter of earnest prayer; and God's promises were sure, whether by life or by death.

And thus, as Harry wrote after the Mutiny, 'he advanced into Oudh on the 29th July with only about 1,200 British determined to do all he could to relieve the pressure upon Lucknow. Every mile of movement towards it would be *some* relief. And he hoped to have the rest of his 2,800 British or even enough to make them up to 2,000 (that is, 800 more) sent on to him immediately'. 'Give us 3,000 Europeans and six horsed guns', Havelock had telegraphed Grant through Tytler, 'and we will smash every rebel force one after the other, and the troops coming up in the rear can settle the country'. To Lucknow he sent a message by Ungud the spy: 'We hope to meet you in five or six days'.

THE WEATHER WAS clear, the sun already high when after three miles the advanced picquet sent back word and Havelock rode up to see the enemy strongly entrenched near a village straddling the Lucknow road shortly before the little town of Unao. As Havelock swept the scene with his glasses he saw how strong was the enemy's position: 'his right was protected', he wrote in his despatch that night, 'by a swamp which could neither be forced nor turned; his advance was drawn in a garden enclosure which in this warlike district had purposely or accidentally assumed the form of a bastion. The rest of his force was posted in and behind a village, the houses of which were loopholed. The passage between the village and the large town of Unao is narrow. The town itself extended three-quarters of a mile to our right. The flooded state of the country precluded the possibility of turning in this direction. The swamp shut us in on the left. Thus an attack in front became unavoidable'.

Havelock ordered the Enfield skirmishers to open the action while he sent for the guns. The main body of the Highlanders were drawn up ready for the assault, but finding themselves under fire from the garden bastion, Colonel Hamilton cantered back to report. 'Remove them out of range till the guns arrive,' answered Havelock. 'Pray, sir,' said Hamilton, 'let them go at the place and have done with it!' Havelock assented, and a few moments later he saw Highlanders and Blue Caps, a blotch of dirty red and dirty white, rush forward with a yell at the garden wall under a withering fire. A Scot climbed up and fell back, shot through the head and chest, a fusilier followed and collapsed, a bayonet wound in his throat. The next man was over, and the garden bastion was carried, though with loss.

The battle swayed forward to the village. The fire from the loopholed houses was murderous and, said Lieutenant Crump of the Gunners, 'fairly astonished the English soldiers'. At Havelock's side his aide-de-camp, Seton, fell wounded. From the end of the street a two-gun battery of Mohammedan Oudh gunners, the smartest in India, poured grape into the mêlée. The town was on fire. Men were being 'pulled out dead and dying from the entrance of houses they were trying in detail to storm'. Havelock sent for the reserve, the 64th. To his disgust, as the 64th, at the double, approached the flames and smoke and heard the shattering reports of the guns echoing in the enclosed space and the screams of men burning to death, they paused and hung back, until one ran forward, an Irish private, and 'was cut literally in pieces by the enemy whilst setting an example of distinguished gallantry'. Shamed thus by Private Cavanagh, the 64th recovered and surged into the fight, their weight proving decisive. The guns were captured after a fierce hand-to-hand struggle.

At that moment, Captain Crommelin, the field engineer of the force, who had been reconnoitring on his own, 'came running back in hot haste with the information that a very large force of infantry, cavalry and guns was rapidly advancing from the other side upon Unao'.

Without hesitation Havelock moved the bulk of his force forward rapidly, leaving some of the Sikhs to clear up the village, and passing Unao on the left extended his line on a firm tongue of land about half a mile wide. The road stretched away from the centre, and either side of it was swamp. Behind him was a thick grove of trees, impassively green. He placed Maude with his guns in front, the two heavy pieces on the road, three on each side, and waited.

Still the enemy came on, trumpets sounding, banners streaming, drums beating. Havelock let them come; his line, British and Sikh, stood silent, the regimental colours hanging limp in the hot, still air. At less than a thousand yards the enemy halted and opened fire. Maude's gunners had the sun behind them and could see their targets clearly; they replied with devastating effect. The enemy recoiled and began to deploy; guns and horse became embroiled in the red-brown mud at the edge of the swamp. Havelock ordered the left flank to wade forward, Maude's guns advancing down the road. 'I declare', wrote one of the gunners, 'the disproportionate idea of such a proceeding seemed almost ludicrous to me, as I looked forward at the vast masses of infantry and cavalry with which the plain swarmed in front, and then backwards at the small, thin line of men struggling on, with sloped arms, knee-deep in swamp. Yet there was not one of those grim-bearded Englishmen that did not *know* we should beat the foe; and a groan ran down the line, "Oh that we had but cavalry to cut the dogs up"'.

When the Enfield riflemen were near enough to open fire and saddle after saddle of the enemy cavalry was emptied, 'the horsemen went threes about – there was a waver amongst the infantry – and then the whole went off pell-mell to a village in the distance across the plain, where we saw them huddled together like a flock of sheep, leaving us masters of the field and fifteen guns'.

It was now two p.m. Havelock halted for three hours; the men had a meal, the wounded and those taken by cholera during the action were placed in the carts. The dead were buried and the captured guns, for which there was no transport, burst. At five p.m. the column continued its advance down the Lucknow road – thirty-seven miles to go.

The next township was Busseratgunj, five miles on: 'it is a walled town', wrote Havelock, 'with wet ditches. The gate is defended by a round tower, on and near which four pieces of cannon were mounted; the adjacent building being loopholed and otherwise strengthened. In the rear of the town is a broad and deep inundation, crossed by a narrow chausée and bridge'.

To deal with this formidable obstacle Havelock planned that during a preliminary bombardment, at steadily decreasing range, the 64th at a given moment should move round to the left flank to distract the enemy and cut him off from the one escape route – the hundred and fifty yards causeway across the water. When the 64th were well on their way the main body led by the Highlanders and Fusilier Blue Caps should assault the gate and town; with the enemy caught between two fires there was considerable hope of his extinction.

The battle opened in fine style: 'the guns pushed on in admirable order, supported by the Fusiliers skirmishing and the 78th Highlanders and 64th Regiment in line. The enemy's cannonade was well sustained; nevertheless our force continued to gain ground'. The 64th set off on their turning movement and the Highlanders and Fusiliers threw themselves on the earthworks with great gallantry, forced the gate and were in the town. The 64th, however, had stopped to return fire from a small building which they should have taken in their stride, and their opportunity was fast disappearing. Havelock ordered Harry, who had just remounted after having a horse shot under him, to take them the peremptory message, 'If you don't go at that village, I'll send men that will, and put an everlasting disgrace on you!' The message, embellished with Harry's choicest oaths, got them on, but the rout of retreating enemy, a jumble of disorganised horse and men, was already gaining the causeway and the 64th reached it too late. The bulk of the sepoys escaped, carrying their wounded, and Havelock's few cavalry could not be used because of the floods. Three more guns were captured.

The short twilight had already closed in. The line was halted on the edge of the water, and bivouacked 'with exhausted frames and minds', as Maude wrote, 'after three actions fought in a July sun'. Havelock rode on over the causeway and personally placed the picquets. Returning he passed along the narrow road towards the town, his horse stepping over recumbent forms of exhausted soldiers. One man rolling out of the way saw who was the horseman and stood up shouting, 'Clear the way for the General!' The cry passed down the line, 'Clear the way for the General!' Havelock reined in, beaming with pleasure, and called out, 'You have done that *well* already, men!' 'Never was compliment more happily timed', wrote Major North in his journal, 'or more warmly appreciated; they were literally transported with delight'. There was a moment's silence and then a spontaneous shout, 'God bless the General!' 'Despite his reserved manner', commented North, 'no man is more capable of conciliating, I had almost said compelling, regard than General Havelock'. North himself had been allotted the defence of the baggage and thus denied the day's battles; Havelock made a point of thanking him personally and North wrote, 'there is pleasure in serving such a general, ever ready courteously to acknowledge a service'.

At his Headquarters bivouac, while Harry made up the lists

of dead, wounded and sick, Havelock drafted a characteristic Order of the Day: 'Soldiers, your General thanks you for your exertions today. You have stormed two fortified villages, and captured nineteen guns. But he is not satisfied with *all* of you. Some of you fought as if the cholera had seized your minds as well as your bodies. There were men among you, however, whom he must praise to the skies...' And he proceeded to list Private Cavanagh, Lieutenant Bogle of the 78th and Major Stephenson and Lieutenant Dangerfield of the Blue Caps.

That night, while the men slept happily, assured of further victories, Havelock faced facts.

'My force is reduced by sickness and repeated combats to 1,364 rank and file, with ten ill-quipped guns. I could not therefore move on Lucknow with any prospect of success', especially as he had no means of crossing the Sai river at Bunni, or the canal at the Char Bagh bridge, Lucknow. Of the 1,000 effective European infantry, as Tytler put it two days later, 'we could only place 850 in line, our numerous sick, wounded and baggage requiring strong guards in this country where every village contains enemies. We were diminishing daily from cholera, diarrhœa and fighting. The Bunni bridge, 120 yards long, strongly entrenched and said to be destroyed, had to be passed. We could not hope to reach Lucknow with 600 effective Europeans; we had then to pass the canal and force one and a half miles of street'. And though 'we thrashed the Oudh people easily in the open', some of the men had shown no taste for carrying fortified buildings.

To add to this, Havelock knew that on his flank was the Nana, and since Busseratgunj could not be garrisoned, his communications with Cawnpore were sure to be cut, while if he was forced to beat a retreat it would be almost impossible to re-cross the swollen Ganges under fire without heavy loss; Neill boasted that his guns covered the further bank but in view of the range, 'his shot would do more harm to us than to the enemy'. Moreover, so Harry said afterwards, 'every single doolie and sick cart was full of sick and wounded and there was no alternative but either to retire temporarily and place them in safety or to leave them by the roadside. We had 125 of them on our hands, and not a single vacant litter or cart for the casualties that must occur in future fights. This consideration imperatively demanded a temporary retirement'.

Yet to decide on retirement, even if temporary, was grievous, requiring far more strength of will than the initial decision to advance into Oudh. Havelock's men had won every battle and thirsted for more; retreat would shake their morale. If they went forward in a desperate attempt to reach Lucknow and perished in the attempt the world would applaud, whereas by retirement Havelock's reputation might suffer as the decision could be misunderstood in Calcutta and England. But this was not a matter for impulse but for cold, clear intellect. Havelock's military knowledge and experience, his years of placing duty before inclination in every aspect of life, his sense of the overriding and abiding presence of Providence – that sense which he had expressed by his words after an earlier action, 'I felt the Lord Jesus was at my side' – led him clearly to his decision.

Having made up his mind Havelock sent for Tytler and asked his opinion 'as to the possibility of at once relieving Lucknow'. Tytler said there was no chance of success, and failure now would seal Lucknow's fate while 'if we waited for reinforcements we might still be in time to save it, as the garrison say they can hold out to the 5th August'.

The next morning the men were resting and discussing the exciting prospects ahead. 'I suppose we shall advance this afternoon', Groom of the Blue Caps was writing to his wife, 'we shall in all probability have one fight tomorrow or tonight, and an awful scrimmage at Lucknow, of course'. In his tent Havelock was reading a despatch just received through Neill stating that the sepoys at Dinapore, far back in Bengal, had mutinied. The new crisis meant a dwindling hope of the reinforcements which he had been promised so glibly when he left Calcutta, where he had urged Grant and Canning to disarm the Dinapore sepoys, only to be assured that the men would never revolt. It was Havelock who now would suffer, for the 90th Foot and 5th Fusiliers which he was expecting would certainly be delayed by the new mutiny. The news clinched his decision to retire temporarily.

In the afternoon the men fell in, their faces towards Lucknow. Havelock gave the order to retire. An astonished, angry murmur of protest ran down the line. 'A man of less genuine mettle than our General', wrote North, 'might be swayed by such demonstrations, but the superiority of his moral courage renders him unassailable, and elevates him far beyond the fear of man which bringeth a snare'.

The column marched back across the battlefields of yesterday, dejected and sullen, sickness increasing. They saw no sign of an enemy and after spending the night at Unao reached their old camping ground at Mungalwar where they again found such shelter as they could in mud huts, for they were, Harry wrote, doing 'what never has been attempted since the time of Clive – campaign without tents and without beds in the height of the rains'.

From Mungalwar Havelock wrote to Grant (the letter to be telegraphed from Cawnpore) informing him of the temporary retirement, and stating, 'a reinforcement of 1,000 British soldiers, from which it would be necessary to make a detachment to defend the bridgehead on this side might yet enable me to obtain great results, but with a smaller addition to my new column little could be effected for the interests of the state'. He also informed Neill of the position and added an urgent request that any reinforcements available should be hurried through.

He wrote to Hannah, 'to tell you that by God's blessing Harry and I are still well and safe. On the 29th I had two more combats at Unao and Busseratgunj in which God gave me the victory, and I captured 19 guns. Harry had a horse badly wounded under him. Lieutenant Seton, who was acting as my aide-de-camp, was shot through the face and his underjaw fractured.

You do not know the lad but may feel for him... What a mercy you did not come out to India! Pray for me and trust in God. PS: My despatches will be published. Read and partly believe them. Believe nothing else'.

Late the following day, August 1st, Havelock was astounded to receive from Neill, his junior officer, 'the most extraordinary letter I have ever perused'. 'I late last night received yours of 6 p.m. yesterday', wrote Neill in his almost illegible hand, exasperating in itself, 'I deeply regret that you have fallen back one foot. The effect on our prestige is very bad indeed. Your camp was not pitched yesterday before all manner of reports were rife in the city – that you had returned to get more guns, having lost all you took with you. In fact the belief amongst all is that you have been defeated and forced back. It has been most unfortunate your not bringing any guns captured from the enemy. The natives will not believe that you have captured one. The effect of your retrograde movement will be very injurious to our cause everywhere...' Sentence by sentence Havelock read on, each increasing his sense of astonishment and fury at Neill's rank insubordination, until he reached the final paragraph: 'when the iron guns are sent to you, also the half-battery and the company of the 84th escorting it, you ought to advance again and not halt until you have rescued, if possible, the garrison of Lucknow. Return here sharp, for there is much to be done, between this and Agra and Delhi'.

Havelock took paper and in no uncertain terms wrote forthwith to Neill: 'There must be an end to these proceedings at once. I wrote to you confidentially on the state of affairs. You send me back a letter of censure of my measures, reproof and advice for the future. I do not want and will not receive any of them from an officer under my command, be his experience what it may. Understand this distinctly; and that a consideration of the obstruction that would arise to the public service at this moment alone prevents me from taking the stronger step of placing you under arrest. You now stand warned. Attempt no further dictation. I have my own reasons, which I will not communicate to anyone, and I alone am responsible for the course which I have pursued'.

ON AUGUST 2ND Havelock received, through Neill, a telegram from the Commander-in-Chief: 'Calcutta, 31st July. Send the following to Havelock and let it be written in Greek or otherwise disguised. Recent events in Bengal make it impossible to send up the 5th and 90th Regiments to Allahabad and it is certain that no other European regiments can reach Allahabad for 2 months. This being the case you cannot be strengthened in Oudh as you desire and it is necessary you should not be influenced in remaining there by a reliance upon early reinforcements. It is particularly desirable that our force should be collected above the line of the trunk road and the Ganges, and therefore if after relieving Lucknow you find that you cannot recross the Ganges bringing with you the Europeans in Lucknow this should be done'. The telegram was a bitter disappointment. Havelock must seek to relieve Lucknow with fewer men than he had started with four days earlier, and they more weakened with sickness and exposure; or abandon the attempt. 'What a feeble rule was that of Pat Grant,' raged Harry, 'why did he not force Birch[1] or Lord Canning to send more men up! Simply because he continued to believe in the sepoys till too late!'

The scanty reinforcements, a company of the 84th and a half battery of two 9-pounders, reached Havelock on August 3rd. Havelock paraded his column and placed the new detachment on the right, the two guns beyond and opposite them their gun lascars who were reported by the battery commander to have shown mutinous tendencies on the march. He addressed the 84th and the gunners and congratulated them 'on having come into a camp of heroic soldiers who had six times met the enemy, and every time defeated him and captured his cannon'. Then he

---

[1]Military secretary and a close friend of Havelock's.

turned to the lascars, 'and told them what miscreants I had this morning discovered them to be, traitors in heart to their fostering government'. He ordered British soldiers to disarm them and march them out of the Camp to return to Cawnpore as labourers under Neill; if they attempted to desert or refused to work they would be punished with death. 'I cannot afford to have a single traitor in camp,' he said.

'We are still in the dark about the General's intentions', wrote Groom that day, 'everybody is frightfully disgusted at his conduct; but he is doubtless acting on the best information, and has very good reasons for his apparent want of energy. News came into camp this morning from Delhi. What it is no one knows. The General only deigns to say "It is good", which I suppose means that we have not been actually yet obliged to raise the siege'.

On August 4th, ignoring a plea from Neill that he would deal with a small sepoy force rumoured to be threatening Cawnpore, Havelock once more set out on the desperate gamble of reaching Lucknow. When the men had fallen in, lined up on the road, he read out telegrams from the Governor-General and Commander-in-Chief congratulating them on their brilliant victory at Cawnpore. 'Men,' he continued, 'yesterday two guns and a small reinforcement joined us and I told them to go from the right down to the left of the line and in every man they would see a hero. You have heard what the Governor-General and Commander-in-Chief have said. I shall have to write to His Excellency again tomorrow; it depends upon you what I write. Tomorrow we meet the rebels again in the field.'

Meanwhile, up the Lucknow road, Ungud the spy was working his way back to the Residency with a cheerful note written by Tytler in minute letters, partly in Greek characters, and folded inside a quill: 'We shall push on as speedily as possible. We hope to reach you in four days at furthest. You must aid us in every way, even to cutting your way out if we can't force our way in. We are only a small force'.

The force bivouacked once again at Unao. Havelock now had a new aide-de-camp, William Hargood of the Blue Caps who, until the end, was to mean much to him. When Hargood was killed, in June 1858, Harry wrote that he had never left Havelock's side 'or was absent from him one hour – I feel his loss as that of a brother. He was the noblest, tenderest friend I ever knew. He had the soul of a hero and the modesty of a girl. My father selected him entirely by accident, but from the day they first came together there was a thorough understanding between them. Hargood seemed framed by nature to suit my father. Day and night he was always by his side ready in the middle of the night to jump up at the slightest word with a cheerful and ready alacrity which often put me to shame'.

The next morning they advanced on Busseratgunj which they knew to be reoccupied by the enemy. Using much the same tactics as before Havelock, after bombardment, led his force, in which cholera was raging, against the walled town. 'I advanced upon it, turned the position by its left and drove the mutineers and rebels out of it with great slaughter'. Yet he gained little. 'When I have overcome the enemy's artillery fire, my wearied infantry can scarcely muster strength to capture their guns; and as I have no cavalry the mutineers resist as long as they have the power and they retire without fear of punishment'. Most of the enemy guns kept at a distance and only two fell into Havelock's hands. He had two men killed and twenty-three wounded, but the one night and a day had cost him nearly one hundred sick and dying of cholera, and the expenditure of a quarter of his gun ammunition.

Havelock made camp on the far side of the causeway, about a mile beyond his final line of July 29th. And then took stock of the position. He had gambled on the chance that the enemy had weakened; to do so had been militarily sound. He now saw that an advance of thirty miles with sick men against a series of strongly held positions with stiff street fighting at the end, would 'involve the loss of this force'. 'The only military question that remains is whether that, or the destruction of the British garrison at Lucknow, would be the greatest calamity to the State in this crisis'. If there was any hope of relieving the pressure sufficiently for the garrison to cut their way out, he should go on. But Inglis – the inexperienced, hesitant commander who had found himself in Lawrence's place – would scarcely succeed, encumbered with women and children, in breaking the ring of mutineers.

If Havelock was annihilated 'in a fruitless attempt to relieve Colonel Inglis' Lucknow would certainly fall. And back behind the Ganges the strong Gwalior contingent was on the move; it had mutinied long since but the Maharajah had held it in check. They now threatened Cawnpore or Agra, and if he was wiped out in Oudh neither city would survive, while every native ruler in the region might come out against the tottering Government.

Yet, even more than on July 29th, it was a cruel decision that Havelock faced while they buried the dead beyond Busseratgunj. Then, a temporary retirement only was in mind; now, having failed with the feeble strength which was all that a supine Government could give him, he might be waiting a whole two months before reinforcements enabled him to advance, too late. His fame as a master of war had spread far and wide in the past month; was all to end in retreat which might be condemned as cowardly? Would it not be finer to die fighting?

Havelock did not take long to reach a decision, 'the most painful I have ever had to form in my life'. Having done so he called together 'the only three staff officers in my force whom I ever consult confidentially, but in whom I entirely confide' – Tytler, Crommelin the Engineer and Harry. Tytler said that to go on would sacrifice the force 'without a chance of benefiting the garrison'. The country was in arms; the mere nine hundred which were all that would be paraded could never force the Sai River or the Char Bagh canal and 'the men are cowed by the number opposed to them, and the endless fighting'. Havelock turned to Harry. Harry was up in arms at once. 'I voted for advancing at all hazards. Tytler and Crommelin, Tytler especially, took me to task severely about this, saying that I was prepared to sacrifice the whole force, and the interest of British India rather than compromise my father's and my own reputation by a retreat. Tytler particularly urged: "You must recollect that this is more than a personal question. However galling it is to the General and you to retire, you must have regard to the interests of the Government". Crommelin agreed with him strongly, and my father then said, "I agree with Tytler"'.

And so, 'with great grief and reluctance', Havelock turned back once more to Mungalwar where he planned to remain, strengthening the position and his communications with Cawnpore, 'in the hope that some error of the enemy may enable me to strike a blow against them and give the garrison an opportunity of blowing up their works and cutting their way out'.

On the Sunday, August 9th, he wrote to Hannah from Mungalwar: 'I know not when I may have leisure to write a line to you again so I will avail myself, not of a Sabbath's rest, for that I have not, but of an incidental cessation of work, to give you my news. I have fought seven fights with the enemy and by God's blessing, have beat them in every one of them. Old Hearsey writes me that all Calcutta is ringing with my praises. I know only that the *Friend of India*, conducted by I know not whom, is abusing me in the most violent manner, which I only mention for the oddness of the thing. The *Englishman* which alone I see and that incidentally, at the same moment tells the world that I am the only conqueror (?) in Upper India. But I will say no more of public matters than that I have everywhere beaten my foes; but that the folly, baseness and selfishness of others has placed everything in the most perilous state. If we succeed at last in restoring anything it will be by God's especial and extraordinary mercy.

'Harry is safe and well. He is my DAAG – and my right arm. His talents, courage, activity and energy exceed everything that

235

I ever witnessed at his age. But his temper more imperious than ever leads him astray perpetually and makes me continually feel that I pay too great a price even for talents like his in having him with me.

'I must now write as one whom you may see no more, for the chances of war are heavy at this crisis.' He added some notes on money matters and ended, 'thank God for my hope in the Saviour. We shall meet in Heaven'.

15

Enforced Delay

In England the news of Havelock's victories, received after some six weeks' delay, broke as sunshine in the darkness.

Since the first announcement of the Meerut mutiny, shock after shock from India had caused consternation more complete than any in living memory. The Indian Mutiny horrified the British public. The Crimea, for all its sufferings, was a professional war, but the revolt in India involved women and children in privation and horrors at a period when women – especially those who could be described as 'ladies' – were honoured and protected as the weaker sex with a chivalry unequalled before or since.

Moreover, the Empire was visibly shaking. India was the chief possession with a predominantly native population and its importance in British prestige and economy made its possible loss an inconceivable disaster. And India was of intimate concern to so many in Britain; scarcely a family in the middle and upper classes did not have a member or connection or friend in the civil or military services, or in trade.

Every day the newspapers were eagerly read by a public not hardened to horrors, and as the summer of 1857 advanced the news seemed steadily worse.

Then, mail by mail, came the victories of Fatehpur, of Aong and the Panda Nudi, and Cawnpore, followed hard by the staggering impact of the massacre of the women and children. Havelock's name, previously unknown except to the small circle of professional soldiers, was at once on every lip. He seemed to personify the hope of England. 'Havelock and his troops', wrote *The Times*, 'fought Plassey five times over between Allahabad and Bithoor. General Havelock's march is the very expression and type of our position in Hindustan. He advances, he fights, he conquers – everything goes down before him as long as he can stand; but it is desperate work to make head against twenty to one'. *The Times* described the attempt to reach Lucknow and the onslaught of cholera, supposed in England to be the main cause of the retirement, and continued, 'a general and an army victorious beyond precedent, marching to assured success and the relief of a long-beleaguered fortress, have been struck by the fatal pestilence, and, by our last accounts, Havelock and the remains of his gallant band, encumbered by their sick comrades, were retracing their steps to Cawnpore... We cannot attempt to express the sympathy which the calamity that has befallen these brave men will excite, not only in England but wherever the tale of their gallantry and their misfortune shall be told'.

The barbarism of the Nana Sahib and others, the fanaticism of the Mohammedans of Lucknow and Delhi, made the Mutiny appear something of a religious conflict to the eyes of an England for which religion was fast becoming the predominant factor of life – scattered bands of Christians were facing hordes of Hindus and Mohammedans; it was a war between light and darkness. And, men now heard, the hope of England was a General unashamedly and unequivocally Christian. 'No soldiers', said one newspaper, 'ever show themselves more invincible than those who can pray as well as fight, nor have any swords proved more resistless than those wielded by the right hands that know their war through dog's-eared Bibles. This is evidently, a Christian warrior of the right breed'. At meetings held up and down the land to raise money for the Indian Relief Fund, Havelock's name was cheered to the echo. 'Men of all ranks and classes', wrote John Marshman, 'the statesman, the noble, the minister of religion, and above all the middle class, who claim him as their own, vied with each other in doing honour to the man who had so nobly maintained the honour of his country; and in a few weeks the "neglected lieutenant" rose by national suffrage to the pinnacle of renown'.

Hannah paid a visit to England from Bonn and thoroughly enjoyed being fêted as a hero's wife.

The War Office awarded Colonel Havelock, CB a Good Conduct pension of £100 per annum ....

Back at Mungalwar, in the steamy August days, Havelock's dwindling force, in intervals of burying the cholera dead, was digging itself in. Havelock ordered the building of a bridge of boats, with a road across the islands which the fall of the river now exposed, and this was pushed forward with remarkable speed.

On all sides bad news – by telegraph from Bengal or trickling in from the upper provinces through spies. From Delhi Havelock learned that the siege of the mutineers in the Fort might be abandoned by Archdale Wilson, from Agra he had repeated cries for help though, as was known afterwards, Agra was never seriously threatened; from Colonel Inglis in Lucknow came an anguished letter, 'if you hope to save this force no time must be lost in pushing forward'. 'In all this', wrote Harry, 'my father never wavered. His soldierly counsel put to shame, and by force of example inspired confidence into the miserable commander of the garrison at Lucknow. He opposed in the strongest terms any abandonment of the siege of Delhi; and throughout, his bearing was as though his sight could pierce the future and see the result'.

To Agra he wrote on August 10th, by hand of a native spy, to Colvin the Lieutenant-Governor: 'You urge me to advance on Agra. I am instructed to relieve Lucknow if possible and then take a position on the Trunk Road. I have not yet been able to relieve Lucknow. I have *nine hundred British Infantry only*[1] and *much* cholera amongst them. I am most anxious to aid you and move on Delhi, but under the circumstances I must wait for further instructions, by which I will be guided and for which I have applied. I cannot in the meantime make disclosures how-

---

[1] The words in italics were written in Greek characters.

ever disguised, which might fall into the hands of the enemy, and bring about the ruin of this force. I have been officially warned to expect *no reinforcements for two months*'.

The loudest alarms were coming from Neill at Cawnpore. Continuing to write disloyally behind Havelock's back about the retirement, he was pleading with him by a succession of notes to return to Cawnpore and rescue him from the threats he believed multiplying on all sides. Havelock was determined to remain in Oudh if possible though offering Neill such help as he could spare. Early on August 11th he received an urgent, breathless call from Neill: 'one of the Sikh scouts I can depend on has just come in and reported that 4,000 men and 5 guns have assembled today at Bithoor and threatens Cawnpore. I cannot stand this. They will enter the town and our communications are gone and if I am not supported I can only hold out here. Can do nothing beyond our entrenchments, all the country between this and Allahabad will be up our powder and ammunition on the way up if the steamer as I feel assured does not start will fall into the hands of the Enemy and we will be in a bad way. In haste'.

That night Havelock sent all his stores and spare ammunition, his sick and wounded across the bridge of boats, just completed. He had no intention of slinking back himself. To ensure an unopposed crossing and to prevent the enemy in Oudh thinking that they had done with him he marched that evening towards Lucknow, determined to deal the sepoys a reeling blow which should leave them immobile during his withdrawal and enable him to leave Oudh still victorious.

The column bivouacked at Unao. It rained hard in the night and on the morning of August 12th 'we advanced', as Major Stephenson of the Blue Caps wrote, 'the small, gaunt, careworn remains of our force, the men almost dropping out in tens from cholera, but with courage as high and as undaunted as of old'. There could be no holding back while Havelock was with them. 'No man who served under my dear Father', Harry once said, 'would have dared show hesitation in the face of the enemy. There was that in the example that feeble old man showed, of patient endurance of exposure and fatigue, and stern determination to do his duty to his country, which strengthened the hearts of the weakest'.

The enemy were reported in strength before Busseratgunj, about a mile and a half in advance of the old battlegrounds. Havelock sent the 78th and the Blue Caps on a flanking movement to the right, to be supported by heavy artillery fire from the front. While the guns were creaking and straining through the stiff glue of the mud the enemy brought their heaviest fire to check the flanking movement. 'I certain was never under so heavy a fire in my life', wrote Crump of the Gunners, 'in five minutes after we came into action every man at the gun I was laying was wounded with grape'. Slowly the steadiness of the British gunners gained the upper hand and then the Highlanders flung themselves at the works in such style that a spontaneous cheer broke from the staff and the reserves, British and Sikh, waiting on the road. 'Oh if you could have seen the Highlanders', wrote Harry to his cousin a few days later, 'a handful – 120 men – overwhelmed almost with shot, shell and grape – up to their middles in swamp – rush with a cheer on two guns behind entrenchments and defended by not less than 2,000 sepoys, and wrest them from them without a second's check – you would have been proud of your countrymen for ever'. The battle ended as the previous actions, with the sepoys crowding in rout through the narrow street of Busseratgunj mown down by musket and rifle fire and hustled across the causeway to the firm ground beyond, where Havelock left them cowed and beaten.

The same afternoon the force retired leisurely to Unao where they cooked a meal and then to Mungalwar. During the night the heavy guns were sent over the bridge of boats and the next morning the force crossed, destroying the bridge behind them, and entered Camp at Cawnpore 'much worn out by fatigue and exposure', to respond to Neill's plea for help.

Cholera spread rapidly. The Camp was one large hospital, echoing with feeble cries of water from the desiccated, dying men, while despite stringent orders the ground between the lines became soiled and foul since dysentery cases could scarcely drag themselves to the latrines. Neill, caught by his own disloyalty, brought a letter from the Commander-in-Chief asking him to discuss with Havelock the feasibility of an immediate advance on Lucknow. With some relish Havelock 'told General Neill that if his Excellency required it absolutely, or he thought it practicable, I would order my bridges over the islands of the Ganges to be restored, and march immediately. He replied that he conceived the attempt without reinforcements could only terminate in disaster, without the possibility of relieving the garrison, which would be injurious to our interests in this part of India. I concurred in this opinion'. Hardly had Neill left when the doctors waited on Havelock and reported that at the present rate of deaths the whole force would have disappeared in six weeks; he must rest them and give them a chance to shake off the epidemic. Havelock replied that he must attack Bithoor and deal with the Nana. 'It is now', he telegraphed the Commander-in-Chief the next day, August 15th, 'that I should report to your Excellency the fearful inroads cholera is making in my little force. The total sick and wounded is 335. The total British strength is 1,415. I do not despond. I must march tomorrow against Bithoor, but it seems advisable to look the evil in the face, for there is no chance but between reinforcements or gradual absorption by disease'.

The same day Harry was writing to his cousin Charley, who had escaped to Benares with forty loyal sowars after most of his native cavalry had mutinied at Dinapore. 'I wish to God', wrote Harry, 'I could send you better news of Mary and her husband than I can, but please God we will get them out yet – in spite of the measures which have made it for a time an impossibility... The Garrison of Lucknow were holding out stoutly four days ago, so that if reinforcements are sent to us any time within a fortnight by God's blessing we may rescue them yet. Every man in the force is living for it. Tired to death, wet, hungry, footsore and half-senseless from the sun – that hope has always been sufficient to keep our men up. But if we had gone – Cawnpore would have gone too, and probably Allahabad after it. So it was cruel necessity that sent us back... If the people at Lucknow perish before we can relieve them, the guilt of their blood will be on the heads of those who for the mere wish to be able to say that 3 regiments of the Bengal army had remained *staunch* – staunch! What cursed folly and imbecility – just to say *that*, cut the means of relieving them from under our feet. But this may yet be remedied if they will send us reinforcements... I am, thank God in the best of health and the Governor bears the fatigue better than any man in Camp. We march out early tomorrow towards Bithoor...'

BITHOOR, WHEN THE column reached it after an exhausting eighteen mile march, Havelock found 'one of the strongest positions I have ever seen'.

Three sepoy infantry regiments, two of cavalry and the Nana's levies made up a force of 4,000 men, some of them rifle companies, with two guns. 'The plain, densely covered with thicket and flanked by villages, has two streams flowing through it, not fordable by troops of any arm and only to be crossed by two narrow bridges, the furthest of which was protected by an entrenchment armed with artillery. The road takes a turn after passing the second bridge, which protects the defenders from direct fire; and behind are the narrow streets and brick houses of Bithoor'.

Havelock's favourite turning movement was impossible because of the streams and his frontal assault was met by fire which, he said, reminded him of Ferozeshah. Despite the weight of metal which Havelock brought on them from his guns the mutineer infantry stood firm and fought harder than in any of the recent actions, so that for the first time since the battle of

Cawnpore the British troops could make effective use of the bayonet. It was all over in an hour although, wrote one of the force, 'the men came into action so fagged with the heavy road and the hot sun that ere half the fight was over they were utterly exhausted and could not do half the execution they would otherwise have done'. 'After a severe struggle', runs Havelock's despatch, 'the enemy were driven back, their guns captured and infantry chased off the field in full retreat towards Seorajpore. Had I possessed cavalry not a rebel or mutineer would have reached that place alive'.

And so once more the little column was victorious. As the general rode down the line they stood up and cheered him, desperately tired as they were. 'Don't cheer me, my men,' he replied, 'you did it all yourselves.'

They spent the night at Bithoor. 'It was really piteous to see our fellows lying disabled in the large enclosed garden of the Residency', wrote Major Stephenson. 'Our doctors are quite overworked, for the cases of acute dysentery are painfully numerous and generally terminate in cholera'. Incursions of rebels were still expected at Cawnpore, so there could be no days rest and the force set off back on the morning of August 17th, leaving the battlefield to the vultures. Man after man dropped out, gripped by dysentery or shaking with fever, to be picked up by the train of tumbrils in the rear. After an hour of furious sunshine a storm broke with such force that the column had to halt and turn their backs against the rain. 'We reached Cawnpore', wrote Ensign Dale who had carried the colours of the Blue Caps, 'wet to the skin'.

Bithoor had completed the work of the third action at Busseratgunj in eliminating any danger that Havelock's withdrawal from Oudh would encourage the rebels; for as Harry wrote, in the light of subsequent events, 'when he retired from Oudh, striking within 96 hours two decisive blows on points separated by twenty-five miles of most difficult country and a rapid river 1,700 yards in breadth, our prestige was increased and not lessened'.

That night Havelock wrote and published the last of the famous Orders of the Day with which he sought to praise and encourage his magnificent troops: 'The Brigadier-General congratulates the troops on the result of their exertions in the combat of yesterday. The enemy were driven, with the loss of 250 killed and wounded, from one of the strongest positions in India, which they obdurately defended. They were the flower of the mutinous soldiery, flushed with the successful defection at Saugor and Fyzabad; yet they stood only one short hour against a handful of soldiers of the State, whose ranks had been thinned by sickness and the sword. May the hopes of treachery and rebellion be ever thus blasted! And if conquest can now be achieved under the most trying circumstances, what will be the triumph and retribution of the time when the armies from China, from the Cape, and from England shall sweep through the land? Soldiers! In that moment, your labours, your privations, your sufferings, and your valour will not be forgotten by a grateful country.[1] You will be acknowledged to have been the stay and prop of British India in the time of her severest trial'.

ON RETURN FROM Bithoor Havelock received the Government *Gazette* for August 4th and in it he read: 'Major-General Sir James Outram KCB, of the Bombay Army, to command the Dinapore and Cawnpore Divisions which are to be combined in one command'.

Thus Havelock would no longer hold an independent command, responsible direct to the Commander-in-Chief, but as soon as Outram joined him would be merged in the restored Cawnpore division. His task of relieving Lucknow would fall to Outram, though there was no one under whom he would rather serve, and Havelock would merely command a wing; the chance of crowning his series of victories by the relief of Lucknow seemed over.

---

[1] This sentence is engraved on the plinth of Havelock's statue in Trafalgar Square.

Neill's friends hinted darkly that this was supersession – as punishment for the withdrawal. Public opinion in India assumed that this was so and 'a feeling of indignation was aroused by the supersession of a General in the midst of his victorious career, and there were some who went so far as to arraign what they considered the injustice of Government in visiting him with their displeasure for not accomplishing an object which could not be accomplished without the reinforcements which that Government had neglected to supply. The supersession likewise created no little disgust in England'. Neither Havelock nor Harry, though disappointed, looked on it as deliberate supersession. Havelock had never held the Cawnpore division, to which his rank did not entitle him. Outram was a senior general, the first to become available, and the Government would naturally make use of him on his arrival from Persia. The news of the temporary retirement of July 30th had not reached Calcutta when Outram arrived on August 1st and despite Neill's disloyal thunderings the Commander-in-Chief approved the measure. Nor, when the appointment was made, did there seem from Calcutta any direct connection between Havelock's operations and the eventual plans of Outram, who had first to deal with the Dinapore mutineers and talked of then moving on Lucknow by a different route from Benares if Havelock had not already effected the relief. Outram was also to take Lawrence's place as Chief Commissioner of Oudh, a post for which he was the obvious choice since he had held it previously until invalided home in 1856; the provinces were under martial law and Outram, like Lawrence, would naturally be given military command as well. 'There was no supersession of Havelock', wrote Birch the Military Secretary, after the Mutiny. '...As to the reason assigned for the alleged supersession, that Government were displeased with him after Unao; the very contrary is the case. His march to Cawnpore from Allahabad had been so brilliant and effective that Government could have no doubt as to the subsequent measures he took, whether to advance into Oudh or to retrace his steps, previous to resuming the offensive. There was but one opinion on the subject and that was confidence in Havelock'.

It was unfortunate that Grant omitted to tell Havelock personally, leaving him to read of the arrangement from the *Gazette*, yet any doubt as to the Government's continued approval was set at rest the next day, August 30th, by the first telegram received from Sir Colin Campbell, the Commander-in-Chief sent out from England immediately on news of Anson's death: 'the sustained energy, promptitude, and vigorous action by which your whole proceedings have been marked during the late difficult operations deserve the highest praise, and it will be a most agreeable duty to me to make known to his Lordship, the Governor-General, the sense I entertain of the able manner in which you have carried out the instructions of General Sir Patrick Grant... I entirely concur in the soundness of the view you have taken of your position in your telegraph of the 6th instant from Mungalwar, and of all the reasons which influenced you to defer for the present active operations... I esteem myself most fortunate in having the benefit of your assistance, and that I should find you in the important situation in which you are placed at the moment'.

THE LAST TEN days of August passed quickly, the troops resting so far as was possible. The lice and rats, the flies by day and the howling of jackals by night made Cawnpore dismal. With the cholera raging and every fit man quite exhausted, discipline might have collapsed without Havelock's iron hand. 'Quite of the old school – severe and precise with his men' – 'he was sterner and more severe than seems to be generally understood' – 'the old man was hard on the men, I think' – such was contemporary opinion, yet without that severity the fighting powers of his force would scarcely have survived these weeks of waiting in Cawnpore.

Havelock ordered bands to play in the gardens, and horse races out beyond the Camp in an effort to take the men's minds off their miseries; funerals were temporarily shorn of full ceremonial since the constant repetition of the *Last Post* and the Volley were too depressing. A chaplain had at last joined the force. Havelock had received a telegram from Tucker the Benares magistrate offering to send up 'a Papist minister' who had volunteered. Since there were a number of Roman Catholics Havelock replied 'Send him up', though disappointed that no Protestant had volunteered. The Reverend John Gregson arrived and Havelock invited him to breakfast – to discover that the native telegraphist had in typical fashion misspelled a word; Gregson was, to Havelock's delight, a Baptist though prepared to do what he could for all irrespective of their persuasions.

Neill's constant hangings, floggings and deliberate breakings of caste had been ended and Havelock refused to allow his troops to play havoc with local sensibilities. 'It having been reported to the General', runs one Order, 'that a soldier while on sentry offered an insult to some object of idolatrous worship in the town of Cawnpore, the troops are warned to abstain from such practices in the case either of Hindu temples or Mohammedan mosques. The brutal villainy of the population of this place has been evinced by their having reduced to ashes and likewise desecrated three Christian churches during the brief licence which supervened on the usurpation of Nana Sahib, happily cut short by our victory at Cawnpore. But we must not imitate these wretches. It has always been the wise policy of the British Government to refrain from interference with the superstitions and false religions of the land, and recent provocations and atrocities must not lead us to depart from this line of conduct. The assertion that Enfield rifle cartridges were given to the native troops with a view of compelling them to violate by their use the rule of caste, is the lying pretext of deliberate mutiny. But *real* cause of jealousy and alarm is afforded to the inhabitants of towns and villages, whenever their idols and their temples (however degraded and vile in themselves) are subjected to wanton insult and outrage'.

All the time Havelock was collecting boats and making preparations for his next move towards Lucknow. To Inglis he sent, on August 24th, an urgent letter by Ungud the spy: 'I have your letter of the 16th inst. I can only say do not *negotiate*[1] but rather perish sword in hand. Sir Colin Campbell, who came out at a day's notice to command upon the news arriving of General Anson's death, promised me *fresh troops*, and you will be my first care. The reinforcements may reach me in from *twenty to twenty-five days*, and I will prepare everything for a march on Lucknow'. Campbell's vigour contrasted with the kindly Grant's dissipation of strength on petty expeditions, and his friendship was as real: 'the interest felt for you', he assured Havelock, 'is of the warmest kind, and for the brave troops who have proved themselves worthy of having you for their chief. May God speed you, my dear General!' Yet the reinforcements still seemed delayed. 'If I had been reinforced as I ought to have been', Havelock wrote to Hannah on August 27th, 'I could have relieved Lucknow and saved the garrison. Now troops are coming up to me but I fear it will be too late. The place will fall before I can re-enter Oudh. The poor girl Mary and her husband are there, and I tremble for them.... This campaigning in the rain is trying work. Cholera carries off my brave British troops, and it is only here that I have been able to give them a little repose from the most harassing duties and operations.'

Around at varying distances were enemy forces, and at one time, with the cholera at its height and before the reinforcements were definitely announced as having started, Havelock even threatened Calcutta that withdrawal to Allahabad might be necessary. But now, 'the cholera has almost left us', and reinforcements were on their way, accompanied by Outram who had abandoned his plans of approaching Lucknow by another route, which Havelock believed impracticable.

Havelock's independent command would soon be over.

---

[1] Words in italics written in Greek characters.

AT A QUARTER to six on the evening of Saturday, August 29th, Havelock received a telegram from Outram at Benares, dated the day previous. 'I arrived here this morning... I expect the 90th and 5th tomorrow, and shall push on at once to Allahabad... My force will... total 1,268, besides what I pick up at Mirzapore and Chunar. This reinforcement will, I trust, enable you to relieve Lucknow'.

And then came an astonishing paragraph unprecedented in any communication from a general in the field to his subordinate: 'I shall join you with the reinforcements, but to you shall be left the glory of relieving Lucknow, for which you have already so nobly struggled. I shall accompany you only in my civil capacity as Commissioner, placing my military services at your disposal should you please to make use of me – serving under you as volunteer'. Outram, with characteristic chivalry, had waived his right to command.

Outram had said he would leave for Cawnpore on September 5th, but troubles at Allahabad delayed him. Charley Havelock with his remnant of native horse was with Outram and on September 10th Harry wrote to him, 'I suppose you will be here about the 15th, the day we expect the 1st reinforcements to reach us. My Governor won't have anything to do with those black soldiers of yours as far as depends on him but Outram may perhaps overrule him in this matter. At any rate you will be able to join our Volunteer Cavalry... We shall probably cross on the 16th and 17th. Those blackguards on the opposite bank are said to muster about 7,000 foot, 1,000 horse and 18 guns. We shall be 2,300 British infantry, 250 Sikh ditto, 80 cavalry, two complete 9-pounder batteries and one heavy battery of 4 24-pounders and 2 8-inch howitzers – with which I hope we shall whop everything that crosses either in front rear or flank. But crossing while opposed will be a difficult job. Mary and her husband were both well by the accounts of messengers up to 16th August and I have no doubt we shall get them out safe and sound. The garrison are holding out like real heroes. And I think the accounts of their being pressed are a *little* exaggerated'.

On September 12th Havelock, who had laid his plans for the advance and had everything in trim for throwing a bridge of boats across the Ganges on the morning after Outram's arrival, found time for a letter to Hannah quite in the old style. 'On the 15th I expect my reinforcements, which Sir James Outram accompanies, and then will commence war's hurry skurry again. With him comes at the head or tail of some Irregular Cavalry young Charles Havelock, which leads me to the subject of old Charles Havelock. I have had misgivings about his protracted stay in Germany. He pays nobody, as you well know; and this is, first, not the habit which I wish my children to learn, and secondly one that will get you into great disgrace at Bonn, where hitherto you have lived in all honour. I think you are not a little to blame in the matter of his long stay. He is good natured, and very indefatigable in his attentions to those he likes, especially of the softer sex; which qualities cover, to an extent they ought not to cover, a multitude of sins. I am helpless in the matter, but will not disguise my sentiments, and cannot part with my money.

'I have a most arduous task before (me) in endeavouring with not any adequate means to set right what poor Henry Lawrence's quixotism set wrong... I will do my best, but the operation is most delicate and there is too great a probability of the Residency falling into the hands of the foe before we can relieve it. The wretches will put everyone to the sword, and the poor girl Mary and her husband are shut up in the place...'

16

Divided Command

Sir James Outram reached Cawnpore at dusk on September 15th with the last of the reinforcements, and went to a house prepared for him next door to Neill's.

On his way from Allahabad Outram had received Havelock's proposed organisation for the advance. Because of the comparatively small numbers Havelock had termed the two subordinate commands composing his force, one under Neill and the other under Colonel Hamilton, not 'brigades', but 'wings'. Outram had written back, 'as I purpose deputing to you the command, until the great object for which you have so long fought is attained, of course I shall leave you unfettered in your arrangements; but I would suggest for your consideration whether, instead of calling your two columns *wings* you should not constitute each a brigade, with a brigade-major to each brigadier, and with a field hospital to each brigade...'

Havelock and Harry went down to meet Outram for dinner at seven p.m. The crossing of the Ganges was to begin the next morning in the normal manner, a covering party to embark at daybreak, dropping down stream to the left, aided by the steamer and, on landing, to take possession of the low sandy hills on the opposite bank to protect the building of the bridge of boats.

After dinner, at about ten p.m. so Harry remembered, 'Sir James told my father that he had decided to throw the bridge across from this bank without any covering party on the other and he therefore desired him to countermand the march of the force for the morrow. My father gave his opinion on the matter but Sir James overruled him'. Havelock therefore ordered Harry to ride down to the camp and issue the countermand. Harry rode off, fuming, convinced that Outram had been persuaded by Neill who still clung to his belief that guns on the Cawnpore bank could dominate the far bank – 'my father was well assured that this opinion was simply absurd; to prove which it is only necessary to take into consideration the distance...'

The next morning Outram issued, in warmest terms, his Divisional Order waiving the command until Lucknow be relieved. Beneath it was published Havelock's reply: 'Brigadier-General Havelock, in making known to the column the kind and generous determination of Major-General Sir James Outram, KCB, to leave to it the task of relieving Lucknow and of rescuing its gallant and enduring garrison, has only to express his hope that the troops will strive by their exemplary and gallant conduct in the field, to justify the confidence thus reposed in them'. When the Commander-in-Chief published these orders in the *Gazette* he added the following minute: 'Seldom – perhaps never – has it occurred to a Commander-in-Chief to publish and confirm such an Order as the following one, proceeding from Major-General Sir James Outram, KCB. With such a reputation as Major-General Sir James Outram has won for himself he can afford to share glory and honour with others. But that does not lessen the value of the sacrifice he has made with such disinterested generosity, in favour of Brigadier-General Havelock, CB, commanding the field force in Oudh'.

By his chivalry, springing from an honest and unbounded admiration for Havelock, Outram ensured that Lucknow and the glory of its relief would be linked imperishably with Havelock and not, in popular imagination, with himself. And since the Government's latest instruction was to evacuate Lucknow and he could not foresee the operations which fell to him after he had resumed command, to the best of his belief he was also sacrificing the probability of a baronetcy and a pension, and the largest share of prize money.

Unfortunately, however, when Outram resigned the command he continued, in Harry's words, 'to direct every detail whenever he pleased just as if he had not resigned it. With this additional disadvantage that as he continued to profess to have deprived himself of it (though giving orders continually on matters of detail as well as of importance) no one in the force knew who actually was commanding, and consequently instead of the prompt and unhesitating obedience and execution of orders which had resulted from my father's acknowledged and prover-bially decisive system of command – short, precise and clear – there arose a hesitancy, tardiness and inexactness of execution which put everything into confusion'.

The countermanding of the order to embark a covering force had already produced a measure of muddle, and when at the first island the coolies making the causeway and lashing to-gether the bridge of boats met 'a few straggling musket shots from the long grass on the left bank' and downed tools, the Engineer demanded a covering party as originally planned, which now could be put only on the second island.

Another dispute arose over the question of tents. Havelock, on Outram's way up, had mentioned that since unseasoned sol-diers would be among the reinforcements he would probably this time take canvas into Oudh instead of putting the men, as before, under trees or in villages. Because of the delay, how-ever, they would now be marching in less torrid weather. Havelock therefore decided after all that the force should travel light. Outram overruled him.

By September 18th – a day before Havelock and the bulk of the troops were to cross the Ganges, the 'confusion resulting from orders and counter orders' seemed so patent to Harry that he 'as DAAG of the old force took upon myself to urge on my father either to ask for an uncontrolled and undivided command or to resign back into Sir James's hands that which was no gift but merely the establishment, under the name of an act of un-paralleled generosity (and possibly with the very highest mo-tives and intentions), of an anarchy, than which nothing could be more fatal to success in military operations. My father felt the force of this most keenly – no man ever having had a more acute sense of the fit and unfit in soldiering. But a false delicacy restrained him. He thought it would seem to have been an ungracious act thus to requite Sir James's kindness. And this, in hopes that Sir James would become aware indirectly of his views and would then adopt a different line, he allowed matters to go on as they were'.

Harry became increasingly impatient. He had not, he said, the firm faith that all would work for the best which restrained his father 'and tempered all things to him'. The Havelocks were living in a large bungalow on the river bank in the centre of the entrenchment, which had belonged to a Prince of Oudh and displayed the arms of Oudh – the fishes – on its walls. At one a.m. on September 19th, Colonel Napier (the future Lord Napier of Magdala), Outram's chief of staff, came down 'with *orders* entirely contradicting some arrangement my father had made'. Harry could stand it no longer and determined to bring matters to a head by the only way open to him. At the first opportunity he sat down and drafted a formal letter requesting his father to lay before Outram 'my application for permission to resign the appointment I now hold as DAAG of the force under Brigadier-General Havelock'. 'My service as a soldier', wrote Harry in this formal letter to be read by Outram, 'is not of sufficient distinction to entitle me to advance my opinion in opposition to that of those senior to me, but of one thing the most inexperienced person can be in no doubt – that the first military principle is violated in the divided command that exists at present in this force. Major-General Outram has with the most generous intentions waived his superior rank in favour of General Havelock – yet he continues to interfere in every detail connected with the movements of the force. Thus the executive power rests with one person, the responsibility with another. I cannot pretend to be a prophet but I plainly foresee that only disaster and disgrace can result from such an arrangement. My responsibility in the matter amounts to nothing, but I claim the right of separating myself from any official participating in a business which must entail the loss of credit to everyone concerned in it. But, too, I have had the honour of serving with this force in the nine engagements in which it has successfully encountered the enemy. I solicit the favour of being permitted to continue with it on its advance into Oudh – as a soldier of the volunteer cavalry'.

The Havelocks were working at a large table in the central room of the bungalow. Harry made a fair copy of his draft, which he 'handed to my father across the table to be forwarded to Sir James. He read it and smiled, saying, "No, Harry, we won't send this but I'll write to him". Accordingly he wrote a letter saying that he "would be glad to have Sir James's orders on a point on which they disagreed connected with the lodgement of troops on the island to assist in throwing the bridge". By this he meant to imply to Sir James that he felt himself entirely to be *acting under orders*. But unfortunately his extreme sensitiveness of disposition prompted him to express this implied remonstrance with such great delicacy that it lost its effect. For I question whether Sir James saw what was passing in his mind and what he intended to imply. Consequently though this letter had the effect of curing Sir James for a few hours to interfere less than he had done (he wrote a copy disclaiming all intention of interfering) – it failed to have any permanent effect, left matters as to the command precisely where they were and the next day Sir James was again issuing directions on all sides as if he had never resigned the command'.

By the evening of that day, September 20th, the whole force including the guns had crossed the Ganges, leaving three hundred men in the entrenchment for the defence of Cawnpore. Enemy opposition had been nominal. All was ready for the sweep forward to Lucknow – under divided command.

Havelock realised that his chief had already 'repented of his hasty generosity'. 'And I can say', wrote Harry in after years, 'that from this time this determination on Outram's part (to exercise the command while he divested himself of all responsibility by his ostensible resignation) became apparent, my father was never the same man. His false position preyed upon him night and day. In place of being prompt, decided and unhesitating he appeared to vacillate and falter, often when asked for orders saying, "You had better go to Sir James first", and otherwise showing that he felt himself hampered and shackled.

'And his was that peculiar form of sensitiveness of mind to which this underhand dealing, as he unquestionably considered it, was not only painful but injurious. He did not complain of it as he never complained of anything, but it rankled in his mind continually and soon began to tell on his health and spirits. Unfortunately his almost morbid regard for superior authority, coupled with the friendship that subsisted between Sir James and himself for so many years, restrained him from acting in this matter with the decision and firmness habitual to him and which a regard for his own reputation demanded. In fact he deliberately sacrificed his fame as a soldier to his desire to avoid the appearance of returning Sir James's professed generosity (which I will not undertake to say was not *bona fide* in *intention*, at the same time as it was fatally mischievous in practice) with coldness and ingratitude. I have no doubt that Colonel Tytler observed this difference in my father's carriage and mode of command as well as myself; in fact we have talked of it often since'.

AFTER HEAVY RAIN in the night Havelock's force moved forward from the Ganges bank early on September 21st.

The enemy were drawn up before the old camping ground at Mungalwar, with six guns behind an entrenchment covering the road – one of the first of their balls tore off half the trunk of a battery elephant which turned, bellowing with pain and rage, and charged the British gunners. Havelock's customary flanking movement, though expected by the enemy, soon had them in flight, the Volunteer Cavalry, now numbering over a hundred, being launched to follow up. Havelock, Outram and Harry joined in the charge, Harry killing five sepoys, Outram, on an enormous Australian waler, not unsheathing his sword but whacking right and left with a gold headed Malacca cane. Havelock, having wider responsibilities, fell back when the charge drew away into the open country. 'Havelock rode straight up to my guns', recalled Maude, 'his horse bleeding copiously from four or five tulwar cuts. As the poor beast commenced to stagger, the General quickly dismounted saying to me, with a proud but melancholy intonation: "that makes the sixth horse I have had killed under me!" and, sure enough, the animal died in a few minutes'.

Once more they passed through Unao and Busseratgunj and over the causeway, bivouacking for the night in an extensive serai beyond, since the tents, as Havelock had predicted, could not come up in time. The survivors of the earlier marches knew that at last Busseratgunj would no longer be their furthest point, and on September 22nd the advance continued through rain, the enemy making no stand, thus proving how swiftly Havelock could have reached Lucknow in July or August had he been given cavalry and the full number of promised troops. Towards evening, marching along the raised road between flooded land, they drew near the Sai River. Boats from the Ganges Canal had been brought with which to cross if the bridge was down, though some delay would be inevitable, but so overwhelmed was the enemy by the strength and speed of advance that the bridge was intact and undefended and that night the triumphant force bivouacked on both sides of the river. Lucknow was sixteen miles away. For the first time the men could hear the distant booming of the guns of the Residency, carried faintly on the wind. Havelock ordered a royal salute, hoping that despite the direction of the wind the sound would carry back to encourage the garrison.

On the morning of September 23rd fine weather returned and the march was unopposed until within a few miles of the city, when the cavalry scouts were fired on by field-guns.

Havelock rode forward to a low hill. Before him, not far distant, was the palace and walled park of the Alam Bagh beautiful with trees. Across the front lay the enemy, estimated at over ten thousand strong, their left resting on the Alam Bagh, their centre on higher ground through which ran the road, their right well protected by swamp.

Havelock sent the second brigade under Colonel Hamilton to turn the enemy right, the swamp involving a lengthy detour through ditches, ploughed fields and marshy ground, while Neill's, the leading brigade, held the front with Eyre's heavy battery brought into action on the enemy emplacements. Once the battle was fairly joined the sepoy line broke under the impact of the howitzers and the threat of Hamilton's flank march, though one of the Oudh field-guns remained, blocking any advance up the road, until Lieutenant Johnson and twenty native troopers of his Irregular Cavalry with great gallantry charged up a thousand yards of open road and silenced the gun. The Highlanders and the 5th Fusiliers cleared the buildings of the Alam Bagh and Outram at the head of the Volunteer Cavalry pursued the fleeing sepoys as far as the heavily defended Char Bagh bridge over the canal, beyond which lay the crowded mass of the great capital city, with its minarets, mosques and palaces. On his return a messenger from Cawnpore handed him the news that Delhi had fallen to Archdale Wilson, which he immediately read out to the men amid cheers.

Once again it rained and most of the men spent the night in the open, the tents being far behind, on a ridge beyond the Alam Bagh after Havelock had carefully placed picquets and guns against possible night attacks. The troops, runs Havelock's despatch, 'had been marching for three days under a perfect deluge of rain, irregularly fed, and badly housed in villages. It was thought necessary to pitch tents and permit them to halt on the 24th. The assault on the city was deferred until the 25th'. Outram brooked no denial of his recommendation in the matter.

Up early on the 24th, Havelock found that the enemy guns

hidden in the gardens near the Char Bagh bridge were too close for comfort in daylight, and withdrew his main line behind the ridge. The baggage convoy began to arrive about eleven a.m. straggling over a mile and a half of road, some of the wagons being caught by a surprise attack of cavalry which had worked round through the thick trees to the rear. The tents were pitched and, despite occasional annoyance from the guns in the garden which could not have been silenced except by a general action, September 24th passed quietly.

THE RESIDENCY COMPOUND lay around a low hill on the far side of the densely populated city. Less than a thousand yards beyond ran the River Gumti, crossed by the Iron Bridge a little way upstream. On the far side of the Gumti was comparatively open country. Havelock had long planned to reach the Residency by a wide detour, leaving the city on his left, marching through the Dilkusha Park, over the Gumti on its southward bend by use of the canal boats, through the open country to the Fyzabad road and so to the Iron Bridge, and the Stone Bridge higher up. This route would cost little in casualties; the river would protect Havelock's flank, he could always rely on trouncing the enemy in open country and he would avoid the murderous fire of loop-holed houses in tall, narrow streets where his men fought at a disadvantage.

Outram went on reconnaissance with the Volunteer Cavalry on the morning of September 24th and came back to report that the heavy rain of the past days had so flooded the land that not even light field-guns could be taken by the planned route, which was thus impossible. Havelock was disappointed but accepted the accuracy of Outram's judgment. Had they been able to wait three days the route might become practicable, but they understood the Residency's need to be pressing. 'I should have hoped from this plan great results', Havelock wrote afterwards to Marshman, 'but it was doomed never to be tried. On the 25th we went to work in quite a different way'.

To go direct across the Char Bagh bridge and up the Cawnpore Road through the centre of the city would be suicidal. A mere handful would reach the Residency alive. The third alternative was to force the Char Bagh bridge but immediately turn off the Cawnpore Road to the right, work through the lanes close to the canal and strike left through the area of palaces, courtyards and gardens where the density of the buildings was less, and thus to the Baillie Guard Gate which was part of the Residency defences.

At two p.m. on September 24th, in the Alam Bagh, Harry as DAAG went to his father to get divisional orders for the attack on Lucknow. Havelock sent him 'to take them from General Outram'. Harry went to Outram and said, rather pointedly, that his father had sent him to get the orders. This as Outram's chance to make plain once for all that these orders were no concern of his since he was under Havelock's command. Instead 'he acquiesced without a remark. I took down roughly Outram's orders for the attack on Lucknow the next day. This was at 2.30 p.m. on the 24th September 1857 in the centre room of the house at the Alam Bagh. I took this rough, then into the next room, drafted the order in full and then came back to Outram and read it out for his approval clause by clause'.

Not until late in the evening did Outram tell Havelock the plan of attack on which he had settled for the morrow. Havelock protested vigorously on one point: Outram wished to leave the heavy guns behind. Havelock, always a strong believer in artillery, foresaw that stiff positions might have to be forced. More especially since, when withdrawing the garrison as planned, there would be no reason against using the Iron Bridge and the Fyzabad road, re-crossing by bridge several miles below the city to return to the Alam Bagh; the heavy guns would be much needed. Outram accepted this decision.

HAVELOCK ROSE BEFORE dawn on September 25th and, as always, read his Bible and spent time in prayer. At sixty-two he faced the hardest day of his life. The whole force 'knew that we had a very nasty day's work in front of us' but Havelock had the full load of responsibility. This day was crucial. Throughout the previous ten weeks had he made a mistake or suffered a severe reverse he would have been able, if with difficulty, to redeem it. On this day, a mistake would be final – not merely for his reputation and, probably, his life, but for the garrison who had held out so long. They reported themselves 'down to our last biscuit', their ammunition was low and defeat of the relieving force, or even temporary reverse, would bring down on them an overwhelming assault.

The responsibility for their relief was his. Yet he was no longer his own master. The last word, whether of veto or of acquiescence lay with Outram, as the past ten days had made plain. For a man who, genius throughout his life, had flourished best when independent, his present position, nominally free and in reality fettered, was almost insupportable.

As at Jalalabad, at Cawnpore and Bithoor and all the battles between, he commended himself, and his troops, to 'the same kind Providence which watched over me'. Then he went to inspect the lines. Only forty-eight hours' rations and ammunition were to be taken. No followers were to come except cooks, doolie bearers and syces for the officers' horses. The tents and camp equipment, the main hospital and the baggage, the elephants and all but a few essential camels were to remain under the baggage guard within the walls of the Alam Bagh. The march was not to start until shortly after eight a.m. in order that the men should be well fed before fighting.

When all was in order, Havelock sat down to breakfast with William Hargood and Harry at a little table placed in the open field outside the Alam Bagh wall. The weather was clear and fine. Shortly before eight Outram rode up with his staff from the Alam Bagh and dismounting told Havelock that he had decided that it was advisable to make a slight alteration to the agreed plans – the two columns had been directed to reach the Char Bagh bridge by different routes, but Outram now wished that both should proceed up the road.

Maps were spread on the table and the generals were bent over them when a 9-pound shot from the battery near the Char Bagh, two thousand yards away, lobbed in straight at the table. It struck the ground five yards short, bounced over their heads and hit a gun bullock, ready limbered, a few dozen yards beyond. 'The shot dropped, completely spent, at the bullock's feet. But as we looked, a large dark lump swelled out on the poor beast's white flank, and in two or three seconds it quietly sank down and died'.

Neill's brigade, with Outram in personal command, led off at about 8.30 a.m. Havelock rode with Hamilton's brigade which was to pass through after Outram and Neill had forced the Char Bagh bridge and lead the assault into the city.

Within a few hundred yards Neill's brigade came under enemy musket and rifle fire from the gardens and sugar-cane on either side of the road and from two guns in front of a large yellow house. Outram received a flesh wound in the arm in the first few minutes. Owing to delay in the rear Havelock sent an order to halt; the infantry deployed and Maude engaged. 'It was indeed most fearful', wrote Shillock, a civilian volunteer, 'the round shot and grape literally tore up the road, cutting the brave fellows to pieces, while the bullets fell among them like a shower of hail. How I escaped I cannot tell'. When Havelock's galloper reappeared a few minutes later with orders to advance, one of Maude's gunners had lost a leg above the thigh, another 'had the whole of his stomach carried away by a round shot' and a third had had his head blown clean off.

Leaving the enemy at the yellow house to be dealt with by the troops behind, the assault column moved on. When the road turned sharp to the left to approach the Char Bagh bridge, visible three hundred yards in front, they ran into even more intense fire. Maude's battery unlimbered, but his leading gun received a murderous discharge of grape which killed or wounded the crew. Volunteers from the infantry were called for to serve it. The Char Bagh bridge lay over a deep, steep-sided canal. Six enemy guns, including a well entrenched 24-pounder sited direct across the bridge, defended the Lucknow side and on either flank were strong, loopholed barricaded houses from which came steady accurate musketry. At 150 yards Maude came into action. Outram took the 5th Fusiliers and disappeared into the gardens to the right to see if he could effectively enfilade the bridge. The Blue Cap riflemen spread out on the canal bank to the left to deal, unsuccessfully, with the fire from the loopholed houses. The road in front of the bridge was becoming a death trap.

Harry and Tytler came up with the leading men of the second brigade. 'Do something in the name of Heaven,' called out Maude. Harry saw 'that the fire was destroying two of Maude's guns which were opposed to it and would have made no impression on the enemy's superior artillery securely covered, if they had fired to Doomsday. There was nothing for it but a rush. Tytler, one of the finest and noblest hearted fellows that ever lived, agreed with me'. Harry rode across through the fire to Neill who was sheltering in a bay of the garden wall waiting for Outram, and urged an assault by the Blue caps. Neill replied, 'I am not in command. I cannot take the responsibility. And Outram must turn up soon.' In a rage Harry cantered back down the road as if to go to his father, turned, and after a suspiciously short interval rode up to Neill, saluted, and said, 'You are to carry the Bridge at once, sir!' 'Get the regiment together, then, and see it formed up,' replied Neill.

Without waiting for the regiment to form, Lieutenant Arnold of the Blue Caps with ten or a dozen of his men ran forward, with Harry and Tytler on their horses beside them. As they came on to the bridge the 24-pounder gun fired at point-blank range. Tytler crashed, his horse dead but himself unwounded. Arnold fell hit in the legs. All the men lay sprawled on the bridge or its approach, save Corporal Jakes and Harry, on his horse in front of the guns, waving his sword to encourage the rest of the Blue Caps to come on, a sitting target for every musket around. 'A sepoy within fifteen yards of me took careful aim at me – and shot me through the cap – the ball grazing my head and cutting off a bit of hair, but a merciful God spared my life'. The gun team were frantically reloading but just as Outram appeared on the canal bank higher up, the Blue Caps and some of the 84th rushed across the prostrate bodies on the bridge and carried the 24-pounder and the other guns under a storm of bullets from the houses. 'The thing was done – and we were *in* Lucknow.'[1]

As Tytler disengaged himself from his dead horse, two hidden guns on the near side of the bridge opened up from the right rear of the column as it moved forward to cross the canal. Tytler saw at once that this fire would bring the advance to a halt. He ran back, and Havelock coming up the road with the second brigade saw him, filthy and out of breath, emerge from the smoke to ask leave to deal with the guns, which could not be reached by artillery. Havelock gave him the 90th Light Infantry and he disappeared again into the trees where the guns lay.

Reaching the bridge Havelock ordered Harry to supervise the crossing of the baggage train – doolies, camels and wagons – while the 78th Highlanders acted as rearguard until all should be across. Placing himself at the head of the column, which had turned to the right beside the canal as ordered, Havelock rode forward into Lucknow, Outram and Neill near him. By the route planned, they had nearly two miles to go.

They advanced slowly through 'long narrow lanes with straggling lines of houses and mud huts' the heavy guns frequently sinking in the wet sand of the road. Opposition was now tri-

---

[1]For this action Sir James Outram insisted that Havelock again recommend Harry for the Victoria Cross. By the time the matter was dealt with by Sir Colin Campbell in 1858, Harry's award for Cawnpore had been gazetted and the 64th were already complaining; Campbell did not recommend a bar to Harry's VC. Harry tried unsuccessfully to get Tytler a VC for this and other actions. Maude received the Cross for his gallantry at Char Bagh and elsewhere.

fling, the route evidently being unexpected, and they debouched into a more open area with the cupolas of the Begum's Palace shimmering on the left and, a little later, a tall white minaret on the right and the King's stables opposite. Under the turreted wall of the Sikandar Bagh their road turned sharp left.

Ahead, on the right as the column moved forward, lay the Moti Mahal with its magnificent pearl-shaped dome while on the left, on higher ground, was the strongly built house, 'a large native building in the shape of a castle' and surrounded by a moat, which had been used as the mess of the 32nd. Beyond and behind the Mess House, a serried mass of courts and buildings, lay the Kaisar Bagh, palace of the former kings of Oudh. As the leading units approached the Moti Mahal, three-quarters of a mile had still to be covered to the Residency. It was already well into the afternoon.

A tremendous fire developed from a battery in the Kaisar Bagh, 'under which', as Havelock described it, 'nothing could live', supported by musketry from the 32nd Mess House. From then on the column had one long battle, each step taking them deeper in among large buildings, garden walls and narrow streets. There could be no attempt at carrying each enemy post as they reached it. The task was not to capture Lucknow but to get through to the Residency. Every step now was opposed. Eyre's heavy guns proved their worth, twice silencing, though temporarily, the battery in the Kaisar Bagh. A high wall gave protection for a while, but Tytler, who had rejoined the main column, fell desperately wounded.

They approached a narrow bridge over a nullah dominated by the fire from the Mess House, and defended by a four-gun battery beyond which wreaked havoc on the column. 'I never saw before or since', wrote Captain Willis of the 84th, 'such a frightful fire as this four-gun battery poured down the road, grape and roundshot'. A rush carried the bridge and very slowly the British force, every minute losing men by death and wounds, edged forward into the inferno. 'A regular fight', as Captain

Willis described it, 'at every cross street guns in position, storming and taking them, and running the gauntlet through streets, the houses of which were all loopholed and full of men... One was worked up to such a state of frenzy and excitement, *nothing* was thought of but our poor countrymen here'.

The battle had become confused and almost impossible to control, yet a wrong turning would have been fatal and constant delays occurred while Havelock, with Outram and Lieutenant Moorsom who knew the ground intimately, consulted the map. Beyond the Kaisar Bagh, where men had to run through the fire to reach the safety of a high wall, Havelock had a horse shot under him once more, but, as usual, he was unhurt. 'A scene of great confusion ensued when we halted – guns and infantry mixed up, soldiers wandering in search of their companions, and the wounded in the doolies carried here and there without orders'.

In the best of circumstances this slogging through an enemy-held city would have been terrible. But the Havelock touch was missing. Left to himself, his wits still as sharp as before the difficulties with Outram, he might have found another, unexpected way. As it was, even subordinate officers noticed the difference. Maude, normally an admirer of Havelock and knowing nothing of the hidden circumstances, wrote that Outram 'having voluntarily subordinated his rank could not take any independent steps without involving a grave breach of discipline, while the General who was nominally in command took no initiative action whatever'.

The Highlanders from the Char Bagh bridge emerged, unexpectedly by a different route. When the column had gone on down the lanes and the baggage began crossing the bridge under Harry's directions, after a short interval the enemy had brought up fresh guns. The Highlanders had covered themselves with glory but as the last wagon crossed the bridge and turned right, so an orderly now told Havelock near the Kaisar Bagh, Harry had fallen badly wounded. He had been carried on in a doolie but the orderly could say nothing of his wound for the Highlanders had been parted from the baggage and rearguard.

Darkness was falling. Beyond the open space, partly sheltered by buildings, where the column was re-forming and the generals already were, a courtyard opened on to a street which led up to the Baillie Guard, only five hundred yards away. Every foot was covered by muskets or field-guns.

Outram now urged on Havelock a halt for the rearguard to close up, and the wounded and stragglers scattered almost the length of the march. Havelock understood that he wanted to halt for the night; 'Sir James wished to put the troops in a palace and rest them; but I strongly represented the necessity of reinforcing the garrison lest it should be attacked and surprised in the darkness'. Outram said afterwards that he had wished only to halt a few hours. As an alternative he offered to try, from his close knowledge of Lucknow, to lead the column through the back streets, but he urged a halt. The men however, were already murmuring at the delay, 'so great was their eagerness to reach our desired goal, the Baillie Guard'.

Havelock said they should go on at once. 'There is the street,' he said, 'we see the worst – we shall be slated, but we can push through and get it over.' 'Then,' said Outram, describing the incident years later, 'my temper got a little the better of me and I replied, "Let us go on then, in God's name!" I have often since asked myself whether I should not then and there have resumed command; and whether I should not have said, "Havelock, we have virtually reached the Residency and I now resume"'. 'It was a foolish thing,' he said at another time, referring to his waiver of command, 'sentiment had obscured duty. Every man should carry out the task assigned to him. I do not know that I could not have got through the streets of Lucknow with less loss of life. At any rate, I ought to have tried what I could do'. But had Outram held to the spirit of the waiver instead of interfering at every step Havelock might have fought the whole battle differently.

The advance being decided on, the Highlanders were given the van, the Sikhs to follow. Havelock mounted another horse and with Outram, Charley Havelock and Lieutenant Hudson, both on Outram's staff, placed himself at the head. They rode forward in the twilight, through the courtyard and out through the archway into the street. A devastating fire opened from the houses on both sides. They 'had to pass under the very walls, while the rebels on the walls hurled down stones and bricks and even spat at our fellows, a fierce fire being kept up at the loop-holes'. On they went, 'under a shower of balls from the houses on each side... a long, wide street with sheets of fire shooting out from the houses', bagpipes skirling, up the hill towards the Baillie Guard. They could hear cheering in front but the fire from the Residency was mingled in the appalling din of the street fight. 'On we charged', wrote Havelock, 'through streets of loopholed houses, fired at perpetually, and over trenches cut in the road'.

They saw the Baillie Guard, a strong but battered bastion of dull red stone 'with folding doors completely riddled with roundshot and musket-balls', figures jumping about and cheering on the rampart. A small opening lay to the left side, half blocked by a low mud wall over which was the muzzle of a gun. As the generals came on, bullets whistling about them, the gun was dragged back from within. Hairy, filthy white men and loyal sepoys pushed their heads over the wall, yelling to them with joy, pulling them in and over the wall, slapping them joyfully on the back, laughing and cheering.

The gates were thrown open and, wrote Martin Gubbins, the senior civilian of the garrison, 'the stream of soldiers entered, heated, worn and dusty; yet they looked robust and healthy, contrasted with the forms and faces within. Nothing could exceed their enthusiasm. The Highlanders stopped every one they met and with repeated questions and exclamations of "Are you one of them?" – "God bless you!" – "We thought to have found only your bones", bore them back towards Dr Fayrer's house, into which the General had entered.' 'The state of joyful confusion and excitement was beyond all description', wrote Mrs Harris, wife of the chaplain of the garrison, 'the big, rough, bearded soldiers were seizing the little children out of our arms, kissing them with tears running down their cheeks, and thanking God that they had come in time to save them from the fate of those at Cawnpore. We were all rushing about to give the poor fellows drinks of water, for they were all perfectly exhausted, and tea was made down in the tyekhana, of which a large party of officers partook without milk or sugar, but we had nothing to give them to eat. Everyone's tongue seemed going at once with so much to ask and to tell and the faces of strangers beamed on each other like those of dear friends and brothers'.

While Outram had his wounds dressed – Dr Fayrer put him to bed at once – Colonel John Inglis bore off Havelock to dinner. 'I was standing outside our door', Mrs Inglis wrote in her diary, 'when Ellicock came rushing in for John's sword and a few minutes later he (John) came to us accompanied by a short, quiet-looking grey-haired man whom I knew at once to be General Havelock. He shook hands with me and said he feared we had suffered a great deal'. Then, somewhat to Havelock's surprise in view of their circumstances as he believed them, they regaled him 'as their deliverer', 'not only with beef cutlets, but with mock-turtle soup and champagne. I had little relish for delicacies, for you can conceive my anxiety about Harry'.

DURING THE NIGHT Moorsom brought in the guns of the main column which had not been able to cross the trenches in the street, finding a way through the palaces and courtyards, the enemy strangely quiet once they had seen that the relieving force and the garrison had joined hands. The wounded, except for some that Johnson had brought in during the night on led horses of the Irregular Cavalry, and the rearguard were still cut off, back beyond the Kaisar Bagh. Harry was with them.

Next morning, Bensley Thornhill, Mary's husband, offered

to go out with an escort to find Harry and the others and bring them in. On his way back, guiding the string of doolies through courts and back passages, he took a wrong turning and led them into a square of enemy occupied houses; Neill had been killed there the night before. They met a murderous fire and the terrified bearers flung down the doolies and left the wounded to be massacred. Thornhill turned back to stop the doolies which were not yet in the square and was hit under the eye while another ball smashed his right arm, but he regained the Residency alive.

Harry, his left arm badly broken by the wound at Char Bagh, and a wounded Highlander lying with him, were in the leading doolie and would have been shot or burned to death had it not been for the bravery of Private Ward of the 78th who forced the bearers to go on and brought them through; he received the Victoria Cross. Nearly fifty wounded were massacred, nine survivors of the escort, under Surgeon Home, holding out in a house for the rest of the day and the next night until rescued at dawn on the 27th. By then, the whole of the rearguard and the rest of the guns had been brought in without further casualty.

Lucknow had been saved. 'Rarely has a commander', wrote the Governor-General in announcing the news in a General Order of October 2nd, 'been so fortunate as to relieve by his success so many aching hearts, or to reap so rich a reward of gratitude as will deservedly be offered to Brigadier-General Havelock and his gallant band, wherever their triumph shall be known'.

17

In Lucknow

General Outram resumed command on the morning of September 26th.

To the garrison, Outram's generosity had provided formal expression of that which they had always felt – that Havelock and no other was their deliverer. It was not merely the final rescue that counted. His name had been in their hearts and on their lips since the start of the siege. 'It is impossible', wrote Martin Gubbins in his diary, 'to over-estimate the value of the services rendered by that gallant officer and the army of heroes which he commanded, at that most critical period of the mutinies, the months of July and August. In braving the inclemency of the season they, as well as the army of Delhi, achieved what it was till then believed that no Englishman or other Europeans could do; and in putting to flight with their small numbers the masses of disciplined troops opposed to them, supported by so powerful an artillery, they taught all British soldiers to despise the foe; and thereafter, whatever the disparity of numbers, they always advanced to assured victory. A corresponding terror was struck into the ranks of the mutineer. As for our garrison, we owe our safety under Providence, I feel assured, to the exploits performed by Havelock's army; for it was the knowledge of what they had effected, viz. the repeated defeats of the Nana and the occupation of Cawnpore, that kept up the heart of our native troops, and prevented their deserting us'.

The relieving force had lost 535 men killed and wounded, and the enemy showed no signs of departing. Outram discovered, in the days following the relief, that the garrison were unable to produce sufficient carts for an evacuation. An attempt to capture the Iron Bridge, which would give access to the open country, failed, and it began to seem that the plan to withdraw the survivors of the garrison could not be carried out. The decisive factor was a surprising discovery. Outram and Havelock had been, as Gubbins wrote, 'under the impression that the garrison was on the point of starvation and that we had been reduced to our last ration. They congratulated themselves, therefore, greatly on having relieved us before it was too late. Gradually, and not until much enquiry had been made, was their mistake, and the actual condition of the garrison in respect of food discovered.' Sir Henry Lawrence as he lay dying in the early days of the siege had urged his successor to keep a daily tally of food and supplies but on the death of the commissariat officers soon afterwards the practice had dropped, and Inglis was unaware of large stores of grain laid in by Lawrence. Thus he had sent his piteous appeals to Havelock. It was now realised that there was sufficient basic food to maintain the greatly augmented garrison for two months on a reduced ration. By the first week of October Outram had decided to hold out in Lucknow until Sir Colin Campbell, with powerful forces now landing from England, should come up country for a final rescue.

The Residency compound was a considerable area, somewhat hilly, of houses, gardens, streets and buildings centring around Sir Henry Lawrence's mansion on the tower of which, night and day since the start of the siege, 'the banner of England flew'. Every building was battered but most, having thick stone walls, were still basically sound. A strong system of earthworks and barricaded houses formed the outer and inner rings of defence. By a series of local actions Outram now extended the defended area to almost three times the size of the previous Residency compound, seizing a length of the river bank, the Palaces of Furrid Buksh and Chota Munzil and some gardens and houses beyond. He then reorganised his command, giving Inglis the original garrison and Havelock the extended territory outside. They then settled down to wait for Campbell.

'We have been more closely blockaded than at Jalalabad',

wrote Havelock to Hannah over a month later, 'we eat a reduced ration of artillery bullock beef, chapatties[1] and rice; but tea, coffee, sugar, soap and candles are unknown luxuries'. All these things, and much more, had been brought from Cawnpore but left at the Alam Bagh in expectation of a quick return and could not now be brought in. Havelock had set up his headquarters at the house of Mr Ommaney the Judicial Commissioner, who had been killed early in the siege. 'Gubbins sent to invite me and all my Staff to come and live in his better house. To this I would not consent, but commended to his care my two wounded officers, Col Tytler and Harry and he has cared for them as if they were his children. I dine with him once a week and he keeps me supplied with excellent sherry, without which it would have gone ill with me, for I find it not so easy to starve at sixty-three as at forty-seven'. Besides lack of food there was in Lucknow, curiously, an added reminder of Jalalabad; Dr Brydon, the survivor of the Kabul massacre, was lying wounded in the Residency hospital.

Havelock's days slipped into a routine. Soon after daybreak he would set off in the faded uniform which was the 'single suit' he had with him and inspect, on foot with his staff, the whole perimeter of his command in the palaces and gardens, a distance of over two miles. On his return he would call in at Gubbins's to report to Outram and see Harry. 'The enemy fire at us perpetually with guns, mortars and musketry', he wrote, 'but our casualties are not very numerous'. There were mining and counter-mining and continual alerts but compared with the past months, both for the Residency garrison and Havelock's men, the exertion was a little less grievous. Later in the day, Havelock, and Outram, would make a round of the hospitals. 'The scenes in this hospital are past belief', wrote Captain Spurgin in his diary, 'two hundreds and upwards lying side by side, sick and wounded, and our poor good ladies are walking

---

[1] Native bread, not easily digested by Europeans. The British bakers had been left at the Alam Bagh.

about bathing the heads of the sick and soothing the dying. God bless them for it... No medicines, no clean rags to dress wounds, so but few can recover'. Bensley Thornhill, his arm amputated, his skull injured, 'lingered many days and then died in the hospital, leaving Mary a young widow. Their only infant had died some time before'. Thus Mary had been rescued by her uncle only to lose her husband in the rescue of his son.

No longer with heavy responsibilities Havelock had considerable leisure. He spent much of it reading. Gubbins had the best library in the Residency and Havelock was free of it and Harry would keep him supplied. 'I have searched carefully through Mr Gubbins's library', runs a note from Harry, 'but cannot find another volume of military biography. If there is another some one has it out. I can send you either a volume of Napier or Gurwood, but don't find anything else you would like. Which shall it be?' 'This passion for history', comments Harry, 'especially military history, clung to him to the last, and this was his only resource during the last weeks of his life when the command had been taken from him'.

His greatest pleasure was to be with Harry. Harry's arm, weak as he was from exposure and loss of blood, and suffering like the rest from under-nutrition, was slow to heal and he was unfit for duty. Havelock urged him to write an account of the campaign, and Harry filled a notebook with jottings. His book was to be given the resounding and suggestive title *Magna est Veritas – et prevalabit*; but the effort to write was too great, and the book went no further than the list of contents.

AS NEVER BEFORE, father and son were drawn to each other. And, at last, in these days in the Residency at Lucknow, occurred the event for which Havelock and Hannah had so long prayed: 'the great work of conversion in Harry's heart'. Harry's resistance to Christ broke down and, following his father thirty-four years earlier, following his brother Jos and his sisters, he gave his heart and will, as his father had so often urged, 'to the God that governs the earth and the Saviour who died for sinners'.

'Take God for your Father and Christ for your Counsellor and Friend', Havelock had besought Harry again and again. 'Regard Jesus Christ as He is, the Friend of sinners; come to Him'. 'There is no middle path... He must have your whole heart.' And now it was done. Havelock's cup of happiness ran over.

When Harry had first come to India as a young officer nearly ten years before, he had considered his father's Christian faith an unnecessary luxury. With all the intolerance of youth he shared the belief that a good Christian cannot be a good soldier and was ashamed of his father's taste for prayer meetings and Bible readings. Even in Persia Harry, though less intolerant, thought his father's insistence on the need of conversion a mere personal fancy, of no close concern to himself, despite Havelock's urging. During the past three months, however, since the day when they marched together from Benares, Havelock had become Harry's hero. Harry was good enough a soldier to recognise military brilliance when he saw it, and it had been the greatest experience of his life to be in such close companionship, 'consulted in everything' with one who was, he was now convinced, the foremost soldier of the age. Harry was aware also how much he had hindered Havelock by impatience and stormy rages and this humbled him and made him realise his need of the inward power which his father so manifestly had. Yet deepest of all lay his admiration for Havelock's courage; not mere physical courage, for Harry himself and many a man as impious as he had that, but moral courage, the courage which had enabled Havelock to turn back at Busseratgunj, and to keep his heart high and his men together when all was black; and, later, to accept full responsibility and go forward without complaint or reproach when Outram was making his task so dangerously difficult. All this, Harry knew, sprang from his father's trust in Christ 'as Counsellor and Friend'. And Harry no longer had the impudence to deny that the One his father needed, he needed too. Intellectual mistrust, of which he had once made much, vanished away; in Lucknow they were faced with reality. Harry Havelock knew perfectly well that he was a sinner. He knew that Christ had died for sinners and lived to forgive and empower them. And at last he yielded.

OCTOBER DRAGGED INTO November. Flies bloated with human blood settled everywhere. The stenches were awful, especially where the enemy had left bodies of their slain outside the defences, lightly covered with earth. 'Lucknow', Henry Moorsom wrote home shortly afterwards, 'ought not to lessen your opinion of us, "so noble, so enduring, so devoted, and so brave", for all these were more fully exhibited there, and without a gloomy face or a grumble too, even when affairs looked gloomiest and the poor fellows were smoking the bark and leaves of trees, drinking only water, and giving six shillings for two pounds of flour. In fact, they starved on three-quarter rations of meat and flour alone; worked like men working for their own and others' lives; were not a night off duty; perished with cold in their scanty summer clothing; and did all, and suffered all, with a cheerful face, inspired by the General whom that two months killed'. For Havelock was slowly getting weaker. Harry, sick himself, did not notice anything serious. 'If he suffered,' he said, 'he suffered uncomplainingly for I was not aware that there was anything wrong with him.' Some, however, were. 'Poor old gentleman', wrote Johnson of the Irregular Horse to his mother, 'I noticed a great change in him about a fortnight before he died'.

On November 10th Havelock was writing a note to Harry about his book. 'Gubbins wrote me this morning about his publication and I have promised to ask John Marshman to carry his work through the press. I am very glad he is going to be the historian, for a gentleman of the Civil Service might be considered more impartial than one of us. I would wish you to give him the most ample information not withholding anything. But this will not prejudice your own publication in any way... I intend to answer Neill's article myself if I can get hold of the paper, and perhaps draw up a little precis when I can get at my correspondence, but not to publish more than a letter in the *Friend*. My advice is, be most explicit with Gubbins but do not refrain from writing yourself. It is at the least good practice for a young man... It would hardly be right for me to write as I was in confidential correspondence with the C-in-C. But there is no reason for your silence'.

That day Kavanagh, a Eurasian clerk in the garrison, was already on his adventurous way, disguised as a native, with a letter from Outram to Campbell, now only a march from the Alam Bagh. Two days later, on November 12th, through binoculars, a semaphore was seen on the roof of the Alam Bagh. The semaphore which Outram had prepared was immediately hoisted on the Residency tower and communication established. Campbell signalled that he would advance on November 14th, making, in hope of avoiding heavy casualties, a wide sweep to the right of the city, through the Dilkusha Park and then by La Martinière boys' school (Outram, as before, having dissuaded against any attempt to cross the Gumti and approach by the Fyzabad road[1]) to the Sikandar Bagh and thus by Havelock's old route. He would be with them, Campbell promised, on the 15th.

To co-operate, Outram decided that Havelock's force should push outwards to seize two buildings nearer the Moti Mahal, thus distracting the enemy while lessening the gap between garrison and relievers, as soon as Campbell reached the Sikandar Bagh. In preparation, mines were tunnelled under the enemy defences on November 13th and were primed.

Throughout November 14th heavy gun fire was heard on the outskirts of the city. In the afternoon Campbell's semaphore was seen on the high crown of La Martinière. On the 15th Campbell was evidently held up by lack of supplies, for it was not until nearly dark that the semaphore waggled and waved the

---

[1]Yet Outram used this route with great success when acting under Campbell at the final capture of Lucknow in March 1858.

signal 'Advance tomorrow'. The night was noisy with the crash and roar of rockets (brought by the Naval Brigade) and balloon shells. Half the city seemed on fire and a great blaze had been lit at Campbell's orders on the plateau.

Early on the morning of Monday November 16th, Outram and Havelock went across to the Chota Munzil palace and sat in an upper storey to watch so far as they could Sir Colin Campbell's advance, that when the time came they might launch their own attack. As the sun came up, smoke drifted across the city and gun fire and an occasional rattle of musketry showed that Campbell was on the move. At about eleven a.m. they realised that his troops were approaching the Sikandar Bagh and through their glasses the generals could soon see the British guns opening on the mansion and garden. Havelock sent the order to detonate the mines. A feeble explosion showed that the day's wait had damped the charges, and the enemy defences had to be breached by gunfire.

At length Outram was able to send Havelock down to launch the planned assault. Havelock's description of the attack, written that night in his official report, was characteristic: 'At half past three the advance sounded. It was impossible to describe the enthusiasm with which this signal was received by the troops. Pent up in inaction for upwards of six weeks, and subjected to constant attacks, they felt that the hour of retribution and glorious exertion had returned. Their cheers echoed through the courts of the palace, responsive to the bugle sound, and on they rushed to assured victory. The enemy could nowhere withstand them. In a few minutes the whole of the buildings were in our possession and have since been armed with cannon, and steadily held against all attacks. It will be seen by the enclosed return that the loss has been small'.

When darkness fell Campbell's and Outram's forces still had not joined hands. At first light on November 17th, watching from the Chota Munzil, Outram and Havelock saw a regimental colour hoisted under fire, on the pinnacle of a building beyond the Moti Mahal and the 32nd Mess House, which now alone were between the two British forces.

The battle was soon in full blast, with a three-hour bombardment of the Mess House by Campbell's artillery. When the bombardment was over Campbell's infantry moved to the assault and Outram and Havelock at length saw a colour hoisted on one of the Mess House turrets. It was knocked down by enemy fire but raised again, and for a third time. Shortly afterwards Campbell's men were in the Moti Mahal opposite, though the intervening space was still swept by enemy guns in the Kaisar Bagh.

Only a series of courts and passages now separated Outram and Havelock from the advancing troops.

The generals came down from the Chota Munzil and prepared to go over to meet Campbell – on foot, since all horses in the garrison were starved. Moorsom had already got across through the fire and had returned with two officers from the relieving force. Harry, his arm in a sling, came with Havelock. William Hargood was close, as always. 'We had to pass,' wrote Harry, 'through narrow passages and very difficult and broken ground. Here my dear father was as active as a younger man. He was worn and pale as all in the garrison were, but apparently in good health, fit for any bodily exertion'. As they walked 'through a narrow passage only ten feet wide with high walls on both sides, a shell came through the wall on the right, struck that on the left, rebounded and remaining for a few seconds in the middle of the road, burst. The concussion knocked off my dear father's cap and threw him to the ground'. Harry had a moment's horror that at last, at the very end and after narrow escapes innumerable, his father had been wounded. 'But to the surprise of every one he was unhurt... the narrowest perhaps of all the escapes he ever experienced.'

They reached the Moti Mahal. Palisser and Drummer Pearson helped Havelock climb through a low breach in the wall. Soon he was surrounded by Campbell's men, among whom he saw privates of his own regiment, the 53rd. A brigadier, Hope Grant, came up to congratulate him on the relief. Havelock 'went up to the men', recorded Grant in his journal, 'who immediately flocked around him and gave him three hearty cheers. This was too much for the fine old General – his breast heaved with emotion, and his eyes filled with tears. He turned to the men and said: "Soldiers, I am happy to see you; soldiers, I am happy to think you have got into this place with a smaller loss than I had". Hearing this I asked him what he supposed our loss amounted to. He answered that he had heard it estimated at 80, and was much surprised and grieved when I told him we had lost about 43 officers and 450 men killed and wounded'.

Sir Colin Campbell was outside the castle-like Mess House on the far side of the open space, twenty-five yards swept by fire from the Kaisar Bagh. The Generals and their staffs, with Hope Grant, prepared to run across.

Hardly had they started when Harry fell. Colonel Napier and another of Outram's staff were hit also, but Outram and Havelock untouched. Hargood, as soon as he saw Havelock was in safety, 'ran back through that terrible fire' to Harry 'and *returned again* through it that he might comfort his general by telling him I was only slightly hurt'.

As the generals approached, Sir Colin Campbell courteously lifted his cap and held out his hand. 'How do you do, Sir James?' he said. And, to Havelock's unfeigned excitement, 'How do you do, *Sir Henry*?'.

18

Triumph

Sir Colin Campbell having decided that Lucknow should be temporarily abandoned, on the evening of November 19th the withdrawal began with the evacuation of the women, children and wounded.

For Havelock the two days since the meeting of the generals had passed in unmitigated delight and excitement. He now knew that not only had he been created Knight Commander of the Bath but promoted Major-General. Campbell had brought a letter from the Duke of Cambridge which pleased Havelock greatly. 'Though not personally acquainted with you', wrote the Duke, 'I cannot deprive myself of the pleasure, as Head of the Army, of informing you that it has given me the greatest possible satisfaction to recommend to Her Majesty that you should be at once made a Major-General in consequence of the brilliant deeds in which you have been and are at this moment engaged. Her Majesty has most cordially responded to the recommendation which indeed, I may add, she herself suggested, and you will find yourself gazetted to the substantive rank as above stated'.

The unstinted congratulations of officers and men, both for his own sake and because every soldier of the force was honoured in the awards to their general, made pleasure all the more complete. The rewards, as he wrote to Hannah on November 19th, were 'for my first three battles; I have fought nine since'. The public had not been slow to express dissatisfaction with the War Office's paltry £100 per annum, and when the Government at length decided to take proper note of Havelock's services it had done so handsomely.

While Havelock in Lucknow was receiving congratulations on his knighthood, in England the news of the September Relief had only lately been received, with national rejoicing, and he could not know that on this very day, November 19th, Lord Palmerston was writing to Hannah to say the Queen was granting a baronetcy, Parliament a few days later voting a pension of £1,000 a year for the lives of Havelock and Harry. What he did know, however, was that his name was now a household word in England. Campbell had brought in newspapers, and they were full of Havelock. For one whose services so long had gone unsung this public acclamation was delectable. More especially, he realised that the nation had taken him to their hearts as the Christian general, the Christian hero. His plain unvarnished witness, his long endurance in face of disappointment and calumny had received the reward he most coveted – a national exaltation of Christ.

Harry, his left arm wounded for the second time, was being sent out after dark with the rest of the disabled and the women and children, to the Dilkusha Park. 'And so the doolie came for me about seven', he wrote to his mother, 'and in passing my father's door I had it stopped to go in and see him. He was sitting with his back to the door I came in by, reading a volume of Macaulay by a dim light – all alone. I shall never forget the tender accent and the loving look as he turned round and said, "My poor boy!" How I should have hung on that parting if I had known it was the last time I should see him as then. As it was, we expected to meet again in the ordinary course of things in a day or two at most and then he showed me no symptoms of being unwell'.

William Hargood, knowing that the convoy would come under fire from enemy guns in the Kaisar Bagh, insisted on accompanying Harry; 'against all my protestations Hargood walked out by my side making the march on foot in the bitter cold night, and then sleeping on the cold ground till daylight came and he could ride back and tell my father I was safe'.

When Hargood returned to Havelock on the morning of the 20th he found him bothered with an attack of diarrhœa and went to find Dr Collinson, Havelock's staff surgeon, who came with medicine which appeared to settle the trouble. During the day, while Peel's guns from time to time were bombarding the Kaisar Bagh in preparation for the general withdrawal, Havelock felt no worse, but in the evening he began passing blood and suffering other symptoms of dysentery. Hargood stayed all night with him and at dawn rode down to the Dilkusha to get arrowroot and sago from Campbell's commissariat to ease Havelock's bowel pains, and Harry 'first heard the sad tidings of my father's illness'.

During November 21st, punctuated by gunfire as Peel covered the withdrawal of the treasure and heavy material, Havelock grew weaker and it was decided to remove him to the Dilkusha where, on the higher ground, the air was better, and he would be further from the head-splitting cracks and vibrations of the guns. The journey was made at dusk. Havelock lying in a doolie which jolted and swayed over the rough ground of the four-mile march to the Dilkusha. Here in the darkness, torches flaming behind them, Harry met him 'faint and moving with difficulty but still able to stand with assistance'.

In an ordinary private's tent, all that was available, Havelock lay down again, the doolie serving as bed, with Harry and Hargood sitting near ready for anything he might want.

He slept better and in the morning of November 22nd was cheerful and talked happily to the two boys, though his voice was weak. The change of air seemed to have done good, yet Havelock told them, to Harry's distress, that he knew he was dying. During the morning a party of the enemy attacked the Dilkusha and bullets fell close to the tent; when the attack was beaten off Havelock was moved to a safer area deeper within the park. Some of the mail which Campbell had left at the Alam Bagh was brought in and Havelock received a whole batch of letters from Hannah and the family in Europe. Harry marvelled at his patience, feeling that if instead of his father he had been lying there he would have chafed and complained that the long looked-for reunion and the enjoyment together of a nation's plaudits were being snatched away.

Hope Grant, the brigadier who, in the Moti Mahal, had been first to congratulate Havelock, came in the cool of the day 'to visit him in his affliction and say a few kind words of comfort. Havelock was lying', wrote Grant, 'in a miserable doolie under some trees, and on my asking him how he felt himself, he said, "the hand of death is upon me. God Almighty has seen fit to afflict me for some good purpose"'.

That night he slept little, and Harry and Hargood maintained their devoted vigil. From the Residency the garrison was withdrawing, Inglis, the last to leave, closing the gates of the Baillie Guard as the clock struck midnight, the enemy remaining unawares and quiet.

Early in the morning of November 23rd Martin Gubbins sought out Havelock to see how he was. 'I was directed', he wrote, 'to a common soldier's tent which was pitched near the one in which we had found shelter. Entering it, I found the General's aide-de-camp, Lieut Hargood, and his medical attendant, Dr Collinson, lying down. They whispered to me in mournful accents the grievous news that Sir Henry's case was worse, and pointed to where he lay. It was in a doolie, which had been brought inside the tent, and served as a bed. The curtain on my side was down. I approached, and found young Havelock seated on the further side, upon the ground by his dying father. His wounded arm still hung in a sling, but with his other he supplied all his father's wants. They told me that the General would allow no one to render him any attendance but his son. I saw that to speak was impossible, and sorrowfully withdrew'. Dr Fayrer had now reached the Dilkusha and, as he noted in his diary, 'I was asked to see him in consultation by his staff surgeon and found him very ill'.

As the day drew on Havelock grew steadily weaker, his malady, as Harry wrote, 'acute dysentery which his constitution, enfeebled to the last degree by the privations which for two months he had shared with the humblest soldier under his command, had not strength to withstand'. He could no longer read but could still speak. He dictated to Harry a list of his funded property. Harry read to him from the 'daily Bible' and the hymn book which had gone with him everywhere. Friends came in – Tytler, Hamilton, as many as the doctor would allow – and Harry heard him murmur repeatedly, 'I die happy and contented'. The sun beat down beyond the shade where the tent was pitched. The parakeets screeched in the eucalyptus trees. In the tent there was peace. Harry and all who called could see without question that for Havelock there was no fear or gloom in prospect of death. And he was dying, as Harry wrote, 'as much in his country's cause as if he had been struck down on the battlefield; and how could a soldier die better than with sympathising comrades surrounding him, with the grateful plaudits of his countrymen ringing in his ears, and the just confidence that his soul would rest with God'.

Sir Colin Campbell was at La Martinière but in the evening Outram came. Havelock received him with 'a tenderness like that of a brother. He told me he was dying, and spoke from the fulness of his honest heart of the feelings which he bore towards me, and of the satisfaction with which he looked back to our past intercourse and service together, which had never been on a single occasion marred by a disagreement of any kind, nor embittered by an angry word'. Harry, remembering all that had passed, and knowing his father's utter truthfulness, was humbled and amazed by this proof of love. Then Havelock said to Outram: 'for forty years I have endeavoured so to rule my life that when death came I might face it without fear'.

During the night, still lying in his one faded uniform, he scarcely slept though suffering little, and his mind clear. When the thirst was bad he would call and Harry would bring him water, his father smiling weakly, abundantly happy that at last they were one in heart and spirit. Once, at about two in the morning, when Harry had fallen asleep, 'worn out by the pain of my wound and the incessant watching of three days and nights – and for a moment I did not hear when my father called – Hargood was up in an instant though lying at the far end of the tent and woke me. Though my father wished no one near him but me and he was therefore denied the pleasure of attending his wants the dear lad could lie awake watching'. Daylight came. Havelock called faintly, 'Harry, Harry'. As Harry answered Havelock looked up, smiling. 'Harry,' he said, 'see how a Christian can die!'

Outside there was bustle, for this was the day when the force were to move to the Alam Bagh. At about eight o'clock Harry and Hargood noticed a sudden change. Sitting down on the doolie Harry gently lifted his father's head and shoulders and held him in his arms. An hour and a half passed. 'His end was so peaceful that I hardly knew when life was extinct.'

At half-past nine, on this Monday, 24th November 1857, Harry laid back the body. 'His end was that of a just man made perfect', so Harry expressed his thoughts to his mother, 'God send that when that day comes to every one of us it may find us equally prepared'.

WHEN THE NEWS was known to the force, it brought, in Major North's words, 'sorrow and consternation to every heart, even to the coldest. Firm and decided, courteous, urbane and gentle', wrote North in his journal, 'he united the fire and spirit of the warrior to the temperance and moderation of the Christian. His every action was ruled by the strictest sense of duty, his valour was only equalled by his prudence, and his goodness was transcendant. But no praise can do justice to motives such as his.'

They were already on the move. Harry had the body lifted in the doolie as it lay. As he walked beside it the three miles to the Alam Bagh he thought of his mother, of them all: 'who will ever fill to us the place of that dear Friend and Adviser we have lost!'.

In the garden of the Alam Bagh, on the Lucknow side not far from the mansion, the grave had been prepared. 'The Commander-in-Chief and many of the comrades who had fought by his side in so many fields followed him to the grave.' Havelock had always wished to be buried without fuss. Now through 'war's hurry skurry' as he had called it, his wish was granted.

After the burial, when the *Last Post* had sounded and the volley had been fired, the grave was carefully levelled lest it should be desecrated after the withdrawal. Close measurements were taken of the spot and, on the fork of a large mango tree which shaded it, Hargood carved the letter 'H'.

As he stood beside the grave, of one thing Harry was sure: 'After events may dim his reputation as a commander, or call in question his judgment or capacity, but that great moral will stand for ever: that he proved in his life that a soldier may yet be a Christian – and that he doubly proved it in his death'.

THE NEWS OF the Second Relief of Lucknow reached England on Christmas Day 1857. The cable announcing Havelock's death followed on January 7th.

Hannah, receiving the news at Bonn by War Office telegram, at first was utterly crushed. Slowly she felt 'an undercurrent of consolation – "He has fought the good fight and is with his glorified Redeemer for ever", rung in my ears so sweetly. And again, "Fear not, believer, I will be thy portion for ever", and "I will be a father to the fatherless and a husband to the widow", all came pouring into my soul with such comfort...' Then Harry's long letter arrived, written from the Alam Bagh on the day after the burial: they had supposed from inaccurate newspaper reports that he had been at Allahabad with the wounded, far from his dying father. Harry wrote, 'would to God I were in my grave if that could restore that dear lost life to you. God's will be done – from Him only can solace and support come in this affliction... that God may bless its effect to each and everyone of us is the earnest prayer of your affectionate son'.

Two realisations buoyed up Hannah in her grief: 'that he has received the "Well done, thou good and faithful servant" of His

Heavenly Lord and Master, His Heavenly Father and Friend. Our loss is his unspeakable great reward'; and, secondly, the national lamentation and sympathy, 'the nation are *bleeding* under their loss'.

Hundreds of letters poured in, many from perfect strangers. She had been told by the Duke of Cambridge, back in November, that Havelock would probably be made a peer, that he would be the next Commander-in-Chief in India, that 'he considered him *equal* and in some instances *superior* to Wellington. He has great work before him yet, my Lady...' Now in her loss and the nation's, she received the rank of a baronet's wife and a pension of £1,000 a year. Coming over to England, she was given a grace and favour residence and devoted herself to the children and to forwarding the causes dear to Havelock – temperance and evangelism in the army.

Jos, who had been in Peshawar throughout the Mutiny and thus in comparative safety, came home in 1858. He married his cousin and boyhood friend Isabella Creak, Aunt Jane's daughter, and they returned together to the Punjab, where as an Assistant Commissioner, still the same bright, humble minded, deeply spiritual and hopelessly untidy Jos, he died of cholera in 1864 at the age of thirty-two. George, only ten at his father's death, went into the Indian Army, serving later in the Indian Police, and he died in 1908.

Harry, now a baronet, with a pension of £1,000 a year, served throughout the Mutiny. His mother had hoped he would return home at once but Harry felt that though this would be to his advantage, he was 'in the strict path of duty in accepting active employment, in which I only follow the example of him who, steadfastly disregarding the sneers of those who for years laughed at his self-denial, received at last that reward beyond all earthly price, which his faith and constancy had earned'.

At Lucknow, during Campbell's siege of the rebels in March 1858, he again distinguished himself on the staff and was later appointed Lieutenant-Colonel in Hodson's Horse. 'Pray for me, all of you at home', he wrote in June 1858, 'that my weakness may be strengthened that I may be taught to withstand temptation, that my steps may be guided aright, above all that I may do my duty which I find the hardest thing of all – to apply diligently and cheerfully to the laborious little things which make the most important part of a staff officer's duty. Pray for me that I may be upheld and strengthened and guided – my pride repressed and that I may have the strength to fight against sloth and procrastination – my besetting sins – and against violence and anger. I feel like a blind man groping for the truth – now that dear guide and counsellor is away – who *always* saw the right, one word from whom moved my difficulties and showed me the path I should follow... Again I say, pray for your son'. Returning to England in 1859, acclaimed as his father's son and as a VC, with the world at his feet, Harry was publicly baptised by immersion, 'the ordinance that seals me as a public professor of Christ before men. Join with me', he wrote to his mother as he went abroad again, 'when I humbly pray to Almighty God that by the grace of His Holy Spirit, sought in the name of His blessed Son, I may be kept in every good word and work to the day when we shall be reunited in His glorious presence to him who has gone before us'.

After service in the Maori Wars and in Canada Harry retired from the active list and entered Parliament in 1873. Whenever a war blew up he would go out, as a correspondent or observer. Lord Wolseley called him 'the bravest Englishman alive'. In 1880 he inherited from a remote cousin, a descendant of Havelock's great-aunt, the property and large fortune of the Allans of Blackwell in Durham; at the time of his father's death in 1857 so many lives lay between Harry and the Allan estate that eventual succession could not have seemed imaginable.

In later years, the effects of the sunstroke of 1848 never quite leaving him, Harry was known more for eccentricities and violence of speech and opinions than for Christian faith. His end was characteristic. As one of the British Parliamentary commission investigating the Afghan boundary question on the North-West Frontier he found his way to join military operations against the Afridis in the Khyber Pass. During a gallop not far from the British lines he was shot by a tribesman and bled to death, on December 30th 1897.

Hannah, a widow at forty-eight, had lived on with Puss, who never married (Nora died at the age of twenty-one), for nearly a quarter of a century, happy in her memories of 'such devoted love, such gentle consideration of my feelings, such soft words even when spoken in reproof, and that how seldom! Such gallant politeness, down to the smallest point of etiquette, such heavenly-minded prayers and such sweet and happy readings together of the Book – *the* Book of all others dearest to him'. She died in 1882 at the age of seventy-three.

AS THE MEMORY of the Indian Mutiny faded Havelock remained in the consciousness of the British public, as a symbol.

New ideals were emerging in the England of the eighteen fifties, when, as never before, Christian faith and ethics were becoming the mainsprings of the lives of the people. Before the Victorian age could be set fully on its course these ideals needed a personal expression, a paragon to be emulated, who could symbolise the goal towards which men and women strove. Havelock became the man, the Christian hero. Had he been well known previously as a general his impact probably would have been less. It was the suddenness of his rise as much as the brilliance of his exploits which made his name ring across the world. And his death in the moment of triumph ensured his position.

As a symbol, Havelock did even more after his death than before. Apart from his contribution to the art of war, his fame greatly advanced the causes he had worked for: temperance in the Armed Services and in the nation, then beginning to deal seriously with the problem of drunkenness; evangelism in the Army – the Garrison Prayer Room movement, the Army Scripture Readers and the Officers Christian Union each revering him as a founder, direct or indirect; and the unashamed support, by officers of the military and civil services, of missionary work among the races of India. But more especially Havelock was the *beau-ideal* of Victorian chivalry for the new generation.

His oft repeated ambition was fulfilled: 'to be surpassed by none in zeal and determination in the path of my duty because I was resolved to put down the vile calumny that a Christian could not be a meritorious soldier'. After Havelock, no one seriously maintained that it was impossible to profess 'to fear God as well as honour the Queen... that no man could at once be a saint and a soldier'.

Yet Havelock's influence went far beyond the Army. He made men of all classes and ages wish to live better lives. He showed what a layman could do, by character, action and word, to extol and extend the Christian faith and the qualities which uplift a nation. And since truth is constant, and since the vast majority of Christians must serve God in their ordinary avocations, the message of Havelock's life remains relevant.

Had he been as Marshman portrayed, of forbidding moral perfection, Havelock would have little meaning for a later age which has no patience with unreality. Havelock was not an angel but a Christian, 'a sinner saved by grace', as he would have said – human, and therefore a sinner to the end. He was not ready made. His personality, as Hannah and Harry put in the long inscription on the monument at Lucknow, was 'the result of the influence of the Holy Spirit on his heart, and a humble reliance on the merits of a Crucified Saviour'. His growth in grace continued to the end and it was the final flowering of character in circumstances of extreme provocation which, more than any other factor, finally won Harry. Havelock was a saint, but he was not an eccentric like Gordon or dour and harsh like Stonewall Jackson, with whom he is most frequently compared. And he was a lovable man.

In a world so different, the values and beliefs for which Havelock stood still stand. 'There is a God that governs the earth', he had written, 'there is a Saviour that died for sinners'. Every man stood to be judged, but every man had been redeemed and set free if he would reject his own claims and by deliberate faith accept the risen Christ into his life: 'contrite and humbled under a sense of his innumerable sins', Havelock's draft for his epitaph had run, 'and trusting for pardon in the blood of Jesus Christ... Calmly trusting for acceptance in his Redeemer's name...' This was the ground of his faith.

Christ was not for eternity only but for this world. 'Christ is the Friend of all sinners', Havelock had so often written and it was thus that he had experienced Him: 'my trust is in the Lord Jesus, my tried and merciful Friend, to whom all power is entrusted in heaven and earth'. Havelock's deepest desire for each of his family and for his men was 'that you may... regard Jesus Christ as personally your Friend and Benefactor'.

The Friendship of Christ was Havelock's secret. And remains his message: 'it is a happy thing beyond description to have a heavenly Father and a powerful Friend in whom to put our trust'.

HAVELOCK'S RELATIONS

(Principal characters in the book shown in capitals)

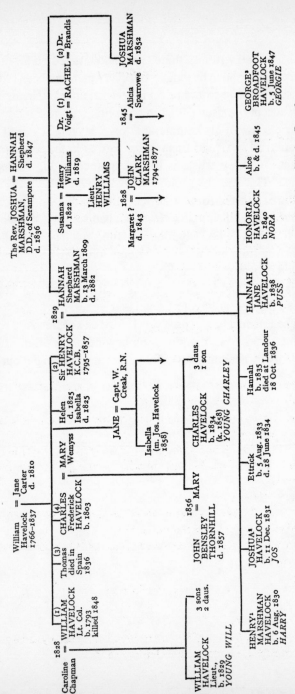

[1] Lt.-Gen. Sir Henry Havelock-Allan, Bart., V.C., K.C.B., G.C.B., M.P. M. (1865) Lady Alice Moreton, and had issue. Killed 30 Dec. 1897.

[2] Capt. Joshua Havelock, Asst. Comm., Punjab. M. Isabella Creak 1858 and had issue. D. 1864.

[3] Col. G. B. Havelock, Bengal Police. Married and had issue. D. 1908.

Authorities

MANUSCRIPT SOURCES

The Havelock Papers
These form a large collection of letters and papers, almost all unpublished. The principal series are:

192 letters from Havelock to his wife, 1829-1857.
108 letters from Havelock to his eldest son, 1843-1857.
23 letters to Havelock from his eldest son.
132 letters between Lady Havelock and her children, selected from a much larger correspondence.
107 private letters, etc, from Havelock to various correspondents.
95 letters from John Clark Marshman to Havelock.
123 Military Papers of the Cawnpore-Lucknow Campaign.
74 Military Papers, miscellaneous.

The important series missing are:

Letters from Havelock to his wife from the Afghan War, and his journal (all evidently lost in his lifetime).
Letters from Lady Havelock to her husband (probably destroyed by her after his death)
Letters from Havelock to John Clark Marshman (lost since the publication in 1860 of the Memoir, in which a number of extracts were published).

WORKS BY HAVELOCK
Memoir of The Three Campaigns of Major-General Sir Archibald Campbell in Ava. 1 vol. Serampore, 1828.
Narrative of the War in Afghanistan in 1838-39. 2 vols. London, Henry Colburn, 1840.

PRINTED SOURCES

LIVES OF HAVELOCK
A Biographical Sketch of Sir Henry Havelock, KCB, by the Reverend William Brock, London, James Nisbet, 1858.

Life of General Havelock, by J T Headley, New York, 1859.

Memoir of Major-General Sir Henry Havelock, KCB, by John Clark Marshman, London, Longmans, Green & Co, 1860.

Havelock, by Archibald Forbes, Macmillan (English Men of Action Series), 1890.

PRINCIPAL OTHER PRINTED SOURCES

Broadfoot, W, *The Career of Major Broadfoot*, 1888.

Burnes, Sir A, *Cabool*, 1842.

Cannon, R, *Historical Record of the 13th Foot*, 1848.

Camp and Barrack Room, by a late Staff-Sergeant of the 13th Light Infantry, 1846.

Davidson, H, *History and Services of the 78th Highlanders (Rosshire Buffs) 1793-1881*, 2 vols, 1901.

Doveton, F B, *Reminiscences of the Burmese War in 1824-6*, 1852.

Edwardes, Sir H, and Merivale, H M, *Life of Sir Henry Lawrence*, 2 vols.

Everett, Sir Henry, *The History of the Somerset Light Infantry*, 1934.

Fayrer, Sir Joseph, *Recollections of My Life*, 1900.

Forrest, Sir George (ed), *Selections from State Papers (Military Department, Government of India) 1857-8*, 3 vols, 1902.

Forrest, Sir George, *A History of the Indian Mutiny*, 2 vols, 1904.

Fortescue, Sir John, *History of the British Army*, Vols XI-XIII.

Gleig, G R, *Sale's Brigade in Afghanistan*, 1846.

Goldsmid, Sir F J, *James Outram*, 2 vols, 1880.

Groom, W J, *With Havelock to Lucknow*, 1894.

Gubbins, M R, *The Mutinies in Oude*, 1858.

Hunt, G H, *Outram's and Havelock's Persian Campaign*, 1858.

Inglis, Lady, *The Siege of Lucknow*.

Johnson, W T, *Twelve Years of a Soldier's Life*, 1897.

Kaye, Sir John, *The War in Afghanistan*, 3 vols, 1874.

Kaye, Sir John, and Malleson, G B, *History of the Indian Mutiny*, 4 vols, 1889.

Lawrence, Sir G, *Forty Three Years in India*, 1874.

Mackenzie, Lady, *Storms and Sunshine of a Soldier's Life*, 2 vols.

Maude, F C M, and Sherer, J W, *Memories of the Mutiny*, 2 vols, 1894.

North, Major, *Journal of an English Officer in India*, 1858.

Sargent, J, *Memoir of Rev Henry Martyn*, 1819.

Scott, Thomas, *The Force of Truth*.

Seaton, Sir Thomas, *From Cadet to Colonel*, 2 vols, 1866.

Smith, George, *Twelve Indian Statesmen*, 1898.

Taylor, William, *Scenes and Adventures in Afghanistan*, 1842.

Teer, Edward, *The Siege of Jellalabad*, 1904.

Wakefield, E, *Some of the Words, Deeds and Success of Havelock in the Cause of Temperance in India*, 1861.

Wilson, H H, *Narrative of the Burmese War in 1824-6*, 1852.

Wylly, H C, *Neill's Blue Caps*, 2 vols, 1926.

Also: *Calcutta Review, Saturday Review, The Friend of India, The Times, Daily Telegraph*, etc.

The First Afghan & The Sikh Wars

North India, Afghanistan & Burma

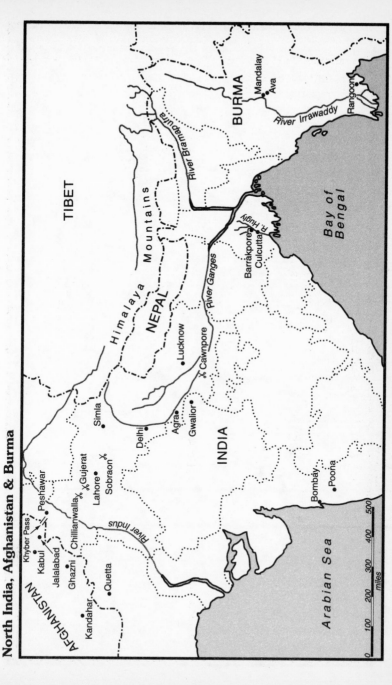

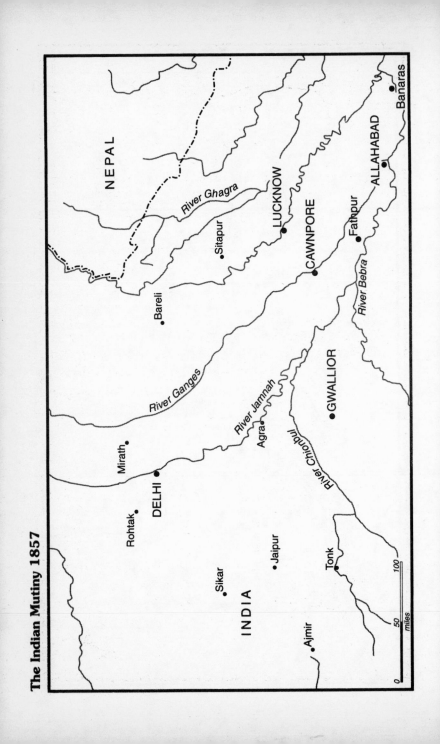

The Indian Mutiny 1857

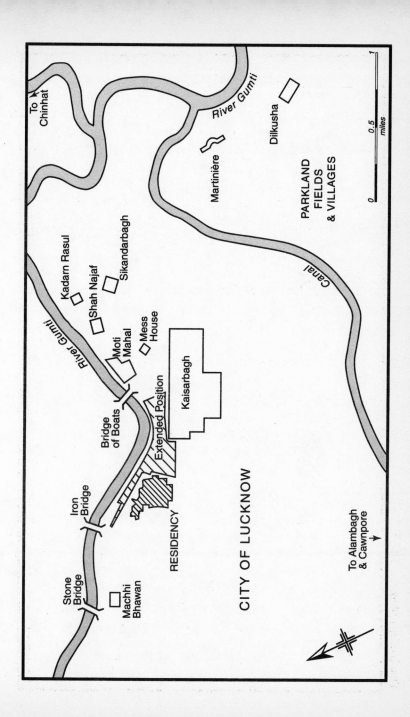

To Chinhat

River Gumti

Martinière

Dilkusha

PARKLAND
FIELDS
& VILLAGES

Canal

Kadarn Rasul

Shah Najaf

Sikandarbagh

River Gumti

Moti Mahal

Mess House

Kaisarbagh

Bridge of Boats

Extended Position

Iron Bridge

RESIDENCY

Stone Bridge

Machhi Bhawan

CITY OF LUCKNOW

To Alambagh & Cawnpore

0   0.5   1
miles